Monogamy

Recent Titles in
Sex, Love, and Psychology
Judy Kuriansky, Series Editor

Relationship Sabotage: Unconscious Factors that Destroy Couples, Marriages, and Family
William J. Matta

The Praeger Handbook of Transsexuality: Changing Gender to Match Mindset
Rachel Ann Heath

America's War on Sex
Marty Klein

Teenagers, HIV, and AIDS: Insights from Youths Living with the Virus
Maureen E. Lyon and Lawrence J. D'Angelo, editors

Rock 'n' Roll Wisdom: What Psychologically Astute Lyrics Teach about Life and Love
Barry A. Farber

Sixty, Sexy, and Successful: A Guide for Aging Male Baby Boomers
Robert Schwalbe, PhD

Managing Menopause Beautifully: Physically, Emotionally, and Sexually
Dona Caine-Francis

New Frontiers in Men's Sexual Health: Understanding Erectile Dysfunction and the
Revolutionary New Treatments
Kamal A. Hanash, MD

Sexuality Education: Past, Present, and Future (4 volumes)
Elizabeth Schroeder, EdD, MSW, and Judy Kuriansky, PhD, editors

Sex When You're Sick: Reclaiming Sexual Health after Illness or Injury
Anne Katz

Secret Suffering: How Women's Sexual and Pelvic Pain Affects Their Relationships
Susan Bilheimer and Robert J. Echenberg, M.D.

Teenage Sex and Pregnancy: Modern Myths, Unsexy Realities
Mike Males

MONOGAMY

The Untold Story

Marianne Brandon

Sex, Love, and Psychology

Judy Kuriansky, Series Editor

 PRAEGER

AN IMPRINT OF ABC-CLIO, LLC
Santa Barbara, California • Denver, Colorado • Oxford, England

Library of Congress Cataloging-in-Publication Data

Brandon, Marianne.
   Monogamy : the untold story / Marianne Brandon.
       p. cm. — (Sex, love, and psychology)
   Includes bibliographical references and index.
   ISBN 978-0-313-38573-5 (hard copy : alk. paper) —
ISBN 978-0-313-38574-2 (ebook)   1. Sex (Psychology)   2. Sex.   3. Marriage.
I. Title.
   BF692.B73   2010
   155.3—dc22   2010020167

ISBN: 978-0-313-38573-5
EISBN: 978-0-313-38574-2

14 13 12 11 10   1 2 3 4 5

This book is also available on the World Wide Web as an eBook.
Visit www.abc-clio.com for details.

Praeger
An Imprint of ABC-CLIO, LLC

ABC-CLIO, LLC
130 Cremona Drive, P.O. Box 1911
Santa Barbara, California 93116-1911

This book is printed on acid-free paper ∞

Manufactured in the United States of America

To my parents

CONTENTS

ACKNOWLEDGMENTS

I am grateful to the two people who helped me realize this dream: my husband, Steve, whose solid and tender support sustained me throughout the project; and Dr. Judith Kuriansky, who continues to believe in my ideas and my work.

SERIES FOREWORD

It is a hotly debated topic: monogamy. Are men—and women—wired to be faithful, or are we expecting too much in our culture for unions to be true to one another 'til death do us part? Since I have been asked that question countless times as a veteran relationship therapist, I am delighted to read Marianne Brandon's book, *Monogamy: The Untold Story*. Having taught about intimacy for years in my course at Columbia University Teachers College, and presented material about the dynamics of love and commitment in my classes and in many workshops around the world, I was exceptionally impressed with Brandon's thorough and intelligent review of the factors that influence fidelity. With academic accuracy, yet in a readable style, she reviews relevant theories about the impact of childhood experiences inherent in Freud's psychoanalytic view, reinforcements according to cognitive and behavioral approaches, role models that underlie social learning, family systems, and (one of my personal favorites) attachment theory, which describes how we are drawn to others. This book presents one of the most comprehensive and valuable reviews of these theoretical bases for not only monogamy, but for attraction in general. Every professional and every couple in a relationship should read these chapters for an understanding of why they pick—and commit to—a partner.

Rarely is there such a depth of psychological theory in a book that also addresses what to do about keeping a relationship going. Indeed, it is this mixture that makes this book unique. In many subsequent chapters, Brandon addresses her readers directly as "gentlemen" and "ladies" as she describes many valuable activities that couples can do to keep monogamy passionate. In these chapters, she includes creative ways to enhance sexual chemistry that are not only useful for couples but also responsibly address benefits to couples, why the technique works, and what critics would say. I was pleased to see the inclusion of Tantra, which is an Eastern approach to intimacy and higher states of enlightenment and ecstasy that I have used with couples for decades, and addressed in my book, *The Complete Idiot's Guide to Tantric Sex*. Brandon's choice of terms and descriptions are creative in and of themselves, as she describes techniques like a "sensing tour."

Professionals will find much for use in this book with its extensive review of theory as well as the techniques for couples they work with to apply in their relationship. As such, clinicians can recommend this valuable book to their clients to read, and then to report back about in sessions. Couples, too, can find much to explore in these pages, as they understand the theories behind fidelity, monogamy, and commitment, and as they try out the techniques in order to achieve intimacy that ultimately will bring the commitment they strive for in love unions.

Dr. Judy Kuriansky

INTRODUCTION

As a clinical psychologist and sex therapist, I have devoted many years to helping people open and feel alive, both emotionally and physically. I myself have
walked the same path I assist others in traveling every day. It is clear to me that
when we are disengaged from any part of ourselves, including our sexuality,
our hearts and bodies close in response. When we close, we stop evolving, and
we no longer live and love to our fullest potential. Our lives lack creativity and
joy, spontaneity and humor. As a culture, we have supported this unfortunate
process in each other by ignoring the realities of our sexual instincts. Conse-
quently, we are disconnected from the core of our sexual selves. It is because of
this widespread and heartbreaking effect of our cultural misunderstanding that
I have chosen to write about monogamy. I have witnessed too many couples
descend into self-criticism, blame, and closure because they misunderstand
their sexuality. Monogamy, as we understand it today, is not necessarily a natural state. At least, not for everyone.

Embracing this truth does not have to be frightening. In fact, my hope is
that it is liberating. After all, it is an unavoidable fact that the better we know
ourselves and understand our motivations, the more control we have over our
behavior and the more powerful we are in the world. Obviously, the alternative—
self-confusion—is never a place of strength. Plus, it is only in understanding our
instincts that we can learn to use them to our advantage.

Monogamy: The Untold Story does not imply the end of marriage as we know
it. It does not mean that lovers cannot bond for a lifetime, nor does it mean
that a happy and sensuous long-term commitment is impossible. It does not

mean the demise of the family unit. And it certainly is not an excuse for men and women to act out sexually in ways that are hurtful to themselves, their partners, or their children. Instead, *Monogamy: The Untold Story* suggests that we recognize the limits of our current understanding of adult sexuality; we honor the truth of our animal heritage; we stop shaming each other for natural instincts and inclinations, and we adjust our understanding of modern-day intimacy to accommodate these realities. In this way, we encourage each other in evolving our feminine natures as well as our masculine sides, we support our biology as well as our intellects, and we embrace rather than pathologize our instincts. It means that monogamy is a choice, not an indisputable fact between lovers. As humans with powerful logical minds and advanced neurophysiology, we don't have to blindly follow our mammalian impulses. We can rise above our more animalistic drives. However, it is only in taking into account these more basic realities that we can stop blaming ourselves—and our partners—when sex loses its luster. We can cease feeling ashamed because of a "low libido." We can put an end to blaming our lover's sexual style for all that's wrong with our sex lives. *Monogamy: The Untold Story* provides an alternative explanation for these practically inevitable challenges of intimacy. With this understanding, we can approach relationships from a new mind-set, armed with powerful techniques aimed at supporting a satisfying sex life over time.

In sum, *Monogamy: The Untold Story* is an exciting invitation to actualize your truest power, and your deepest gifts of love. When we manifest our potential, in touch with our loving hearts and our instinctive physical drives, men and women feel satisfied and joyful. It is from this place that we become able to offer our lovers the most succulent juice of life. And it is here that we are able to experience the sexual bliss that is our birthright. Living well, joyfully, and passionately is all about loving well. In doing our best to love well, we can only benefit everyone we interact with. For most of us, myself included, this is a lifelong practice of unfolding.

Please note that the concepts in this book are universal, in that they apply to both heterosexual as well as homosexual partnerships. Human beings are quite similar when it comes to these very basic laws of Mother Nature. I also want to note that the stories in this book are based on fictional characters that represent composites of patients. These people do not exist in real life—although, in a sense, they live in each of us.

Part I

THE TRUTH ABOUT MONOGAMY

Chapter One

THE MONOGAMY ILLUSION

Most humans aren't naturally monogamous. Monogamy is actually extraordinarily rare among mammals. We know this from studying animals: less than 15 percent of primates and 3 percent of mammals are monogamous.[1] We know this from studying humans: of 185 societies, only 29 formally restricted their members to monogamy.[2] And in those societies that consider themselves monogamous, affairs and extramarital liaisons occur regularly.[3] Even the human body offers clues to our natural mating patterns: many of our sex characteristics conflict with those of monogamous species. In fact, there is no evidence from biology or anthropology that monogamy is natural or normal for humans![4]

In spite of these statistics, few topics generate as much controversy and emotional exchange amongst lay people and professionals alike. Thus far, the monogamy debate has been largely focused as a moral issue, and everyone has an opinion. It's a cutthroat moral battle out there.

Some say those who aren't monogamous:

are selfish.
want too much out of sex and marriage.
have no will power, no integrity, or no morals.
think sex is too important or overrated.
don't care about their children.

In contrast, others say:

people change over time, and marriage to one person for a lifetime can interfere with
    self-growth.

people can continue to love each other, but not desire each other sexually.

people stay together because they are dependent on one another, not because they love one another.

people embrace monogamy because they don't believe they could find another partner.

sex is difficult to enjoy with the same partner over time.

Who is right?

After researching this topic for years, I boldly answer, "No one." This complex and controversial issue does not lend itself to a single understanding. There is variability within a species for all attributes—and sexual behavior is no exception. So, some people feel monogamous and behave that way. Many more people feel capable of monogamy but believe they are with the wrong partner to enjoy it. Others adapt to monogamy very well—with some effort. In actuality, there are couples who enjoy monogamy, couples who tolerate it, and couples who struggle with it.

Most mammals, it seems, don't even attempt it. In fact, research demonstrates that many of the animal species we classify as monogamous actually have more varied sex lives than we once believed.[5] We now know that even mammals once thought to be monogamous are more likely to be serially monogamous or faithful to one mate for a distinct period of time. Penguins are a case in point—they have enjoyed an excellent sexual reputation for being monogamous. We are charmed by the male penguin's dedication to his offspring. He fights harsh arctic conditions to keep the egg he fertilized warm for several long winter months. His is a beautiful and courageous love story. In reality, however, penguins are dedicated parents, but their coupling dissolves after each mating period. Penguins are monogamous for only one season—enough time to fertilize and hatch their baby. This is not exactly how most Westerners define monogamy.

Even the rare mammals considered monogamous have unique living arrangements that few humans would choose to emulate. The gibbon is one such example. Gibbons are monogamous primates—they mate for life. That's the good news. The bad news is that they have sex only when the female is fertile, which typically occurs every several years. Plus, they live in seclusion—so far away from other gibbons that most don't interact with another potential partner in their lifetime. For the gibbon, monogamy is a natural adaptation to their unique environment.

In spite of the evidence, the debate rages on. In our rapidly changing culture, the dilemma of monogamy is only becoming more heated. In fact, this is the first time in history that we are so blatantly faced with the monogamy dilemma! That's because up until recently, a woman's desire for sex was essentially irrelevant. The feminist movement only raised the possibility of female sexual pleasure a few decades ago. And it has taken this long for women (and now men) to overcome feelings of shame and embarrassment in order to deal with these issues more publicly. This open discussion of sexual pleasure and satisfaction has paved the way to explore the feasibility of monogamy as a long-term mating strategy in the 21st century. But while monogamy remains our cultural ideal, science and social statistics demonstrate that it is not a likely mating pattern for humans. Instead, the majority of Westerners either divorce, have affairs, struggle in their sexual relationship, or live in sexless marriages.

In spite of these challenges, we are a romantic culture that admires great love stories. We adore the idea of long-term love. And that's a beautiful thing, because monogamy remains a great idea. Whether or not monogamy is natural, there are numerous benefits to a long-term coupling—and the majority of couples strive for it. In fact, keeping a marriage faithful is a reason many couples find themselves in my therapy room. I have spent many years helping my patients achieve these goals. Making monogamy work is challenging in part because, as a culture, we approach it unrealistically. That is, when we assume it's natural, we do not make space for the inevitable struggles inherent in an unnatural process. And this is why I wrote this book. In acknowledging the realities of monogamy, I hope you will be better equipped to achieve it.

In these pages, I will lead you through the same process through which I lead couples in my therapy practice who want to stay monogamous and enjoy it. In the first part of this book, I explain what we know about monogamy from a psychological and a biological perspective. I describe the instinct to organize into hierarchies, and how this relates to sexual relationships. I explain the difference between masculine and feminine instincts, and the key role these energies play in a long-term monogamous relationship. In the second part of the book, I teach how to use your sexual instincts to your advantage. I explain how to highlight your sexual chemistry with your partner and improve your technique at making love. I describe the skills that make for great sex. And I give you lots and lots of homework, because practice makes perfect!

Until now, our nonmonogamous instincts have been largely ignored. The importance of our innate masculine and feminine sexual instincts has been downplayed. The unfortunate result has been a mass of confusion about our sexual natures. But intimacy involves a complex combination of emotions, neurochemicals, early childhood relationships, culture, environment, genetics, and yes, *instincts*. Like a fingerprint, this combination is unique for every man and woman. For some people, instincts play a larger role in their sexual experience than for others. As a result, this book may resonate more for those who feel particularly connected to their instinctual sexual nature. However, it may be most helpful for those who do not, as these people may find the most sexual boost from discovering previously ignored aspects of their sexual experience.

Possible Challenges of Monogamy

- Diane and Greg were married for four years when she "lost her sex drive." Their marriage was good and they clearly loved each other. But Diane was tortured by the fact that she didn't want to make love. Sometimes she masturbated, but for the most part she really couldn't care less if they had sex again.

- Rick and Linda had a lot in common and their marriage went along pretty smoothly. But Linda became unglued when she realized that Rick was looking at porn on the Internet almost every night after she went to sleep. Later, Rick guiltily admitted that he regularly went to strip clubs while on business trips. Linda felt completely betrayed.
- Kim and Jeff had a great sex life until they had children. After that, Kim was just too tired and worn out to be interested. They had very little time alone as it was. Kim had so much physical contact with the children, when they were in bed she just wanted to be left alone. But Jeff missed their sexual relationship, and his sex drive remained strong. He didn't want to cheat on Kim, but he didn't know what else to do.
- Carol couldn't understand why John never came on to her anymore. His lack of interest in sex was alarming to her. All of her friends were complaining that their husbands wanted too much sex. Carol was ashamed to admit she had the opposite struggle with John.
- Rachael ignored the truth for years. She pretended that as long as she didn't have sex with her coworker, Ed, it wasn't an affair. When her friend finally challenged her about the emotional affair, Rachael had to admit it. But now what was she going to do about it? She couldn't imagine life without Ed.

THE WESTERN LIFE PLAN

Most of us try our best to follow the plan. But for many men and women, it's not working as smoothly as we expected.

We get through school. We fall in love. We marry a beloved mate and start a family. We try hard to create a good life for ourselves and our family. And then . . . slowly but surely, it all starts to unravel. She loses her sex drive. He has an affair. She becomes irritable and depressed. He shuts down emotionally. Sometimes there is talk of separation. Oftentimes they divorce. The children adapt; they have no choice. Everyone picks up the pieces of life and tries again. He remarries sooner, and to a woman younger than his first wife. She tries to use what she learned to avoid the same mistakes in her next relationship. They pray their children won't be destined to repeat this miserable pattern.

But of course, the cycle continues.

The confusion repeats itself, generation after generation. Despite everyone's best efforts, marriage and sexual monogamy challenges the majority of men and women. Great thinkers have offered up a variety of explanations for this dilemma. Perhaps people have such massive intimacy issues leftover from troubled childhoods that it becomes extremely challenging to keep a marriage healthy. Maybe our judgment is so poor that we consistently marry partners with our parents' bad habits. Possibly we are so sexually repressed as a society that we are too overwhelmed by shame and discomfort for intimacy to thrive in a long-term relationship. Plus, our cultural support of self-growth doesn't seem to support long-term commitment. We are terrible communicators, and we don't know how to talk about sex. Or for some mysterious reason, a significant number of people have such imbalanced sex hormones that they no longer want or enjoy sex. These are some of the explanations we've been taught, and of course they *are* true for some people. But for many of my patients, I've found these hypotheses to be severely lacking. In fact, they are often of little use to me as I assist patients seeking a better sex life with their long-term partners. In truth, even after we analyze their sexual histories, work with their intimacy issues, improve communication skills, balance their hormones, and explore their shame, many monogamous people still find their sex lives inherently lacking. And this leads to additional difficulties. For many of these men and women, their sexual struggle impacts many aspects of their lives even beyond sex—such as their feelings of intimacy with their partner, their sense of themselves as a man or woman, and their experience of personal power in life.

It's time to look at a bigger picture.

Our species, Homo sapiens, loves to analyze, critique, and solve dilemmas. We want to make sense of troubled intimate lives by further analyzing personal histories, sexual fears and anxieties, and emotional issues. Of course, these are all valid and necessary steps in our understanding. However, sometimes they are overkill. When we actively seek out problems, we can always find some. But that doesn't mean that these problems directly cause monogamy to be so challenging—at least, not always, which is why resolving these problems in therapy doesn't necessarily make monogamy work. In fact, our understanding of love and making love has become much more complex than it needs to be.

Instead, we would be better served to take a breath and comprehend love, attachment, and mating via the more fundamental aspects of human nature. We are mammals. Sex is an experience we share with our primate ancestors. In fact, men and women describe memorable, exciting sex as a primal act—a letting go into something deeper, more purely emotional, or more animalistic. That is because in accessing our more primal instinctual nature, sex becomes more of what we want it to be. And the more ancient parts of our brains are the vehicles that can take us there. It is time to simplify this sexual mystery, and get back to basics. This process will involve taking a look at our belief systems, our environment, our biology, *and our animal nature*. But first, let's take a closer look at monogamy, our favorite sexual illusion.

WHAT IS MONOGAMY?

Most of us define monogamy as being sexually faithful to one partner for a lifetime. But this is actually not the true definition! Quite literally, monogamy means to be *married* to one person—nothing more, nothing less. Marriage is defined as a social institution involving a legal commitment between two people. It is fascinating that neither of these definitions mentions love or sex. Yet love, and making love, are what marriage and monogamy are ultimately all about—aren't they?

Apparently not.

At least, not according to our dictionaries. And not according to the behavior of much of the society in which we live. Adultery has occurred in all cultures across time, and estimates of cheating in America have ranged from 20 to 50 percent.[6] Approximately 20 percent of marriages are sexless.[7] And of the married people who are having sex regularly, many are not satisfied.[8] With time, research indicates that most marriages actually become sexually[9] and emotionally[10] *less* gratifying. And this appears to be a cross-culturally universal phenomenon.[11] Ultimately, the sad reality is that in spite of everyone's best efforts, about half of all marriages end in divorce. And of those who don't split up, many couples appear less alive. Despite the fact that faithfulness and a satisfying sexual relationship are considered by most people to be a necessary and very important ingredient for a happy marriage,[12] this scenario is not most people's reality. As a sex therapist in the business of helping couples enjoy their sex lives, these statistics distressed me. It seemed that the odds were against me in helping people reach their marital and sexual goals.

THE MARRIAGE IDEAL

In spite of what the dictionary says, in its ideal, marriage represents much more to us than a legal commitment between two people. We marry for a multitude of reasons, some logical, some economical, and some emotional. We marry in an effort to enhance our lives. We marry to create children and enable a part of us to live on even after we have died. We marry to complete ourselves, to unite with another because we can achieve more together than we can individually. We marry to love more fully, and to experience life more richly. However, marrying for love is a more recent luxury of the 21st century. For most of modern history, marriages were arranged for political, religious, financial, or other reasons. Thus, we may marry for love, but it is not what marriage was designed for. And as much as we wish it to be, this is not necessarily the typical outcome of marriage. Monogamy, the state of being married to one person, is often not the pleasurable journey newlyweds joyfully anticipate when they say, "I do." Monogamy is actually much more challenging than we like to admit.

"I Don't"

Who really is naturally monogamous? Anthropologists, who specialize in studying human mammals in all their varieties, inform us that only 16 percent of the world's societies remain exclusively monogamous.[13] Most people in most societies are not sexually monogamous for life. Divorce appears to be a cross-cultural phenomenon.[14] In fact, anthropologist Helen Fisher found that there is a trend across cultures that couples stay together for about four years. She believes there is an evolutionary reason for this time frame—long enough to successfully mate and raise a child to toddlerhood. But this is clearly not the intention of newlyweds walking down the aisle. It's only years later, after practicing sexual monogamy for a while, that people feel the true complexity of monogamy—because that is often when people's natural sexual inclinations start making themselves known.

ORIGINS OF MONOGAMY

Where did the ideal of sexual monogamy originate? If it's so hard to attain, why did we idealize it in the first place? After all, most of us don't attempt to beat the odds and achieve such extraordinary tasks on a regular basis in other aspects of our lives.

We can gain clues to answer this question by observing the animal kingdom. Short-term monogamy is a very good idea from an evolutionary perspective. Mammals that give birth to helpless infants require a lasting parental partnership for their offspring's survival past infancy. In these species, like birds, wolves, and humans, mothers cannot feed and protect themselves and their helpless infants without assistance. Active and involved fathers are necessary for offspring survival. Obviously, infant survival is imperative—if babies don't survive, neither does the species. As Charles Darwin, the original evolutionist, explained many years ago, most animals innately behave in ways that encourage their own survival, as well as the survival of their offspring. In humans, this translates to a father participating in the family unit for at least several years after a baby's birth. Pair bonding, or the development of an attachment with one romantic partner, best supports survival of the young. This sets the stage for the institution of marriage, with all its accompanying ideals.

And marriage has served us well.

But humans have interpreted marriage—and monogamy—very differently than Mother Nature did. And that's because humans have consciousness, integrity, and compassion. Ending love relationships every few years feels heartless and cruel—not to mention the fact that lovers often remain emotionally attached, even though they may not be passionately attached or still in love. As a result, humans took Mother Nature's masterful short-term mating strategy and turned it into a long-term one. We changed the rules on Mother Nature. Rather than being monogamous for just a few years, we became monogamous for life! And up until recently, lifelong monogamy has been a magnificent solution. Marriage has helped evolve our societies into the thriving metropolises we enjoy today. It has been an amazingly efficient and effective way for our species to prosper. The family unit provides a safe and secure home base for all its members to thrive. However, while this remains true, societies continue to change and grow, and in some ways the dynamics of life and love have become more complex. Unlike husbands of years ago, most men do not farm their land for a living. Women are no longer dependent on men to care for their young. As our social needs change, we are no longer required to marry to ensure our off-spring's survival. Today, we *want* marriage rather than *need* it. And as a result of our social growth and the opportunities now presenting themselves, maintain-ing a monogamous relationship has become more complex as well. The stage has been set for our instinctual processes to bubble to the surface in a new way, consciously and unconsciously. And they are quickly interfering with our best-laid plans!

INSTINCTS AND YOUR UNCONSCIOUS MIND

Instincts are innate responses. They are inherited from generation to gener-ation because they assist the survival of the species. Human instincts are easi-est to observe in our core emotions and bodily functions such as the needs for sleep, sex, and food. Interestingly, the more evolved we become as a species, the more we try to rise above or control our instincts. For example, we attempt to ad-just our sleeping and eating patterns based on conscious desires rather than re-specting our natural physiological drives. We do the same with sex, by expecting ourselves to comfortably adjust to monogamy.

However, though we may not agree with our instincts, that doesn't mean we can change them. Most of us aren't successful at controlling our drives for food, sex, or sleep. That is, we cannot will ourselves to want more or less of them. We cannot strong-arm ourselves into preferring apples for dessert rather than chocolate. Those of us who are night owls cannot strong-arm ourselves into falling asleep early. We cannot will ourselves to fall in love with men if we in-nately respond to women, or vice-versa. Nonetheless, our conscious minds en-gage in power plays with our innate responses. But, when our minds pick a fight with our bodies, our bodies typically win in the end. Thus, when our in-stincts, drives, and inclinations are deemed unacceptable, they don't dissolve. In-stead, one of several outcomes is likely to occur. They can resurface in the mind, such as in the form of obsession. This phenomenon is called the suppression effect. It refers to the paradox that when we try to stop an internal process, it of-ten intensifies, and we simply become even more focused on it.[15] Otherwise, when we try to suppress our drives or inclinations, they can resurface physically in the form of a bodily symptom. Either way, when we attempt to consciously control unconscious processes, we risk a potent battle of wills. Natural yearn-ings and proclivities can exert a powerful influence over our emotions and behavior; and they can cause us to feel and act in ways that are contrary to what we want to believe about ourselves. So what *is* our unconscious mind, and how does it play a role in our sexual experience?

The Adaptive Unconscious

Your unconscious mind is that part of your brain that processes all the information that doesn't reach your conscious awareness. It includes a vast array of mental processes that influence your feelings and behaviors. Amazingly enough, this represents much more information than ever reaches your conscious thought. For example, your five senses alone receive over 10,000,000 bits of information per second. However, most people can only consciously process about 40 bits of information per second. That leaves your unconscious mind to wade through over 9,999,960 bits of information per second from your senses alone![16] Considering the amount of information we are bombarded with every moment, it is adaptive that we have unconscious minds in the first place— otherwise, we'd be so burdened by information that we'd never be able to manage daily life. Hence, the more recently coined term "adaptive unconscious."[17] The adaptive unconscious mind helps the conscious mind function effectively.

Ultimately, most of our thoughts and behaviors are probably the result of *both* our conscious and unconscious processing. This complicates matters, because our conscious and unconscious minds don't necessarily agree, or embrace the same goals for our behavior. But even though our conscious and unconscious minds are often at odds, they both still exert a powerful influence over us. Because of this, when we ignore our unconscious minds, we ignore a significant proportion of the input infusing our brains. This puts us at a disadvantage, as it becomes difficult if not impossible to understand ourselves with access to only part of our brain function. This is why we will act in ways we don't understand—like eat when we aren't hungry, or pick a fight with our partner when we really want to be loved. With regard to sex, this means that a vast array of sexual feelings and behaviors may fall outside our full understanding.

Monogamy is a case in point. When we expect sexual monogamy to be a natural and comfortable way of life, we force many of our animal instincts into unconscious seclusion. Sex loses its zest, because the raw material for great sex is largely generated from this animalistic place—the more primal part of our psyches. As much as we try, humans cannot necessarily will themselves to enjoy sexual monogamy by simply controlling their sexual inclinations. Over time, many monogamous couple's sex lives naturally dry up. People lose contact with the flow of their sexual life force. Eventually, life itself becomes less juicy. Because people don't understand the process that is unfolding, they seek intellectual explanations for these changes. They become more focused on their partner's idiosyncrasies and blame their partner. They become obsessed with their own less than desirable traits and they blame themselves. They look for medical diagnoses—low libido, hormone imbalances, or maybe depression. While these medical diagnoses may be very real, they may also be intertwined or even accelerated by symptoms of an even greater problem—the fact that, for many people, monogamy simply isn't natural. It is possible that until we address this issue consciously as a culture, many sexual therapies will fail in the long term, and people's sexual concerns will continue. And this does seem to be exactly what is happening. The research on sexual dysfunction speaks for itself. What is probably the most quoted survey research in sexual health suggests that 43 percent of women and 31 percent of men report a sexual dysfunction![18]

When Unconscious Desires Collide with Conscious Ideals

Most of us want to do our best in the world. We want to care well for the people we love, and to feel good about ourselves and our behavior. We don't like believing that our private feelings and inclinations would hurt our loved ones or conflict with culturally acceptable behavior. We want to trust that we are normal and our behavior is appropriate. There is peace of mind in knowing that we feel and act in socially acceptable ways. Most of the time, this evaluation by cultural custom is a good thing because our cultural understanding of what may be termed normal is a reasonable barometer of satisfactory human behavior. However, we make trouble for ourselves when societal expectancies are actually *not* natural human behavior. This is true when it comes to sex. Here, what is natural and what is normal can be at odds. Our conscious minds are well versed in culturally acceptable goals and behavior. But our unconscious minds don't trouble themselves with cultural ideals. They get their marching orders in much more basic ways—including our instincts.

Thus, our unconscious minds endorse their own set of relationship rules that defy our earthly laws of space and time. And of course, this complicates things, because we have no control over our unconscious minds. There is little that we dislike more than not having control of something, particularly something about our minds and bodies. This creates psychic conflicts that we deem unacceptable. Because solutions aren't easily evident, we may try to ignore the matter. But in ignoring the contents of our unconscious minds, we lose in the end. Our thoughts, feelings, and behaviors become difficult, if not impossible, to make sense of. By keeping our instinctual motivations locked tight in our unconscious minds, our sexual selves are hindered. For many couples, sex becomes a controlled, monotonous, routine, robotic show of affection—rather than the juicy, sensual, flowing intimate exchange that we long for.

The obvious solution to this dilemma is to improve our awareness of the material in our unconscious minds. People whose unconscious and conscious motivations are in sync tend to enjoy greater well-being.[19] Because they know themselves at a deeper level, they are able to make better decisions that more accurately reflect what they want and need. Interestingly, however, few of us enjoy this synchrony of conscious and unconscious mind. And this is especially true when it comes to sex. We are all pretty confused. And our massive misunderstanding is made even more challenging by the changes rapidly occurring in Western culture. Years ago, ignoring our sexual instincts was an easier proposition than it is today.

THE EVOLUTION OF MARRIAGE AND OUR SEXUALIZED CULTURE

One hundred years ago, it was highly atypical to consider the quality of a marriage. Even several decades ago, divorce was unusual and generally frowned upon. The roles for men and women in a family unit were more defined, and much less challenged. Men worked outside the home, women inside. Sex was understood as a man's right and a woman's duty. People expected that sex was a part of married life, but they didn't expect it to be fabulous sex. Porn and prostitutes existed but were not nearly as available as they are today. Intimate relationships could not be created on Web sites, and prime time TV shows didn't highlight sex scenes. It was a very different world. And in that world, monogamy was essential. Men depended on women to care for their children. Women depended on men to provide money and stability to raise children. The sexes needed each other to survive and to raise families. Monogamy was an integral part of this balance, this interdependency among the sexes. Humans believed in it, because it worked. It accomplished what they expected it to. But most people and cultures seem to naturally evolve with time. Societies transform and progress in knowledge, skills, and emotional development. And this is exactly what's happening now, in Western culture.

Fast forward to 2010. The realities of living in the 21st century place new challenges on our sexual selves. Life in Western culture becomes more sexualized every year. Television shows offer sexual images in unprecedented amounts. In fact, now the majority of evening TV shows have sexual content, so people are constantly being reminded about hot sex—who's having it, and who isn't. Our newspapers are filled with stories about the sex lives of politicians and famous people. Women's fashion magazines and advertisements symbolize raw sex acts to sell everything from jeans to hair products. Billboard ads depict youthful adolescent bodies in sensual poses. Access to pornography is totally free and available 24/7 on the Internet. Americans are flooded with sexual images more than ever before in history. Multiple references to sex are part of any normal day, and access to sexually related media is effortless. This immersion in sexual imagery makes its way into the public's conscious and unconscious minds. People are stimulated by cues about sexual intercourse without even realizing it. Research demonstrates that our brains can feel the impact of the environment without our conscious awareness.[20] Thus, even though people may believe they are not focusing on the sexual images presented to them, it is unlikely that they are truly not impacted by such dramatic imagery. As a result, while Western culture supported monogamy in the past, times have changed. Our daily lives are inundated with invitations to waken and engage our sexual energy.

In addition, we are living in an unprecedented time in history for information exchange. Men and women have unparalleled opportunities to cultivate intimate relationships through social networking via the Internet. No longer are we limited to socialize only with the people in our communities. We can develop intimate relationships with anyone in front of a computer, anywhere around the globe. These changes in our access to information and people impacts sexual expression. Married as well as single people may take advantage of these opportunities to engage others in emotionally, intellectually, and sometimes even physically intimate contact.

But the Internet and the media are not the only ways 21st-century folks receive sexual stimulation. In just the last few decades, women's participation in the work force has skyrocketed. This trend alone results in significantly more intimate opportunities for both men and women. For some people, simply having access to others is a primary reason for having an affair. Affairs and intimate relationships cannot happen if there is no opportunity for them. Thus, men and women interacting regularly in sometimes confidential work situations results in many more prospects for everyone's sexual expression.

The feminist movement influences our intimate relationships in other ways as well. Women's evolution has itself presented more opportunity for the sexual expression of both men and women. As women have left behind a passive role in society, they are more actively seeking sexual relationships and a satisfying sex life. This shift means that women are now enthusiastically pursuing sexual relationships for the first time in history. With both sexes feeling comfortable initiating dating and sex, opportunities for intimate activity only increase for everyone.

The reasons we have sex are evolving, too. These numerous social changes have impacted our sex lives even more directly. Sex is not just about procreation anymore. In fact, evolutionary biologists suggest that if sex were only about reproduction, then the human body would have evolved very differently. They determine this by comparing the ways a human body functions to animals that have sex only to propagate their species. For example, if sex were only about procreation, then human females in heat would be easily identifiable—males would know automatically which females could be fertilized.[21] In this way, males would not be in a position to waste semen in a female who was unable to conceive. In addition, females would only be receptive to sex when they were fertile.[22] Otherwise, there would be no motivation for her to be sexual. In fact, she'd be actively motivated *not* to have sex at other times in order to avoid expending valuable energy on a meaningless task. However, this is obviously not typical intimate behavior for our species. Instead, humans endorse a variety of reasons for having sex, including for physical pleasure, to please their partner, to boost their self-esteem, and to enhance their emotional connection with their partner.[23] As our species evolves, the reasons to make love become more diverse. This wide variety of conscious motives for having sex make sexual relationships more complex, and make sexual monogamy that much more challenging.

The reality is that we live in a time of great social change. The strength of women, the increased opportunities for sexual activity because of women in the work force, developments in technology, and the changes in the media with regard to sexual expression all add up to a culture that is inundated with sexual stimuli and opportunity. These changes impact everyone's sex life in some way. As a result, we no longer have the luxury of ignoring key aspects of human sexual motivation such as our nonmonogamous instincts. In fact, consciously ignoring our sexual truths only makes humans more vulnerable to the opportunities and changes that are occurring around them. And research shows us this may be exactly what is happening. More people than ever are accessing pornography on the Internet.[24] The statistics on sexual affairs suggest that women are having more of them, rapidly approaching frequencies comparable to men.[25] Strip clubs are big business, as is prostitution. These more superficial expressions of sexuality upset many people, but they are not going away. People who develop a greater understanding of their sexuality may be better equipped to consciously deepen their sexual connection with one partner rather than disperse it in a multitude of directions—that is, to channel their sexual energies back into their intimate relationship if they so desire.

MARRIAGE—A GREAT IDEA

Marriage and monogamy exist because they are great ideas. Sexual monogamy offers real and significant rewards for those who practice it, as well as for our culture. The advantages to children are perhaps the most obvious. Children reared in two-parent homes enjoy numerous benefits. They tend to be better adjusted emotionally, intellectually, sexually, and physically. In contrast, children of divorced parents show greater challenges in all of these areas.[26] They reach puberty earlier, have sex sooner than their peers, and over time they have more sex partners.[27]

But children are not the only beneficiaries of monogamy. Mothers and fathers profit emotionally, physically, legally, and financially from marriage. They generally find co-parenting easier and more enjoyable than single-parenting from all these perspectives. Married people have less physical and emotional illness, and they practice healthier lifestyles.[28] Couples enjoy greater efficiency in their daily lives by dividing parenting, financial, and household responsibilities. The financial benefits of marriage are very real. The pooling of two people's resources enables everyone to enjoy a higher quality of life. Marriage also offers the potential of additional support from extended family members. In many ways, marriage provides a safe haven in an often overwhelming world. Within the safe confines of a sexually monogamous marriage, couples enjoy the comfort of a consistent, reliable partner dedicated to caring for them. People have the benefit of a live-in sexual partner. Socially, even our culture benefits from the institution of marriage. Without monogamy, venereal disease would become even more of a public health crisis than it already is. Yes, sexual monogamy in a long-term relationship is undoubtedly worth fighting for.

WHY WE HOLD ON

The reality of our nonmonogamous instincts isn't really earth-shattering information. We know we are descendents of more primal beings. We acknowledge that marriage is a legal concept, not necessarily an innate one. Most people at least recognize this possibility, all the while hoping that their marriage is somehow immune to the laws of nature. Why do we hold on so tightly to our monogamy illusion, even when we suspect it is not accurate?

First, because the reality that monogamy isn't natural doesn't mean there are great alternatives. There is no easy solution to the predicament our sexual instincts present. Many creative solutions have been tried and failed. Humans have experimented with a variety of alternatives to a sexually monogamous family unit—harems, communes, polyamory, and swinging, to name a few. While these approaches work for some people some of the time, none of them have provided a reasonable solution for the majority of couples.

Secondly, women are instinctively motivated to find a partner, nest, and have babies. If we expect that her marriage will split up after a few years, we acknowledge that families are often left in the lurch with a multitude of serious issues, including parenting and financial concerns. What a harsh realization! But in truth, this really does seem to be happening. People are marrying later in life and having more children outside of wedlock. For example, the majority of births to 20–24-year-olds are now outside of marriage![29] So, while out-of-wedlock birthing is the reality for many families today, it is certainly not the one most parents are hoping for when they start a family. In fact, "staying together for the children" is a primary reason cited by couples who have chosen to stay married even when they feel their marriages are failing.

Third, falling in love is a very powerful, magical experience. It is so all-consuming that it becomes hard to believe the feelings are temporary. It is easy for lovers to imagine they have found the special true love that everyone seeks, and that their relationship is unique and protected from a painful demise. Lovers want to believe that they will be able to maintain the intensity of their love over time. When a relationship is new, the sheer strength of the attraction allows couples to conclude that they can gain conscious control over their sexual selves and live happily ever after.

WHAT ABOUT THE CHILDREN?

Monogamy is obviously a provocative topic that elicits an emotional reaction from just about everyone. The question that gets raised more than any other relates to the impact on our children of embracing human nonmonogamous instincts. Certainly this is a challenging issue to explore. However, not dealing with it is no panacea because denial brings its own set of difficulties. That is, ignoring problems just gives them space to grow. Plus, not acknowledging our instincts leaves us less in tune with our own sexual nature. And we know that such a lack of self-awareness is never a place of personal strength.

Because we are not publicly acknowledging human nonmonogamous nature, children, young adults, and even mature adults are encouraged to believe an illusion about their bodies and their instincts. Young adults are encouraged to attempt to live up to sexual expectations that their parents themselves usually cannot meet. In this way, young people are set up to believe in a notion about intimacy that will only become more difficult to enact as time passes. That is because the sexualization of our culture is only intensifying, so sexual issues are even more apparent. Thus, what is a challenging struggle for parents will become in a few more decades an even greater struggle for growing children if they are not armed with the truth about their bodies. But there is an alternative. As our children grow into adulthood and fall in love, why not empower them with insight into the nature of their sexual urges? In this way, they may be more prepared for the challenges of intimacy that await them. Perhaps, armed with the truth, they will be in a better place to cooperate with their beloved and work together to create the life they envision for themselves and their family. Challenging? Of course. But the alternative of denial will probably not serve them any more than it did their parents. It appears to be time for a new approach.

SUPPORTING MONOGAMY

In sum, it is clear that there are many benefits to monogamy, even though this mating style contradicts many people's natural instincts. Monogamy is what the majority of couples want for themselves. On the bright side, humans have several natural inclinations that support monogamy. One is the desire to pair-bond with one romantic partner. Most humans start to experience this pull in adolescence. As their bodies awaken sexually, the evolutionary drive to pair up is intense and captivating. And secondly, most of us have an innate drive for long-term companionate love. That is, we have a strong longing to maintain our attachment over time. So in spite of our primal sexual instincts, we have two very powerful drives that support monogamy. In the next chapter, we will explore these issues further by reviewing current psychological thinking and research relating to our drive to love.

Chapter Two

HOW CHILDHOOD RELATIONSHIPS AFFECT ADULT SEXUALITY

Beth had been in therapy for several years before she called me at her therapist's suggestion. On the phone, Beth told me she had been in individual and couples therapy several times over the last six years to work on relationship issues with her husband Rob. She described her previous therapies as very helpful, but a major problem remained. In spite of all their work on communicating, and exploring issues from their childhoods that negatively impacted their intimate relationship, Beth still didn't want to have sex with Rob. Rob was at his wits' end. Their therapist wasn't sure how to proceed.

When I met with Beth for the first time, she was unsuccessfully trying to hold back tears. She clearly loved Rob, and Rob loved her. He was a good husband. They had two children and lived in a charming waterfront community. All appeared perfect to an outsider looking in. But Beth was struggling sexually, and she felt ashamed. Her gynecologist said her hormone levels looked fine. There was no physical reason for her lack of interest in sex. Beth wasn't sure how she would be able to keep her marriage together if something didn't change. She still had sex with Rob, but she didn't enjoy it. This fact was supremely evident to him, which made him lose interest in her. It was a bad situation that seemed to be getting worse as the years went by.

We started by reviewing the great work she had done with her last therapists. Beth described the different therapies she and Rob had tried. She had done individual therapy where they focused on what she learned about sex while growing up—including the negative messages she received from her family, and her first sexual experiences, which were uncomfortable for her. She and Rob did couples therapy with a focus on communication. They also worked with another therapist who focused on basic sex therapy techniques, such as sensual body massage (sensate focus), and then some work with fantasies. Beth then returned to her first therapist for a second round of individual therapy to address her body image issues and more unresolved feelings from her childhood that had gotten stirred up in their couple's therapy. She and Rob had done good personal growth work over the years. But sex remained an issue.

It quickly became clear to me that there was no longer any glaring psychological dysfunction for us to conquer. I suggested to Beth that her lack of interest in sex might be her natural instincts kicking in. We discussed the research indicating that monogamy isn't natural for all humans. Beth's eyes became wide and her speech more rapid. She acknowledged that she would probably feel interest in another man if she didn't feel so guilty about the thought of cheating on Rob. She thought she may even enjoy masturbating if she didn't feel uncomfortable when fantasizing about other men. She cried again, this time with relief that there was nothing inherently wrong with her. It was a powerful moment for us both.

For most of us, to love well is one of the greatest challenges of our lifetime. Like all goals worth attaining, loving well can be exhausting and unrelenting at times, both emotionally and physically. In Western culture, an important part of loving well is remaining faithful to one's partner. But loving an intimate partner is about much more than just being monogamous. Most of us consider monogamy a necessary, but not sufficient, aspect of a strong intimate relationship. Mature love is also about caring, compassion, understanding, and connection. Our ability to love strongly influences our desire for monogamy, and our skill at making relationships work. The way we attach emotionally with our partner affects relationship quality, which then impacts our sex life.[1]

While most mammals form some level of attachment to their parent (or primary caregiver) in infancy, humans are the only mammals that exhibit attachment behaviors in adult romantic relationships.[2] That is, swans and chimps and dogs have sex, but they do not fall in love, or make love. Only humans have this unique and powerful gift. Still, there is variability within the human capacity to love, emotionally and sexually. What enables some people to offer more warm, tender affection than others? What makes some men and women more successful at monogamy than others? Our answers to these questions have thus far primarily been found in psychological literature. From a psychological perspective, success with monogamy as an adult has largely been understood as an outgrowth of attachment history. That is, the quality of a child's attachment bond with parents impacts how they later experience love relationships as adults. However, as was evident in Beth and Rob's experience, this conceptualization of intimacy is often lacking, and patients are frequently left struggling with sexual issues.

In this chapter, we explore what psychology understands about the link between love, sex, and monogamy. First, we review what the major psychological theories suggest or imply regarding this complex interrelationship. In the second half of the chapter, we look at the current research findings on attachment and sexuality. Finally, we consider some of the ways these issues manifest sexually for couples attempting to maintain a passionate monogamous connection in a long-term relationship. It will become clear that no single psychological theory satisfactorily explains monogamous behavior in humans. Current research on attachment theory also fails to predict success with monogamy in long-term relationships. We will see that until human instinctual behavior is considered, our theories and research will not succeed in explaining all of humanity's complex sexual behavior. If you are a therapist, you'll enjoy this review of our current knowledge. If you are not a therapist, what follows may be a bit technical for your taste. But the subsequent chapters will help you digest this information and make it usable for your own sex life.

MAJOR PSYCHOLOGICAL THEORIES AND THEIR IMPLICATIONS FOR MONOGAMY

We traditionally turn to psychological theory to understand human sexual behavior, including monogamy. The primary theories that have influenced our interpretation of intimate behavior are identified below. This list is an attempt to review only the major theories that have impacted our mindset about intimacy and monogamy. It is not intended to be an exhaustive or comprehensive analysis. Instead, it is a very brief overview of the theoretical contributions to our current cultural mindset regarding monogamy.

Writing this section has been a challenging task because, for the most part, our psychological theories do not address monogamy directly. That is because throughout history, monogamy was assumed to be a natural, realistic, and necessary goal for intimate relationships. Failures of monogamy are therefore typically understood as pathology, and generally referred to as "intimacy issues" by the mental health professions. This conceptualization is certainly valid as a crucial component of monogamy, and it has served us well in our understanding of intimacy. However, we will also explore how our current theories fail to account for all of the challenges inherent in monogamous relationships.

To aid in understanding the differences among the theories, we will explore two failures of monogamy from each theory's perspective. The first example is Alex, a 45-year-old married man who frequents strip clubs without his wife's consent. While this is not technically an example of nonmonogamy, many married women consider this a clear breach of their marriage contract and a serious violation of trust. The second example is Claire, a 33-year-old married woman having an affair with a coworker.

Alex and Tamara were married 23 years and had three children. Alex was very proud of his family. He was a hard-working computer programmer and he made a good living. Alex loved his wife and he wanted more of a sex life with her. However, ever since their third child was born, Tamara seemed to have lost interest in sex. She had gained weight with each pregnancy and was self-conscious about her body. Alex didn't mind her additional weight, but she did. After some years of trying to resurrect their intimate life, Alex held less and less hope that their sex life would become fulfilling again. When they did have sex, Tamara was pretty motionless and uninterested. In the past, Alex had gone to strip clubs with his colleagues when on business trips. But in the last few years, he took to going more regularly after work, telling Tamara he had to work late. He tried not to think about it much to avoid feeling guilty. He knew Tamara would be very hurt if she found out, so he was careful to hide it from her.

Claire and Tim had been married three years. Claire wasn't yet sure about having children. She worked as an emergency room doctor and life was busy enough as it was. She had met Tim in medical school, and he was now a radiologist. Claire worked long shifts and she became close with the other physicians in the ER. Over time, Claire became more and more smitten by her colleague Steve. When they were working late one evening, Steve kissed her. Claire initially resisted him but found his touch alluring. She and Steve started meeting secretly after work. Before she knew it, she had fallen in love. But Claire still loved Tim and she didn't know what to do. She would tell herself to end it with Steve but then she'd see him and she'd forget her promises to herself. Claire was at a loss as to how to handle her situation.

PSYCHOANALYTIC THEORY

Psychoanalytic theory is the oldest psychological theory, developed by Sigmund Freud beginning in the late 1800s. Freud presented the first conceptualization of the psyche as being composed of both conscious and unconscious processes. He offered other innovative concepts as well, such as the belief that human personality develops in the first years of life. Freud hypothesized that humans are motivated by a drive toward pleasure. Biological needs, such as hunger and thirst, are thus primary motivators since their satiation offers much pleasure. Freud's pleasure principle also addressed the sexual drive, or libido, as a primary motivating force for children and adults. He recognized that libido is wild and primal. Freud believed that this animalistic sexual energy had to be appropriately managed and contained for a person to successfully negotiate intimate relationships.

Like his peers and followers, Freud assumed that monogamy was the obvious outcome of a healthy, mature intimate relationship. He believed that those who were unable to maintain monogamous relationships had difficulties resolving their sexual feelings toward their first romantic love—their mothers if they were male, or their fathers if they were female. Children's sexuality could thus become fixated at a developmental phase, leaving an adult unable to express mature sexuality with a monogamous partner. In the therapy room, challenges with monogamy could be resolved through the use of free association on the part of a therapy patient, and correct and timely interpretation on the part of the analyst. For example, Alex's regular attendance at a strip club could be traced back to his anger at a withholding mother which got transferred onto his wife. This anger was then expressed unconsciously by his degradation of women. Alternately, Alex may have felt so belittled by his father that he now felt unworthy of intimacy with a woman. He thus accepted only superficial intimacy through contact with women at strip clubs. Claire's sexual affair can be traced back to her emotionally unavailable father, who left her feeling empty and needy throughout her life. This resulted in an insatiable need as an adult for masculine attention and adoration.

Today varied theories exist as offshoots of psychoanalytic thought, including object relations and ego psychology. These theories maintain a common denominator that adult sexual relationships are significantly impacted by infants' and young children's experiences of relationships with their primary caregivers.

Psychodynamic theory has contributed much in our understanding of intimacy and sexuality. However, like all theories, it fails to explain the entire spectrum of issues relating to monogamy. For example, people can identify and resolve childhood emotional scars, yet still struggle with intimacy in relationships. Sometimes therapists are left wondering if there was repressed trauma in someone's past, as their history does not appear to support the level of sexual issues challenging a particular adult. Alternately, parent/child relationships are never perfect, so most adults carry some psychological wounds from childhood. However, not everyone feels challenged by intimacy. Thus, while psychodynamic theory offers us much in our understanding of adult sexuality, it does not offer an absolute explanation for the challenges of intimacy and monogamy in long term relationships.

BEHAVIORAL AND COGNITIVE-BEHAVIORAL PSYCHOLOGY

Behaviorism was developed in response to the deterministic views of psychoanalytic thought. Led by John Watson in the early decades of the 1900s, behaviorists hypothesized that any behavior could be learned through conditioning. That is, all behaviors were either reinforced with rewards and punishments, or learned through associations between two stimuli. In this viewpoint, internal mental states such as thoughts and emotions were inconsequential and could essentially be ignored. Decades later, cognitive-behavioral theory took strict behaviorism to a more complex level by addressing internal mental states, including thoughts and feelings. Cognitive-behavioral therapy employs techniques to assist people in logically evaluating and managing their thoughts and emotions.

A cognitive behaviorist could understand Alex's repeated trips to a strip club as inherently reinforcing—he enjoyed the attention of attractive women and the sexually stimulating atmosphere, and this enjoyment increased his chances of attending again. Claire's affair could be similarly conceptualized—she enjoyed the attention and affection of her lover, which reinforced her illicit behavior. These hypotheses do make sense, and are likely to play a significant role in human sexual expression. However, once again these theories do not account for all aspects of complex sexual behaviors. While Claire may find time with her lover to be inherently reinforcing, she is likely to experience other sensations that are much less positive—such as guilt, jealousy, or shame. Similarly, Alex may feel guilty knowing that his wife would consider his behavior a violation of their monogamous relationship, and he might also berate himself for the money he frivolously spends on women who are manipulating him for their financial gain. Yet both individuals continue to engage in these violations of monogamy. Behavioral and cognitive-behavioral theories neglect the impact of the unconscious mind, thus overlooking what many therapists understand as a missing link in conceptualizing unwanted or undesirable behaviors.

SOCIAL LEARNING THEORY

Social learning theories are based on the premise that humans learn via observation of the environment. This learning can take place in a variety of ways, and ultimately can translate into one's own thoughts, feelings, and behavior. Albert Bandura was a leading proponent of social learning theory in the 1980s. He stressed that learning could take place by watching actual role models, such as parents or sports figures, as well as through reading and pictures, such as information in the media. Like all behavior, sexual behaviors were learned through observation. A person's receptivity to learning was related to a variety of characteristics in the person as well as the learning stimulus. Bandura believed that not everything we observed would translate into learning, and just because something was learned didn't necessarily mean it was acted upon.

Social learning theory did not address the issue of monogamy per se. However, social learning theorists would stress that parents are children's primary role models with regard to sexual behavior. Modern social learning theorists would also address the increasingly sexualized media that children are now exposed to at very early ages. Alex could be seen as acting out an understanding of masculine sexuality learned from his father, peers, the Internet, and/or nightly TV—that men need a variety of sexual outlets and are rarely satisfied in monogamous relationships. Social learning theorists might understand Claire's affair in a similar way—perhaps the repeated sensual interaction with Steve, coupled with the fact that her friend was also having an affair, made this seem like a reasonable course of action for the moment.

Social learning theories have shed light on the ways we absorb learning, both consciously and unconsciously, from our surroundings. It has helped us understand the great importance our environment, including people other than parents, can play in the sexual learning process. Certainly the ways our families and culture depict the challenges of monogamy will affect each individual's experience of their intimate relationship. However, not all aspects of monogamy can be understood in this way. For example, there are many individuals who are surrounded by family and religious teachings in support of monogamy but who still fail to achieve this goal. In addition, anthropologists have shown us that monogamy is challenging for the vast majority of human cultures.[3] That fact alone means that the sexualized Western media, and thus social learning, is not the primary influence on adult attitudes and behaviors with regard to monogamy.

FAMILY SYSTEMS THEORY

Family systems theory understands an individual's behavior in relationship to the emotional system created and maintained by the family unit. Murray Bowen proposed this theory in the 1960s. Bowen was influenced by evolutionary theory in that he believed the goal of the family is ultimately the survival of its members. A family unit can be made up of two people in a committed relationship, or it may include other family members such as children, siblings, and parents. Bowen's theory also stresses the primacy of emotions in influencing human behavior. In family systems, the emotions of all family members are considered influential for each individual member. The family strives to reduce tension and maintain the stability of the family unit, and families engage in repetitive patterns in an effort to achieve these goals. Self-differentiation from the family is considered a key challenge in order for an individual to experience healthy, as opposed to enmeshed, relationships as adults. Achieving this level of differentiation is a lifelong effort for many couples. For example, when couples are not differentiated, men and women can become overly concerned with seeking approval or minimizing tension in the relationship, and not focused enough on their own sense of identity. Unhealthy dependencies and anger are often the result.

Unlike the other theories presented thus far, modern family systems theory does directly address the issue of fidelity in relationships.[4] From a family systems perspective, maintaining fidelity in a passionate committed relationship can be a major emotional challenge of adulthood. It is suggested that if a person has not differentiated appropriately from his family of origin, these issues will surface again in his marriage and have a negative impact on a couple's sex life. Family systems would conceptualize both Alex and Claire to be undifferentiated in their marriages. As a result of not feeling their identity within their partnership, they act out sexually. This serves a purpose in their psyche of expressing sexual feelings and behaviors that they are not bringing to the relationship. For example, for Alex it may be a way to express anger or assert his independence. For Claire, her affair may offer a safe place to be sexually open and vulnerable.

Family systems theory does offer tremendous wisdom and understanding for couples struggling with monogamy. However, without acknowledging that monogamy is unnatural for mammals, this approach still implies that with enough effort, couples can and perhaps should work to achieve it. But for some couples, this mental health goal of differentiation may be lofty and unrealistic. Thus, it may have the impact of adding pressure and shame for a couple already significantly challenged by the goal of monogamy. Many people do not have the financial and emotional resources, as well as the motivation for years of hard therapy work, to attempt self-differentiation. Most couples find themselves struggling with life, stressed and overwhelmed with too many priorities, and unable to do the therapeutic work to achieve differentiation. But perhaps more importantly, not all couples who create an emotionally individuated partnership feel sexual desire for each other. For some couples, no amount of therapeutic work makes monogamy a satisfying experience. In addition, when couples seek counseling to deal with sexual issues, it is probably rarely addressed that what they are attempting to do is not necessarily natural.

ATTACHMENT THEORY

Attachment theory was developed in the 1950s by John Bowlby. Attachment theory conceptualizes adult intimate behavior as the by-product of early attachment relationships with primary caregivers. Bowlby proposed that love/ attachment and sexuality are overlapping but separate systems within the human psyche. He suggested that they interrelate to such a degree that they can be difficult to tease apart. Each system shifts in importance and influence depending on a person's developmental stage and environment. Bowlby believed that both of these systems are instinctually based, serving the evolutionary function of survival and ultimately the propagation of our species. In order to stay alive, an infant must have a relationship with her caregiver. To meet her survival needs, an infant develops one of several relationship strategies based on her caregiver's behavior. Many scientists believe that the infant starts to learn within the first few months after birth which attachment strategies offer her the most protection from adversity combined with the most receptivity to available rewards. In fact, some researchers believe the infant receives cues about the environment in utero, and thus begins this process even before birth. Attachment theorists have identified two basic classifications of strategies, hyperactivating and deactivating. Hyperactivating strategies involve moving toward the parent or love object. This movement involves any strategy of reaching out, emotionally or physically, to get the care needed to survive. Deactivating strategies create distance with the love object. The goal of a deactivating strategy is to not agitate or irritate the caregiver and thus encourage the caregiver's support.

Attachment behaviors are further classified into four main subtypes: secure, avoidant/dismissing, anxious/preoccupied, and disorganized. If a child experiences an attentive, loving caregiver who is attuned and responsive to her needs—particularly in times of stress—then she grows up to be a securely attached adult. Securely attached adults have the most stable intimate relationships, both emotionally and sexually. It is estimated that approximately 60 percent of adults are securely attached.[5] Alternately, children whose parents are unavailable, unreliable, or hurtful develop emotional strategies to cope with these challenges. These relationship strategies are generally classified as avoidant, anxious, or disorganized attachment styles. Children become avoidantly attached with their caregivers when they use emotional detachment to cope. That is, they attempt to disconnect emotionally from their caregiver in an effort to protect themselves from rejection and emotional pain. Anxious attachment results in children being emotionally or physically needy or clinging to caregivers. These children respond to discomfort in their primary relationships by grasping at their parents. Disorganized attachment results when a child's relationships are a chaotic mix of anxiety and avoidance. These children want closeness and fear it at the same time. We will explore attachment styles more in depth later in this chapter.

Clearly, each of these attachment styles significantly impacts an adult's sexual style and relationship. A likely understanding of Alex might be that he was avoidantly attached to his partner and found sexual gratification comfortable only when there was no emotional relationship involved—such as in a strip club. Claire would probably be considered anxiously attached—vulnerable to seeking approval and love from another partner because she constantly felt needy and unfulfilled in her committed relationship.

Attachment theory has offered much to our understanding of adult sexual relationships. While this theory does not explore the challenge of monogamy directly, issues of fidelity are addressed. Like family systems theory, attachment theory was greatly influenced by evolutionary theory and an understanding of basic emotional instincts that support survival. However, as with the other psychological theories discussed thus far, biological sexual instincts have been largely ignored by attachment literature.

EVOLUTIONARY PSYCHOLOGY

Evolutionary psychology offers the most recent theory (of those we are reviewing here) to hit the psychological scene. Adapted from evolutionary theory, it does not offer a detailed psychological perspective such as those explained above. Instead, it suggests a broader approach to understanding human behavior from an instinctual, survival perspective. That is, all human behavior is believed to be an adaptation to the environment with the goal of perpetuating our genes.

Evolutionary theory, and in particular the concept of natural selection, was developed by Charles Darwin in the late 1850s. After studying a variety of animals, he determined that all characteristics of a species could be understood in their relationship to survival of the organism. Those traits or behaviors that increased the chances of survival would be naturally selected, or inherited, from generation to generation. Darwin determined that natural selection occurs when an inherited trait results in enhanced reproductive success. Thus his theory eventually evolved to encompass not just species survival but successful mating strategies—also referred to as sexual selection. It was determined that the goal of mating was of primary importance because successful mating behavior was required for gene propagation. Thus, it is ultimately those traits that support successful mating which have the highest likelihood of being passed on from generation to generation. In a sense, Darwin cut through all the secondary explanations of human characteristics, behaviors, and emotions. He offered us a bottom line: if it assists with mating, the trait will continue—and in fact gain momentum—with time.

Modern evolutionists refine Darwin's ideas. They work to explain traits that seem to survive natural selection processes yet appear to oppose species survival—such as overeating in humans, or with regard to sex, females not always orgasming during intercourse. Some traits are considered old adaptations that are misplaced in today's environment, while others are believed to be mutations. One current evolutionist suggests that the cutthroat competition for survival actually takes place at a level even more microscopic than reproduction—at the level of the genes themselves.[6]

Today, researchers are demonstrating that our lives, including our sex lives, are actually much more influenced by instincts and sexual selection than we previously realized. As we will discuss in chapter 4, instincts play a role in everything from the amount we tip to the foods we choose to eat. For example, strippers that are ovulating make more tips then strippers not ovulating.[7] This means that men unconsciously find ovulating women more alluring! This innate knowing enables a man to identify the most fertile women to copulate with, thus increasing the odds that he will pass on his genes. But men are not alone in their ability to make instinctual judgments about the opposite sex. Women demonstrate their own instinctual sexual selection techniques. For example, when ovulating, women rate photographs of men high in testosterone as more attractive. This is because men whose testosterone levels are high also tend to have strong immune systems. Men who have strong immune systems are likely to offer high-quality sperm. Thus, women instinctively prefer men with strong immune systems during the fertile time of their menstrual cycle.[8]

Returning to Alex and Claire, evolutionary psychology would offer a unique understanding of their sexual exploits. Alex would find his behavior compelling because he is instinctively oriented to find fertile, receptive, physically healthy women alluring. Such women would likely be the most willing to mate, and also be in the best position to become pregnant and carry on the species. Alex's mating goal would probably be unconscious, but still influential in his behavior. Claire's affair could be understood as her attempt to "mate up" and become impregnated with the highest-quality genetics available to her.[9] In contrast to men, who tend to have affairs with all types of women, women almost exclusively have affairs with men they consider to be socially, physically, or emotionally more dominant than their partner. In sum, consciously or not, women want to mate with more dominant men, while men are more concerned with mating young, fertile women.[10]

Of course, there is much more to us than our biology. Our instincts may set us up for certain behavioral patterns, but we also have conscious, higher-level processing brains that are capable of self-control and creative adaptations to instincts and needs. Our frontal lobes and ability for conscious thought set us apart from all other species on the planet. These abilities play a huge role in who we are as human beings. It is impossible to imagine that the *only* reason a man would attend a strip club is to gawk at fertile women, and the *only* reason a woman would have an affair is to gain access to higher-quality sperm. No, these would certainly not be complete explanations for Alex's and Claire's behavior. But for many men and women, they are nonetheless influential—important enough to be considered as one piece of the puzzle in our quest to understand people's complex and often inappropriate sexual behavior.

WHAT ANTHROPOLOGY HAS TO SAY

Dr. Helen Fisher is a modern-day anthropologist who offers a fascinating theory of love. She explains that love is actually a complex neurochemical process with three distinct stages—sex drive, attraction, and attachment—that occur in a predictable sequence. Dr. Fisher hypothesized that these phases are distinct, biologically based evolutionary processes. She came to that conclusion after identifying similar trends among peoples of various cultures, and observing actual brain changes on MRI scans in individuals actively experiencing these different phases of love. She suggests that love occurs in stages because it supports procreation and the continuation of our species.

Dr. Fisher explains that sex drive is the inherent drive to have sex, and it is the initial stage or precursor to attachment. It is experienced by humans primarily during the fertile years of life. Sex drive varies in intensity from person to person, but is part of a human's biological makeup. This drive to procreate ensures the survival of our species.

Attraction is the second stage of love. It occurs when an individual identifies someone with whom he wants to be intimate. We call this phase of love *lust*. It is that intoxicating combination of feelings and sensations that occur when falling in love. Brain scans reveal that attraction has an impact on the brain comparable to cocaine or stimulants.

The third phase of love is attachment, or companionate love. This is the stage of love addressed by the theories presented at the beginning of this chapter. Attachment is the experience of longer-term bonding with another in a nurturing, safe, stable, loving connection. It is this stage that couples transition into if/when the exciting lustful attraction phase comes to an end, which according to one MRI study it seems to do for about 90 percent of couples.[11] A loving bond and a passionate bond are two different neurochemical events, each able to exist independently of the other. Attachment results in a secure, predictable, supportive love environment.

Dr. Fisher's research is compatible with many people's experience of love. The first stage, sex drive, has a natural ebb and flow within each person. It tends to diminish at times, such as for a woman after giving birth, or after menopause. Men generally seem to have a stronger natural sex drive than women which is likely to be an evolutionarily selected trait.[12] For both women and men, sex drive may be reduced by a variety of factors, such as stress, depression, medications, and painful emotions such as anger. I coauthored a book, *Reclaiming Desire: 4 Keys for Finding Your Lost Libido*, which explores women's relationship to their sex drive in much more detail.

The second phase, attraction, is the result of a complex neurotransmitter brain bath. It is experienced as an emotional state specific to the person we love rather than a neurochemical state supported by our biology. It is such a strong sensation that it feels like it will never end. It has a natural several-year course,[13] and couples are shocked when their brains return to normal homeostasis and their intense attraction diminishes over time. Unlike sex drive, which tends to appear stronger in men, both men and women seem to have relatively equal predispositions for attraction. It is attraction that becomes the glue that keeps a couple intimately connected for at least a few years. From an evolutionary perspective, this means that a man is oriented to remain a part of the family unit long enough to support a woman and child until the child becomes at least a toddler, able to move about without assistance.[14]

Attraction can be emphasized and supported over time. Sadly, attraction suffers when individuals do not care well for themselves and their intimate relationship. As a result, if couples aren't actively working to support their levels of attraction, their sexual experience tends to wane. The second half of this book is dedicated to teaching you how to consciously manipulate this instinctual attraction process so that you can maintain an exciting sexually monogamous intimate relationship over time.

The third stage of love, attachment, provides the bond that keeps couples together over time. Women seem to be particularly oriented toward this phase of love. That is probably because women tend to be the primary caregivers of children, and thus the female brain more easily and comfortably rests in this state of stable, nurturing connection. We see this difference between men and women acted out with matrimonial engagements. Women more stereotypically seek marital commitments, while men often seem less persistent about making intimate relationships legally binding. It has been suggested that men are less naturally inclined toward attachment because of their innate, unconscious desire to sexually engage a variety of partners, thus shuffling DNA and mixing up the gene pool.[15] Paradoxically, just as women are more likely to initiate marriage, they are also more likely to instigate divorce.[16] This may be because women are more sensitive to the quality of their attachment relationship, and thus more apt to feel the impact if a relationship deteriorates emotionally over time.

Some couples make the transition from an attraction-driven intimacy to a more emotionally bonded connection with little difficulty. Sometimes their work or family responsibilities simply take precedence over their intimate relationship. For other couples, physical expression of their love is simply less important than other forms of intimacy. However, in many couples, one or both spouses feel the loss of their lusty union. It is these couples who find themselves less sexually satisfied, and who are likely to benefit the most from the second part of this book.

Anthropological theories offer interesting additions to psychological theories. However, they neglect to account for how each individual's psyche and personal history contributes to sexual behavior. For example, in returning to Claire and Alex, anthropologists might suggest that Alex's tendency to frequent strip clubs offers him an outlet for his sex drive that wasn't being met at home. He and his wife experienced attachment love but Tamara didn't enjoy making love. They also would say that because humans are oriented toward serial monogamy, perhaps Alex and his wife were avoiding intimacy altogether for fear they would feel their lack of passion more acutely and decide to separate. Neither of them wanted to end their marriage and break up their family. Anthropologists would say that Claire and her husband were experiencing companionate love as well. But Claire longed to feel the lusty thrill of attraction, and found this intoxicating sensation with her lover.

SUMMING IT UP—A THEORY OF REALISM

In sum, each of these theories stands on its own in deepening our understanding of human behavior and sexuality. However, no single theory is capable of explaining all of humanity's complex behavior—sexual or otherwise. In reality, most therapists are well aware of this fact, and as a result, the majority consider themselves to be eclectic in their therapeutic style. This basically means they take what they consider to be the best of every theory and combine the information creatively for each client's unique needs. However, despite access to numerous insightful psychological theories, therapists still struggle in assisting their clients with the challenges of intimacy. Clients still divorce, have affairs, or remain monogamous in sexless marriages. Clearly, in spite of our best efforts, we are still missing key information about sex in long-term relationships.

Enter instincts. Even though our sexual instincts are inconvenient at best, and destructive at worst, they should not be ignored or underestimated in our understanding of human sexual behavior. We do not attempt to override other basic animal instincts—such as a woman's drive to have a baby. In fact, we often encourage this mating instinct, even when it flies in the face of reason. "There's never a good time to have a baby, you just do it" is common cultural wisdom. I am not at all suggesting that our instincts toward nonmonogamy ought to be supported in the way we support and even encourage pregnancy. These are very different instincts, with hugely different implications. I am, however, suggesting that human instincts are very real and powerful, and we cannot continue to ignore sexual instincts as a pivotal motivator of human behavior.

RESEARCH: INTIMACY, SEXUALITY, AND MONOGAMY

We've just reviewed what the major psychological theories suggest about monogamy and mating behavior. Now we will review the current psychological research relating to these themes. While monogamy itself has not been a popular research topic, intimacy and attachment have caught researcher's attention for decades. Below is a brief summary of the current knowledge of themes indirectly related to monogamy. We will then explore possible associations between this research and monogamy.

ATTACHMENT, FIDELITY, AND ROMANTIC LOVE

In spite of the dictionary definition of monogamy that we discussed in chapter 1, when we speak of monogamy we are typically referring to faithfulness to one sexual partner. But most applicable psychological research regarding fidelity relates to issues of emotional attachment, that is, the study of how infants initially attach to caregivers, and how this translates later in life into emotional intimacy between adults. At this time we are only able to make indirect links and inferences regarding how childhood emotional experiences relate to monogamy in adulthood. I highlight attachment research here because of the quantity of relevant psychological research available as well as clinicians' general recognition that attachment theory offers rich information about adult sexual behavior.

Attachment research is based on the premise that adults project their original family issues onto their romantic partner. To review, there are four major attachment styles: secure, avoidant, anxious, and disorganized. Of course, adult attachment is quite complex, so this link is not direct or clearly evidenced in our existing research. For example, people don't respond the same way in all their relationships. A person can appear securely attached with one partner but anxiously attached with another. In addition, it appears that stress can mediate whether a child's attachment style is carried into adulthood. Healing experiences can lead to emotional growth with time, just as traumatic experiences can lead to emotional decompensation. As a result, more recent theorists have suggested that these subtypes are oversimplified, and perhaps more accurate is a classification based on two dimensions: avoidance and anxiety.

Secure adults score low on both anxiety and avoidance. Securely attached children feel loved, valued, and respected by their parents. They trust that the world is generally a safe place. These children mature into adults who are trusting of their romantic partner. They expect love and adult attachments to feel good, and they reach toward their partner to give and receive love.

> Sara and Don were celebrating another anniversary—the years were starting to add up! Sara was proud of her marriage and her family. She and Don had succeeded in creating a warm family environment similar to that of her childhood. As Sara and Don toasted each other, they talked about some of the ups and downs in their lives together. They had come through a lot—the challenges of rearing twins, their mutual dissatisfaction in their marriage which led to a course of couples therapy, and their family business failing. Nonetheless, Sara felt optimistic about where they were headed. She believed that they could weather any storm.

Securely attached people approach their intimate relationships with a sense of empowerment and trust.

Avoidantly attached people score high on dismissing/avoidant and low on anxiety. Avoidantly attached adults expect intimacy to feel uncomfortable, as it did when they were younger. They may have had parents who were emotionally unavailable and thus never taught them the skills to love others. Alternately, they could have had a parent who was enmeshed and demanding, leaving them experiencing intimacy as a burden and not worth the effort. For example, Bill is a 40-year-old single male:

> Life as a child was not easy for Bill. His father was frequently away on business trips, leaving him alone with his mother for weeks at a time. Bill's mother was lonely and she relied on Bill for emotional support, even when he was very young. Bill came to feel that intimacy with a woman was taxing and burdensome. As an adult, he preferred to keep his relationships with women light and superficial. Sex for Bill wasn't an emotional connection, but more of a physical release. When his partner showed signs of wanting more with him, he moved on. Bill liked sex, but it certainly wasn't worth the struggles of intimacy to have it.

Avoidantly attached people distance themselves from others in intimate re-lationships.

Anxiously attached folks are high on anxiety and low on avoidance. They seek committed relationships and they relish attention. They can be needy and demanding of their partners, requiring reassurance because of their abandon-ment fears. As children, they may have perceived their parents as unavailable or undependable. This lack of emotional connection continues to be perceived in adult relationships as well. Leslie is an example of an anxiously attached woman:

> Leslie grew up in a busy household run by parents who owned a small business. Her parents worked long hours and Leslie often spent her afternoons in their office, wait-ing for one of her parents to take her home and make dinner. Leslie tried to get their attention by misbehaving or crying but it rarely worked. As an adult, Leslie longed for a lasting intimate relationship although her clinginess made relationships tricky for her lovers. When she did get married, Leslie had difficulty trusting her husband. Her constant questions and demands for his attention stressed their intimate con-nection. When she was worried about their relationship, Leslie would use sex to re-connect. When their sex life was going well, Leslie felt more confident of her husband's love. When her husband was working late, Leslie would have fantasies about having an affair with a neighbor who at least was around in the evenings.

Anxiously attached people reach out to their partners, but sometimes in a smothering way.

Disorganized individuals are high on both anxiety and avoidance. Disorga-nized attachment is the challenging state of both longing for love and fearing it. These children were significantly troubled by fears of being hurt by their primary caregiver, coupled with a longing for closeness and love. Adults with disorganized attachment still long for intimacy but they don't experience oth-ers as safe and trustworthy. Meet Mark, a 29-year-old engineer:

> Mark grew up with a depressed, alcoholic mom. Mark felt he couldn't initiate much interaction with his mother for fear she'd berate him for bothering her. As a result, Mark spent much of his childhood alone in his bedroom. As an adult, Mark longed to get married and have a family, but he had difficulty opening up to women out of fears of being rejected. He wasn't very comfortable in social situations so it was hard for him to meet people. When Mark did marry, he remained emotionally distant from his wife in spite of his desire to be close to her. Making love was challenging for him because of his anxieties about pleasing his wife, coupled with his fears about being close to her. Mark rarely initiated sex due to fears of rejection. Additionally, Mark felt inadequate about how to be a good lover.

Disorganized adults want to reach out but have a very difficult time doing so.

ATTACHMENT AND SEXUAL BEHAVIOR

Researchers have identified correlations between attachment styles and certain sexual behaviors. This research does not address monogamy directly. However, it does offer further insight into our understanding of adult sexual behavior.

Securely attached adults are believed to be the most comfortable with intimacy and closeness. Of all the attachment styles, they are most apt to perceive their mate as dependable and their relationships as safe and secure. Thus, securely attached people are probably most able to weather the pain that is unavoidable in love relationships. I tell my patients that if they are loving well, their relationship will occasionally bring them to their knees. People with secure attachment are more likely to tolerate this level of tension. Secure adults approach intimacy from an "I'm okay, you're okay" perspective. They are less likely to have sex outside of their relationship. Plus, they are also most likely to enjoy bodily contact that is both physical, such as cuddling and holding, and sexual.[17] They are probably more emotionally mature, a key ingredient for satisfying long-term intimate connection. Maturity allows people to show up and be seen more fully, as well as see their partners for who they are—both their light and dark sides. Mature passion is so ecstatic because people feel seen and loved anyway, in spite of their very human flaws. Finally, securely attached people are probably most suited to enjoy the sexual emotions like passion and longing because they are less threatened by emotional intensity.

Preoccupied/anxiously attached adults exhibit an "I'm not okay, I need you" attitude in their intimate relationships. They desire sexual closeness but this is often in a bid for security rather than a desire for sexual connection.[18] Preoccupied/anxiously attached adults have low self-esteem. They can become dependent on their romantic partners, but at the same time have difficulty trusting them. They may be hypervigilant about a partner's behavior, which can result in even more tension between the two partners. The anxiously attached are overreactive to situations that represent a perceived challenge or threat to their intimate connection. These individuals experience their sexual bond with their partners as a strong indication of their relationship's quality,[19] and they are more likely to have sex to please their partners.[20] Thus, preoccupied/anxiously attached adults are more prone to using sex to increase closeness,[21] and less likely to have sex for physical pleasure.[22] Preoccupied women may be more likely to have affairs, probably because of their high need for approval and attention, and their tendency to seek support from people outside of their romantic relationship. They are also attracted to more intense sexual practices such as exhibitionism, voyeurism, and domination/bondage, as well as the more intimate aspects of sex like touching, and kissing.[23] Preoccupied men tend to have less frequent sexual activity than their more secure counterparts.[24] Their nediness seems to interfere with their sexual longing. Because of their tendencies toward dependency, they may be more interested in long-term relationships.[25] Anxiously attached people tend to exhibit more of the personality traits that predispose people to be attracted to others, which are a high desire for intimacy, low self-esteem, and high sociability.[26] Anxiously attached people may crave and/or find comfort in sexual emotions like passion, but have a harder time managing the tension and anxiety inherent in longing.

Dismissing/avoidantly attached men and women tend to be mistrusting of others and prefer distance in their romantic relationships. They have more difficulty with commitment as they perceive less value for themselves in intimate relationships. They approach relationships more from an "I'm okay, you're not safe" viewpoint. Dismissing/avoidant individuals may be less comforted by touch as an intimate exchange. However, they may be more likely to engage in extramarital sex and one-night stands as these outlets offer sexual contact without intense emotional connection. They seem to have the most difficulty integrating sexual feelings and loving feelings toward their spouses. They are more attracted to solitary sexual activities, such as masturbation[27] and nonintimate sexual experiences.[28] They will have sex for motives that use others, such as to gain power or status.[29] Avoidantly attached adults would find the sexual emotions of passion and longing threatening and uncomfortable.

People with a disorganized attachment style are the most challenged by intimate relationships. They have the low self-esteem of anxiously attached folks, and lack trust and feelings of safety with others similar to avoidantly attached individuals. Thus they exhibit many of the characteristics of both anxiously attached and avoidantly attached people. They exhibit an "I'm not okay, you're not safe" perspective on intimate relationships. They do long for touch and love like anxiously attached individuals, but they lack healthy strategies for negotiating intimate relationships. For example, they have difficulty conversing in social situations, and thus communicating in intimate situations is that much more challenging for them. Disorganized adults would probably find the sexual emotions of passion and longing overwhelming, as they might feel threatened by these feelings and be the least equipped people to cope with them.

IMPLICATIONS FOR MONOGAMY

It is likely that attachment styles influence people's interest in monogamy and their ability to remain faithful. However, more research is needed before we can make definitive statements in this arena. It seems likely that attachment styles may correlate with the reasons people either enjoy monogamous relationships, or choose affairs. For example, secure adults could enjoy monogamy because of the potential for deep intimacy. But, they could also have an affair because they fall in love without intending to. Avoidant individuals might take pleasure in monogamy if their partners are comfortably distant and give them emotional space. But, they might seek one-night stands as a way to get anonymous sexual release. Anxiously attached people may prefer monogamy because it allows them to develop an intense emotional connection. But they could have an affair to bolster their self-esteem. Finally, disorganized people might favor monogamy because it enables them to feel more secure with their loved ones. At the same time, they might seek a prostitute to experience sexual pleasure without an emotional attachment.

Thus, there are numerous reasons why people choose monogamy, and countless reasons people don't. Attachment styles are one important variable playing a role in these decisions. In my working with many couples over the years, it appears difficult for people to predict how monogamy will feel to them as the years go by. I have worked with many people who were in love and determined to be monogamous, but were unsuccessful at achieving their goal. Some people seem to become more in touch with their sexual instincts with time, others much less so. Others are more vulnerable to influences in the environment and outside opportunities. Some individuals value the security of a long-term relationship more than the passion of a new love. Others value passion more than security. People change and grow with time, and so do their preferences and desires. Indeed, predicting monogamous behavior is a very complex, if not impossible, task.

WHAT IS PROBABLY TRUE: HOW ATTACHMENT CAN SUPPORT MONOGAMY

While attachment research does not address monogamy directly, we can use the above research to make some educated guesses about how attachment tendencies can support the goal of monogamy. First, for many people, a satisfying sexual relationship is largely dependent upon their own ability to attach and love. Thus, men and women who wish to enjoy monogamy will be well served by resolving any emotional residue that interferes with their ability to give and receive love. Second, most people usually need to feel intimate with their partner in order to enjoy passionate monogamy in a long-term relationship. When people avoid intimacy, sex becomes rote and boring. For most of us, allowing loved ones to come close involves a constant effort to stay open and accessible to our partners. Third, our ability to know and love ourselves is necessary for enjoying a deep passionate connection with another. It is only in being comfortable with oneself that surrendering to one's passion and one's partner is possible. Finally, secure attachment is largely based on feelings of security and stability. Passion, in contrast, is based on novelty, adventure, and the unknown. This inherent conflict can present challenges for couples wishing to maintain a satisfying monogamous relationship. Finding the delicate balance that allows both forces to flow is an ongoing endeavor. It is my hope that the second part of this book will assist couples in achieving just that.

Chapter Three

THE HUMAN SEXUAL ANIMAL: HOW OUR BRAINS AND BIOLOGY AFFECT INTIMACY

Sex is the original mind-body experience. No experience so profoundly integrates our body and biology with our thoughts and feelings. Considering how many systems feed into a single act of making love, it is amazing that we succeed as often as we do. But Mother Nature has made sex pleasurable so that we feel compelled to keep having it. In this chapter, we explore those aspects of our biology that influence our desire for sex, and how these may relate to monogamy.

It is important to note that this chapter necessarily oversimplifies an exceedingly complex interplay between the body, brain, and environment. Attempting to clarify what we know inevitably results in errors and misunderstandings, because the complex business of the body lends itself poorly to concrete generalizations. For example, it is almost impossible to tease out the role of culture from the role of biology.[1] That is because cultures of people pass on similar genetic adaptations to their environment. This makes it difficult to determine if a particular behavior pattern is biologically based, or is environmentally based and stems from societal morals.

Similarly, the argument of nature versus nurture is outdated—it's more how nature and nurture intermingle to produce sexual feelings and behavior. For example, romantic relationships can trigger changes in the endocrine balance of the brain, just as hormones and neurotransmitters can trigger changes in romantic relationships. In our attempts to simplify this discussion by making it a black and white issue, we risk a loss of accuracy.

The attachment literature that we explored in chapter 2 approaches the concept of monogamy differently than the biological perspective we are now reviewing. For the most part, the attachment literature assumes that monogamy is how emotionally healthy people conduct relationships. A long-term monogamous relationship is considered the natural, mature goal for adult intimacy. We now turn to a school of thought that works from a different set of assumptions. While biological researchers may agree that a long-term monogamous relationship is a desirable goal for intimate relationships, they generally do not consider this a natural—or even expected—process for humans. Instead, the brain and body researchers tend to recognize our physiology as strikingly similar to that of our primate cousins. They explain human sexual behavior with words like "oriented towards monogamy," "generally monogamous," or "monogamous with occasional intimate relationships on the side." These are gentle terms that nonetheless acknowledge the harsh reality that humans are not naturally monogamous for a lifetime.

We now explore the various ways biologists, zoologists, endocrinologists, and neuropsychiatrists relate the brain and body to human sexuality.

THE BRAIN AND SEX

In many ways, our brains really are our most powerful sex organ. Making love is a brain experience first, before it becomes a genital experience. This means that our brains receive and react to stimuli before our genitals have the opportunity to respond. In fact, the genitals receive marching orders from the brain. Remarkably, in spite of our impressive neurological development, many aspects of the human brain still resemble those of chimps—particularly the areas devoted to the more basic drives and instincts such as arousal, homeostasis, and—you guessed it—reproduction. For many of us, this fact creates mayhem in our minds, and sometimes even in our sexual relationships.

One neurologist, Dr. Paul MacLean, constructed a simplified theory that explains human brain development in relation to evolution. This *triune brain theory* defines three basic brain structures and explains how they developed sequentially over time to sustain the evolution of modern man.[2] These three brain systems include the reptilian brain, the limbic system, and the neocortex. Each brain region has its own purpose and ambition distinct from the others. And since these systems can work in conjunction but not necessarily in agreement with each other, their agendas can and often do clash as humans go about the business of daily living. The unfortunate result is that one part of the brain may strongly encourage a particular goal (such as monogamy), while another part of the brain promotes an altogether different plan with an equal amount of gusto.

The reptilian brain is the oldest and least evolved area of our brain. It is command central for vital functions that do not require conscious control such as breathing, balance, basic reproduction, and muscle tone. Because it assists with self-preservation and aggression, it actually can have a significant amount of influence over our behavior. It processes information much faster than the more evolved areas of our brain. For example, it takes 500–600 milliseconds for our neocortex to consciously process an experience. In contrast, our reptilian brain can process a potential threat in about 20 percent of that time![3] Thus, well before we are consciously aware of a potentially threatening situation, our primitive brain has already processed it and initiated a reaction.

The second area of the brain to develop evolutionarily is the limbic system. This comprises the emotional areas of the brain, including emotions relating to sex and attachment. The limbic system is ultimately concerned with the avoidance of pain and the repetition of pleasure.

Finally, our modernized neocortex encompasses our higher cortical processes. This is where we analyze, synthesize, and organize information. It is our language center and it helps us plan for the future—including planning for sex. Luckily for us it represents the vast majority of our brain space. Our superior brain development is what sets us apart from other animals and makes us human. However, it creates unique challenges for us when it clashes with the best-laid plans of our more primitive brain.

When people fall in love, they enjoy the luxury of all brain centers working together toward common goals—sex, attachment, and probably monogamy. In this situation, their reptilian drive for reproduction matches their limbic system's desire for a particular partner, which complements the neocortex's plans for marriage and monogamy. However, an example of dissension among the parts of the triune brain is related to expectations of sexual pleasure. The expectation of a reward from sex—whether it be in physical pleasure, romantic connection, or stress relief—occurs in the limbic region, an area of the brain that is outside of conscious control. Thus, we humans can't consciously decide what will feel rewarding and pleasurable to us. Instead, our brains respond to rewards in spite of our conscious intentions. For example, a young woman cannot find medical school rewarding just because her parents find the thought of her being a physician rewarding. While her parents may feel much pleasure from contemplating her impending profession, and she can logically acknowledge the benefits of this choice for her future, she cannot make herself feel pleasure about it. A similar kind of dilemma can happen with regard to sex—just because we *want* sex with a particular person to feel pleasurable, doesn't mean that it *will* feel this way. This helps to explain why someone, in spite of consciously wanting to make love to a partner, may not find the experience enjoyable or rewarding.

Of course, sexual behavior is complex and multidetermined. Brain biology is not the only explanation for behavior. But it does represent one piece of the monogamy puzzle that therapists and researchers are attempting to unravel. The choice to remain monogamous is *impacted* by brain structures, although clearly not *determined* by them. Each individual must weigh conscious intentions and beliefs about monogamy against unconscious sexual impulses generated by the reproductive desires of their reptilian brain. In recognizing this process, it becomes easier to understand how conscious intentions can mutate into the complex sexual behaviors of adulthood.

THE BODY AND MONOGAMY

We can garner clues about a species' mating habits just by looking at their bodies. This is because certain parallels exist among the physiques of animals that are generally monogamous as opposed to those who are polygynous. (Scientists typically consider polygyny, or a male mating with several females, as the opposite of monogamy since polygyny is so very prevalent in mammalian species). Animals that are more dimorphic, or exhibit obvious distinctions between the males and females of the species, tend to be more polygynous. For example, animals in which the males are significantly larger in stature than females are considered more dimorphic. In these species, the male's size appears to serve a variety of functions. For example, it supports mate competition in that the largest and strongest males typically gain access to the most sexual partners, thus passing on their genes to future generations. In this way, the strongest males generate the most offspring.

On the other hand, more monogamous species tend to be less dimorphic—that is, males and females are more similar in appearance. In some animals, it can be challenging to tell the males and females apart. In these species, males and females have more equal access to prospective mates—that is, one male mates with only one female and vice versa. Male size is less important because male-to-male competition is not as much of an issue since mates are chosen once in a lifetime.

So the obvious question is, are humans considered dimorphic? And the general scientific consensus is, sort of.[4] An unsatisfying conclusion, but realistic nonetheless. In sum, human males are moderately larger than females. This means that humans are considered to be less oriented toward monogamy than we have tended to believe.

It has been noted that the human male and female size difference has been slowly depreciating in the last several thousand years. That is, men and women are gradually becoming less dimorphic. This would support the notion that our culture is transitioning from polygamy (having more than one sexual partner at a time) to monogamy. A transition to monogamy from polygamy could make sense in that monogamy ensures that infants receive more paternal care when they are in their most vulnerable stages of life. Interestingly, in support of this theory, it is speculated that growth of technology reduces the value of sexual dimorphism in our culture.[5] This is because different masculine and feminine skill sets are not required in a social system that is not based on hunting and gathering. If it were the case that we are a species in transition toward monogamy, then sexual selection for unique traits of masculine and feminine—that is, the traits of dimorphism—would be less imperative for the survival of the species. Ultimately then, the traditional traits such as muscle strength in men and nurturing in women could be more equally shared between the sexes. This fascinating concept of a human transition toward monogamy remains controversial, and it certainly will be many years before the answer is evident.

Body size differences are not the only biological indicator of the mating strategies of a species. The size and shape of genitalia offer other clues to mating behavior—that is, a tendency toward monogamy or polygamy. For example, the relative size of testes as compared to body size is one such measure in men. Relatively larger testes size occurs in species that are polygynous. This makes sense, because of the importance of sperm competition in polygynous males. That is, polygynous males are better served to have access to abundant semen so that they can impregnate more females in a short period of time. Larger testes are required for more sperm production. In contrast, monogamous species are not as concerned about sperm competition among males, so they do not need such extensive sperm-making capability. And again we ask the question of where human primates fall on this continuum of genital size. And again we find a similar answer—human testes size as compared to total body size falls somewhere in the middle of this range. This suggests a general middle ground, a tendency away from polygamy. As described by one author, human average testes size is representative of a species that maintains a generally monogamous mating system with occasional extra-bond liaisons.[6] Of course, this description well represents much of Western culture's mating habits—the common practice of serial monogamy, with intermittent affairs on the side.

Another physical indicator of mating strategy in mammals is the existence of secondary sex characteristics. These are obvious physical signs of masculinity or femininity. In peacocks, the males strut their plumage. In roosters, the males crow to attract hens. In humans, male secondary sex characteristics include broad shoulders, a deep voice, and a square jaw. In women, they include breasts and a significant waist-hip ratio. Secondary sex characteristics serve the function of attracting potential mates. They help advertise sexual fitness to the opposite sex. Where do humans fall on this rating scale of mating strategies? Once again, humans demonstrate moderate secondary sex characteristics— more than typically monogamous species, but less then polygynous species.[7]

Body size and shape are not the only physical indicators of mating strategy. The timing of male puberty as compared to females has also been considered an indicator of polygamy. Human males are physically slower to mature than females. The delayed physical maturation of boys versus girls is indicative of the challenges boys must be prepared to face as adults. Specifically, it suggests that boys require more time to physically mature in preparation for the inevitable competition against other males for females.[8] On this measure, humans fall toward the polygamy end of the rating scale. However, this result is confounded by an opposing piece of evidence, which is that both boys *and* girls ultimately require a significant amount of parental care and attention to reach maturity. This intensive need for caretaking, preferably the care of two parents, is indicative of more monogamous styles where a father remains connected to the family unit for at least a period of time.[9] In Western cultures, this is a tendency to remain together long enough for the children to reach at least the age of toddlerhood, supporting the serial monogamous mating pattern seen so frequently today. In contrast, in polygynous mating systems, a father typically does not remain in a caretaking position after the female is impregnated.[10]

Finally, women's bodies throw an interesting curve ball into this exploration of human mating strategies. Unlike our primate relatives, it is not obvious to males when human females are ovulating. This means that men have no visible way of knowing when women are fertile. In contrast, the genitals of female chimps and other primates swell, offering males a clear indication of fertility. The fact that there is no visible way for human males to know when a woman is fertile (even without clothing there are no visible clues) presents an interesting question in this discussion of mating strategies. Obvious female fertility signs assist polygamous males in determining which females will make the best use of their sperm. Thus, their mating efforts can be much more efficient. Concealed ovulation, on the other hand, puts males at a disadvantage in that they are unable to determine when a female is able to conceive. This may support more of a monogamous or serial monogamous style, as a man probably has to have sex repeatedly with the same partner in order to achieve her impregnation. Instead, if he were to move frequently from partner to partner, he might be less successful in passing on his genes. Some scientists suggest that the fact that women enjoy sex at all phases of their menstrual cycle further supports this monogamy hypothesis, as it is consistent with this more steady male mating strategy. However, in contrast to that opinion, it has also been suggested that if faithfulness had been nature's goal, women would only have sex during their fertile period.[11] Clearly, research conclusions about the body and monogamy are not entirely clear-cut.

GENETICS AND MONOGAMY

Anatomically, modern humans emerged about 100,000 years ago, although our brains became human-like in just the last 50,000 years.[12] Amazingly enough, less than 2 percent of our genome has changed during our evolution from chimp lineages![13] However, it is argued that many of the genes included in this less than 2 percent actually control whole networks of other genes, and thus this low percentage can be deceiving.[14] Considering how much more advanced we have become than our primate counterparts, our evolution has been extraordinarily rapid.

Just as we continue to search for the genetic components to a wide variety of human traits and characteristics, the question remains whether monogamy has a genetic element in humans. Animal studies offer clues to the possible genetic influence on monogamy. Most interesting is the finding that even animals that were believed to be monogamous typically do cheat on their mates occasionally. For example, studies have shown that even birds believed to be monogamous will scurry away with someone else's mate for a brief rendezvous behind the bushes![15] But one species that truly does appear to be monogamous is the prairie vole. (Voles, by the way, look sort of like fat mice.) Unlike the montane voles, known to be promiscuous, prairie voles mate for life. This is believed to be an adaptation to their unique geological environments, and seems to be directed by a particular gene. The gene works by inserting receptors for oxytocin and vasopressin in the reward and recognition circuitry of the brain. Thus, when prairie voles mate with their long-term partner, they experience a reward in the form of a pleasurable sensation. In contrast, the montane voles' oxytocin and vasopressin receptors are not located in the reward circuitry of the brain. As a result, they receive their sexual pleasure reward by mating with new partners.

Scientists now believe that the human brain may work similarly—that is, some humans will experience a familiar partner as more rewarding than others, based on where their oxytocin and vasopressin receptors lie. Twin studies in Sweden indicate that men who lacked a particular allele (an allele is a variant of a gene) were more likely to be loyal husbands. Men with two copies of the variant allele were more than twice as likely to describe serious relationship problems.[16] This fascinating research continues and may shed further light on why some individuals seem more challenged by monogamy than others.

Researchers are also exploring a possible genetic link to other human behaviors indirectly related to monogamy, such as a tendency toward divorce, never marrying, or pair-bonding. The likely inheritable trait is not the behavior itself, but rather certain personality characteristics that are correlated with these behaviors.[17] Thus, rather than inheriting a tendency to divorce, people may inherit a tendency to be challenged by interpersonal conflict or a high need for change and excitement.

But the genetic influence on our mating behavior is even more complex than this. Genetics play other intricate roles in sexual motivation and behavior, which can ultimately impact success with monogamy. For example, genetics appear to play a role in whom we find attractive! People prefer body odors of potential mates who have complementary immune systems to their own.[18]

Specifically, women preferred T-shirts worn by men who had a complimentary set of MHC genes. (MHC stands for major histocompatibility complex and represents a group of 100 different genes that encode proteins involved in our immune responses.) Having complementary genes means that the partner's immune systems (and thus genetics) are similar, but not overly similar because that increases susceptibility to infection. Amazingly enough, women consistently choose T-shirts of men whose genetics were different enough to offer variety for their potential offspring, but not so dissimilar as to become overly complex.[19] In fact, one researcher determined that as the numbers of similar MHC genes increased between lovers, the more likely they would cheat on each other![20] It is amazing to consider the potential impact this could have on monogamous behavior.

Similarly, both animals and humans seem to find new sexual partners more desirable than familiar ones. This tendency is known as the Coolidge effect, referring to a story told about the former president and Mrs. Coolidge:

> One day the President and Mrs. Coolidge were visiting a government farm. Soon after their arrival, they were taken off on separate tours. When Mrs. Coolidge passed the chicken pens she paused to ask the man in charge if the rooster copulates more than once each day. "Dozens of times," was the reply. "Please tell that to the President," Mrs. Coolidge requested. When the President passed the pens and was told about the rooster, he asked, "Same hen every time?" "Oh no, Mr. President, a different one each time." The President nodded slowly, then said, "Tell that to Mrs. Coolidge."[21] (Bermant, 1976, pp. 76–77)

Exploring the genetic contribution to monogamy brings up the age-old controversy of nature versus nurture. But it is important to note that isolating genes that influence human mating behavior is not an argument *for* biology and *against* environment. As noted earlier in this chapter, these variables are constantly intertwined, and human behavior is always influenced by both perspectives. For example, the environment can program permanent changes into DNA, which can then get passed down to future generations. In this way, people inherit adaptations to their environment, and a species evolves. Scientists are thus learning that DNA can be modified just like any other molecule. Genes are not as inflexible as we once believed.

NEUROCHEMISTRY AND SEX

The neurochemicals within our brains are constantly engaged in extraordinarily complex chemical interchanges with our bodies and our emotions. For example, emotions impact thoughts, which influence neurochemistry, which then impacts physical and emotional responses, including sexual reactions.[22] And then of course, the feedback loop also flows back in the other direction. In this section, we will explore some of the hormones and neurotransmitters that have a more influential effect on human sexual behavior.

Neurotransmitters are chemicals released from nerve terminals that signal other nerves. Because of their cell-to-cell mode of transmission, their impact is perceived much faster than hormones. Several neurotransmitters are primarily responsible for our sexual motivations and behaviors. Dopamine is the neurochemical released when we positively anticipate something—whether it be food, sex, or a vacation. It stimulates the brain's reward circuitry, which makes us feel good. As a result, humans are intrinsically motivated to engage in behaviors that cause its release. Some situations seem to further intensify the release of dopamine, such as when something exceeds our expectations, or pleasantly surprises us. Dopamine is the primary neurotransmitter associated with the state of feeling attracted.[23] It is dopamine, along with norepinephrine, that helps to bring about the ecstatic feelings when falling in love.[24] Dopamine is released when we are experiencing something rewarding and new—such as intercourse with a new sexual partner, or a new sexual experience. When couples are in a long-term relationship, less dopamine may be released during sex because making love can become routine. This is why doing something new, like going away for the weekend, or making love in a new place, can momentarily spice up a dragging sex life.

Hormones are chemicals released into the bloodstream from the endocrine glands. They can have a very significant, yet indirect, influence on behavior. That is, hormones themselves are not responsible for certain behaviors. Instead, they influence behavior via their impact on other variables such as attention, concentration, energy level, and emotions like boldness or fearfulness.[25] In this way, hormones correlate with certain sex-typed behaviors (such as aggression in men and nurturance in women), but they do not directly cause these behaviors. Nonetheless, these correlations can be dramatic. For example, researchers have found that even a single sublingual dose of testosterone to young women can have measurable effects such as a decrease in fear-based behavior (a decreased startle response) and a decrease in empathic behavior (a decreased tendency to mimic facial expressions of others).[26]

Testosterone is a sex hormone that gets the most press and seems to generate the most public interest as well as professional controversy. It is the primary hormone we associate with sex drive. Research on testosterone in men reveals that "higher testosterone levels may be associated with male-male competition and mate seeking, and lower testosterone levels may be associated with affiliative pair-bonding and paternal care" (Gray and Campbell [2009], p. 291).[27] This suggests that men with higher testosterone are more prone to mating and dominance behaviors, and men with lower testosterone are more prone to long-term attachment and fathering. In further support of this hypothesis, men with lower testosterone levels were associated with better father-child relationships and better parenting responsiveness.[28] Women actually know this innately, as research suggests that women are more likely to marry men with lower sex hormone levels, but have extramarital sex with men higher in testosterone.[29]

Research demonstrates a correlation between testosterone levels and marital status in men. Married men tend to have lower testosterone levels than single men, and married men with children have lower testosterone levels still.[30] Men with higher testosterone levels have been linked with more sexual partners, and more extramarital sex.[31] One study found higher testosterone levels to be correlated with increased probability of divorce.[32] Men who considered themselves polyamorous were found to have higher testosterone levels as opposed to men who considered themselves monogamous.[33] It is unclear however if this distinction causes their mating choice, or is the result of it. That is, do men lower in testosterone gravitate to long-term relationships and fatherhood (thus lower testosterone is an enduring trait), or do long-term relationships and fatherhood result in decreased testosterone (making lower testosterone a state that is responsive to their environment)? At the moment, the verdict is out on this controversy. One theory has been proposed called the challenge hypothesis.[34] The challenge hypothesis suggests that androgen levels increase in times of social challenge, such as when seeking a mate or engaged in some form of male-male competition. When the social climate is more tranquil, a male need not produce as much testosterone, thus taxing his body less. From this perspective, married men are no longer engaged in mate competition, and thus do not tax their system with unneeded testosterone. On the other hand, men who are dating require higher levels of testosterone to attract potential mates, so their bodies are willing to tolerate the stress of additional sex hormone.

While most of the testosterone research has been conducted on men, there has been some research exploring testosterone levels in women. As with men, testosterone levels in women are associated with relationship status. One study found that women without partners have higher testosterone levels than those with partners.[35] Relatedly, women who considered themselves polyamorous had higher testosterone levels than monogamous women.

It is important to note that conclusions from testosterone studies are still considered preliminary. There remains controversy over collection procedures, such as the time of day that hormone levels are collected. There is even speculation that hormone levels drawn in the lab are not applicable to hormone levels in natural situations that occur outside of a clinic setting—such as in a bedroom.[36]

Oxytocin and vasopressin are two peptides, or amino acid chains, that are related to pair-bonding and parenting behaviors.[37] Vasopressin is essentially the male equivalent of the female's oxytocin. They have received more press recently as they have been identified as the "cuddle hormones." Their release during sexual activity seems to promote the development of a preference for that sexual partner. Oxytocin is also released during touch, even when touching pets. This is at least part of the reason why pets make people feel good. The release of oxytocin while breast feeding is believed to support the maternal-infant bond. Thus, oxytocin plays a role in a variety of loving, tender exchanges.

Oxytocin also plays a role in sexual arousal and orgasm. If dopamine is considered the neurochemical of lust, then oxytocin would be the neurochemical of attachment. In an intimate relationship, oxytocin release isn't just confined to the bedroom. Research demonstrated that women experienced a significant rise in blood levels of oxytocin when they received verbal support from their partner in a laboratory setting. Of interest is the fact that this oxytocin rise was independent of relationship quality. Thus, regardless of how trusting, passionate, or committed the partners reportedly felt, the woman's body responded to her partner's support with the release of oxytocin.[38] Perhaps this is why women claim that when men do the dishes, it makes them more interested in making love! Oxytocin has other benefits as well. It seems to suppress anxiety.[39] This may be why it is released during sexual activity—since it inhibits the stress response, it probably facilitates orgasm. The opposite is true as well—stress hormones block the effects of oxytocin. Thus, if a person is anxious, it can impact the desire for touch and sex.[40]

NEUROCHEMISTRY, SEX, AND MONOGAMY

While the studies reviewed above are not direct indicators of monogamous behavior, they do offer us some clues as to its possible indirect correlates. It seems that certain levels of hormones and neurotransmitters could influence an individual's sexual decisions and choices regarding monogamy. This fascinating field of study will likely provide us with more information about human mating behavior in the coming years.

SEX DIFFERENCES AND MONOGAMY

Are men and women more alike than they are different? Probably so. Yet there do exist significant differences between the sexes, some of which relate to sexual behavior and ultimately perhaps even monogamy. Males and females exhibit clear sex differences from a surprisingly young age. Infant girls ages 3–8 *months* demonstrated a preference for looking at a doll rather than a toy truck![41] It is suspected that these differences reflect girls' preferences for social stimuli (eyes and faces).[42] Perhaps even more amazing, these same toy preferences were found in monkeys,[43] suggesting that more than cultural influence plays into these predilections. Sex differences have also been measured in infant temperament along two dimensions, fearfulness/aversion to novelty, and motor activity level. Girls score higher in fearfulness, which is measured by their response to new or uncomfortable situations. Boys score higher in motor activity level, which is evident even while the infant remains in utero.[44]

Boys and girls do not simply grow out of their sex differences. But there is much debate over the degree and significance of these sex differences in adults. Certainly cultural factors play a huge role in male and female sex-typed behavior. However, subtle as true sex differences may be, they are most evident physically. This fact is obvious in any yoga class, where women's bodies are so much more flexible than men's. It is equally glaring at the gym, where men are markedly stronger than women. Plus, most importantly, men and women do have very dissimilar genitalia. Since our most intimate, authentic, uncensored moments occur when making love, it makes logical sense that even slight gender differences would be obvious in human sexual behavior. And research does support this.

Research on adults demonstrates a variety of sex differences. For example, men are more oriented toward dominance behaviors than women. In recorded history, there is no society where women exhibited more violence than men.[45] Sex differences are clearly evident in men's and women's sexual behavior as well. Across a variety of cultures, men are more positive about casual sex than women, and they place more importance on the physical appearance of their sex partner.[46] Traditionally, men have had more extramarital affairs, although this disparity is shrinking, particularly among the younger generations of women. Men acknowledge a preference for more sexual partners, and on average, men want more frequent sex. Men masturbate more, and they watch more porn. Men spend more money on prostitutes and they are much more willing to pay for phone sex. Of course, the argument remains that many of these sex differences are the result of acculturation. However, research demonstrates that men's and women's brain physiology is different when it comes to sex. Men have more brain space devoted to sex, while women have more brain space devoted to emotions and language.[47] This seems to result in men having many more sex-related thoughts than women.[48] All of this is particularly interesting in light of the fact that is it actually *women's* bodies that seem more designed for sexual pleasure![49] Women are capable of more orgasms than men per sexual encounter, and a woman's orgasms have more contractions than her partner's. A woman can even mate with as many partners as she chooses in a defined period of time—while nature forces men to take a break after climaxing.

A new theory regarding a major difference in the sexual expression of men and women was recently hypothesized. Dr. Rosemary Basson suggested that women's sexual desire is more typically responsive, as compared to men's more spontaneous experience of desire.[50] That is, some if not many women in long-term relationships do not necessarily experience a spontaneous need to have sex, so much as they may be responsive to their partner's attempts at initiation. This hypothesis represents a major shift in our understanding of normative female sexual function as compared to men.

Men and women demonstrate other behavioral differences as well. From an evolutionary perspective, men and women channel their energies into different priorities. These sex-typed preferences reflect behaviors that most support the continued development of our species. Men are generally more focused than women on their next sexual experience. In this way, men continue to seek opportunities to mate. Women, on the other hand, are more focused on the care of their offspring. It is less typical to hear a woman speak of her continued desire for new sex partners, or men speak of their enduring desire to have and care for more children. Thus it becomes clearer why, when women feel stressed or challenged by life, they may prioritize their children over their romantic relationships. However, when men become more stressed by life, they are more likely to find a haven in sex.

Another fascinating difference between the sexes relates to the different reproductive needs of men and women. The term *sexually antagonistic coevolution* [51] refers to an innate mating conflict between the sexes. It is antagonistic because men's and women's evolutionary mating goals are somewhat at odds with each other, thus producing a conflict of interest. "Reproduction should not be thought of as a purely cooperative enterprise between mates. . . . The events that would optimize one partner's reproductive outcomes do not perfectly match those that would optimize the other's" (Gangestad et al., 2005).[52] It is in men's genetic interest to mate often and with new sexual partners. In contrast, it is in women's genetic interest to mate with the strongest masculine partner she can find, and then secure his help in raising their offspring. The process of natural selection results in these traits being sexually selected because they increase the chances that a parent's offspring will survive to maturity (so that they, too, can reproduce). Thus, it seems that humans genetically select for men who spread their genes around and women who tend toward serial monogamy, as these strategies most support offspring survival. Oftentimes, this sexual mismatch becomes an emotional battleground that couples do not understand and feel powerless to rectify.

In sum, a variety of evolutionary differences between men and women can play a role in a predilection toward monogamy. Based on women's reproductive needs, we would expect them to be more in support of monogamy than men—at least, in support of serial monogamy. Women may be as predisposed to enjoying multiple partners as men, but they are also more inclined to maintain a monogamous relationship for a period of time as it supports offspring survival.

A FRAMEWORK FOR UNDERSTANDING

Human sexual behavior is complex and multidetermined. It would surely be almost impossible to identify a sole reason why a particular person would choose monogamy or not. The contributions of the brain and body to an individual's sexual style are just one facet of this complicated life decision. It is likely that each individual must make this choice repeatedly throughout his or her lifetime—some on a daily basis, some on a yearly basis, and some once in a lifetime.

We have identified evidence for and against the natural practice of monogamy in humans. "One way to reconcile these apparently contradictory findings is to acknowledge that humans are designed and adapted for more than one mating strategy" (Schmitt, 2005, p. 268).[53] But even if we assume that the balance of evidence supports a more complex sexual strategy than monogamy for a lifetime, simply being biologically predisposed to a mating pattern doesn't make it a reality for an entire species. There will always be mating variation within a species as complex as ours. Some people will always feel more naturally monogamous, and others will not be so inclined. That is the beauty of our complexity, this diversity that has helped us evolve so rapidly into a species so different from the very primates with whom we share much of our DNA.

Chapter Four

PASSIONATE PACK ANIMALS: MAKING YOUR INSTINCTS WORK FOR YOU

Human primates are social creatures at the core. Very few of us choose to live in isolated locations without human contact. Those among us who do live in seclusion are considered the fringe of society. They make the rest of us anxious because we don't understand their motivations for living in isolation and we tend to assume the worst. That is because we know innately that humans are meant to exist in packs—whether it's the small pack of a family unit, the larger pack of an extended family, or the even larger pack of a community.

Humans are driven to connect. Our social needs are believed to be evolutionarily based for several reasons. One, there is safety in numbers. We are better able to stay alive and care for ourselves when we can assist and be assisted by others. Second, our innate desire to develop partnerships with the opposite sex results in a secure environment for raising children, thus enabling the continuation of our species. If our infants don't survive, neither does our species. Partnership helps to ensure everyone's evolution.

The idea that humans are social and meant to live in packs is not new to us. However, using what we know about pack behavior to understand and improve our sex lives is a relatively new concept, and the subject of the next two chapters.

THE PRIMATE PACK

Because we share about 98 percent of our DNA with our primate cousins, we have learned much about our instinctive behavior by observing how chimp and ape communities function. While there is a variety of primate species, with each group maintaining a unique structure, there are also consistencies between groups. For example, animal packs establish hierarchies. In fact, dominance hierarchies are evident in most nonmonogamous species.[1] Even tiny insects such as ants and bees follow social rules of etiquette that enable their packs to function efficiently. Chickens exhibit a pecking order, in which the stronger animals are able to garner resources such as better food from their weaker peers. This establishment of a hierarchy is believed to be evolutionarily based for creatures great and small. When a community of animals exists within the confines of an established order, they are likely to fight less and cooperate more. Thus, a dominance hierarchy supports evolution by maintaining a level of group cooperation that is good for the species at large, even though it is challenging for the weaker members of the community. Dominance hierarchies may not be fair, but they enable a more efficient system. The alternative to having no one in charge is usually undesirable for all involved. Consider a human example—an extended family vacation without a group leader. Readers who have not experienced this frustration can certainly imagine it. Such a group setting comprises a variety of individuals, all with unique agendas, and all attempting to reach the common goal of enjoyment. Without a leader, this situation can result in endless discussion over even minute details such as when and where to have breakfast. Ultimately, little gets accomplished with lots of wasted time in the process. Here, fairness comes at the cost of enjoyment. Or, consider the example of a leaderless business meeting. Again, many diverse individuals are attempting a common goal. But without a leader, endless discussion would lead to relatively little achievement. In this situation, fairness comes at the price of productivity.

Dominance hierarchies have evolutionary benefits to the species as well. They ensure that the strongest males have the most opportunity to reproduce, thus increasing the chances of healthy, powerful offspring being available to lead the group in coming generations. Thus, violent as dominance behaviors may appear to us, they ultimately support evolution of the species by reproducing the strongest and probably the healthiest animals within the pack. Remember, evolution's purpose isn't to support equality or justice among a species. And unfortunately for us, it's not even to promote happiness. The sole goal of evolution is ensuring the survival of a species.

Researchers studying primate packs describe social hierarchies that are distinct and apparent to observers. Chimpanzees in particular form an obvious dominance structure that appears violent at times. Alpha males harass weaker males and expect the pack to act submissively in their presence. But while alpha males enjoy such perks as better food and sexual access to females, their lives are not always pleasant. It is typical for the dominant male to be challenged by younger males entering adulthood. More skillful alpha males use a variety of techniques, not just brute strength, to obtain and maintain their power. For example, some alphas utilize social skills to enlist the support of other male pack members and thus strengthen their position as leader. They engage an "I'll scratch your back if you scratch mine" approach. Nondominant males (both ape and human) who cannot compete with brute strength will vie for females through other strategies such as friendship or courtship.[2]

Interestingly, it is not just the male pack members that function within a hierarchy. Female primates have their own prevailing hierarchies, which enable them access to stronger males for reproduction, protection, and better food. However, female primates express their opinions verbally or via body language rather than with brute force. Females and males serve different functions within the pack and their hierarchies support cooperation both between and within the sexes.

THE MARITAL PACK

> Lucille adored Brian. She felt so safe and protected around him. He was secure and self-assured in any situation. Plus, he seemed to always be aware of her and what she needed. And making love with him was so exquisite! Brian was so confident when he touched her body. His attention felt like pure gold pouring over her heart and soul.

In humans, packs are further subdivided into pair-bonds. Instinctual desires for love and sex bring couples together in marital packs. As we've discussed, most females are unconsciously and consciously attracted to more powerful men; consciously such men are experienced as most eligible, though unconsciously they likely have the best genes and make the best protectors of offspring. Female animals, including human females, express this instinct via their drive to yield to a dominant male.[3] It is suggested that this drive emanates from the more primitive brain regions.[4] Research supports this tendency in women. For example, in many studies, dominant males have the most reproductive success, thus implying that they are the most popular among the ladies. Some women's tendency to pursue relationships with men who "only want sex" and who are obviously not good candidates for deeper intimate connection also supports this observation. In one study, college men with the lowest dominance scores were more likely to be virgins,[5] thus further supporting women's choice for more dominant male personality traits.

It is not only women who are attracted to the leaders of the pack. Hierarchies are also important to male suitors, although female hierarchies are measured very differently. Instead of strength, women have traditionally been appraised by various qualities that point toward their capacity to procreate. For example, symmetrical facial structure, youth, and large waist-to-hip ratio unconsciously signal female health and fertility to males. While men recognize these characteristics as physically attractive, it is unlikely that they are consciously aware of their motivational drive to connect with the most fertile female. Just as women flock to powerful men, men flock to fertile women. For both men and women, these tendencies seem politically incorrect, and can feel irritating and sometimes even downright degrading. Shouldn't men be more interested in a woman's intelligence than her body? Shouldn't women be more interested in a man's compassion than his checkbook? Most of us want to rise above such superficial qualities when choosing a mate. However, from an evolutionary perspective, they make perfect sense. Again this is an example of how evolution is geared toward one thing only—the survival of the species, which can occur at the cost of human contentment or happiness.

But it is also true that animals adapt to changing environments over time. And as a result, the expression of primal instincts can be modified to current life circumstances. In this way, evolution *and* adaptation leaves their mark on instinct. For example, today women experience masculine dominance as compelling when it is manifested by strength *and* tenderness. That is, women want *loving* strength in their partners, not absolute rulers. This distinction is critical to understanding how sexual instincts manifest in modern romantic relationships. In the past, men have clearly misused their dominance position in the marital relationship, often making marriage unpleasant for women. Coming from an authoritarian and harsh rather than a loving place, the role of a dominant group leader can easily be perverted into an unhealthy dictatorship. Leadership from such a base perspective fails human primates, whether it be within a marital pack or a nation. Unfortunately, this type of harmful, authoritative rule sabotages the potential positive aspects of mating hierarchies. Instead of loving, smoothly functioning systems, they can become tyrannical. This distortion of the family hierarchy helped motivate women to reclaim their masculine sides during the feminist movement. Sadly, harsh authoritarian rule of women remains strong in many less modernized cultures today, and women suffer greatly as a result. Thankfully, women's efforts have successfully resolved much of this negativity in Western cultures. Both women and men have cooperated in their efforts to moderate this extreme tendency, resulting in egalitarian marital packs that are more pleasing to women. But as we will explore, when egalitarian becomes equivalent to androgyny, loss of sexual passion is the price lovers pay. However, the good news is that sexual passion is preserved, and in fact amplified, when a "different but equal" approach is supported—that is, when men and women are equally respected and appreciated for their unique gifts and distinct sexual energies.

FORMING HUMAN DOMINANCE HIERARCHIES

It was Chuck's first day in high school. As he sat for the morning school assembly, he felt something lightly touch the back of his neck. This continued on and off until he turned around. Some jerk was entertaining his friends by tickling him with a piece of paper. Chuck tried to ignore the irritation but it got progressively worse. He knew he had to do something or it wouldn't stop. Chuck took a deep breath, swung around in his seat, and smashed his fist into the guy's face. Everyone in the meeting hall became silent and held their breath. Chuck had won his first and only battle with the upperclassmen. It was a day he would think back on with pride, and never forget.

Carol was in the same auditorium, and also a freshman. She searched the crowd to figure out what the popular girls looked like—how they wore their hair, and what they were wearing. She was humiliated when she realized she had it all wrong. Why did she wear these shoes? And cut her hair when the pretty girls all had long hair? The girls around her were whispering and laughing about someone up front. She wanted to be in on the joke, but no one was talking to her. Carol was becoming more anxious by the minute. She feared it was going to be a long year.

Dominance hierarchies are formed extremely quickly. Research has shown that when placed in groups of three, people will naturally form their own dominance structure in a matter of minutes—sometimes even seconds![6] We assess the hierarchical status of others in a process that can occur largely outside of our conscious awareness, and begins immediately upon meeting someone for the first time. Strength and dominance in human males is measured not just in physical power but also in financial power, intelligence, and access to resources. We form judgments based on how wealthy men appear, how confidently they present themselves via eye contact and body language, and how attractive they are. One author makes a parallel between dominance and submission to a pride-shame dimension. That is, proud people display open, relaxed body language and they maintain direct eye contact.[7] Similarly, dominant people tend to welcome challenges, seek out others, persist at tasks, exercise leadership, discipline subordinates, and command attention.[8] But dominant males have more in common than just behavior. They share biological similarities as well, in that they have distinct hormonal profiles. Specifically, they typically have higher levels of both testosterone and serotonin.[9]

It is not just how a person acts that determines dominance status. Access to material goods, such as their car and the quality of their clothes, are taken into consideration. Members of their peer group, including the social status of their spouse and extended family, also play a role in our assessment of others. Our first impressions can be amazingly accurate.[10] We take them very seriously, and they can have a powerful impact on our opinions both of the person we are critiquing as well as ourselves. That is because we use our evaluations of others to measure our own status within the social system, and these judgments of others offer comparisons to establish our own self-worth. Of course, logically we know that self-worth is not determined according to our status in a social hierarchy. Nonetheless, we are still driven to calculate these judgments about ourselves and others. Conscious or not, this automatic process plays a pivotal role in all our social interactions. Some people find this incessant measuring and critiquing process so intolerable that they attempt to avoid this interchange completely by embracing a socially alternative lifestyle. But even alternative groups establish hierarchies within themselves; the hierarchies are just likely to be based on different criteria than those of the majority pack being escaped from.

Social packs are not the only grouping that humans form—nor are they the most important. When men and women enter romantic relationships, the dyad becomes a small social pack with all the issues inherent in a larger social system. Of course, these dyads become part of two larger extended family systems, which also follow the rules inherent in animal pack behavior. Most marital packs eventually create their own members by giving birth, and with time the dyad slowly grows into a larger social system. Family packs, and marital packs in particular, are the focus of the rest of this chapter. You will soon see how this conceptualization clarifies sexual struggles inherent in monogamous relationships. Strange as it may seem, our evolution as conscious beings with higher-order thought does not shelter us from the laws of nature and the realities of our primate heritage. This may be especially true when it comes to sex, because at its core, sex is one of our more animalistic, base drives.

CHALLENGING THE FAMILY DOMINANCE HIERARCHY

Brent found himself staying at the office later and later. He really didn't mind hanging out there—he was well liked and respected. Going home was a different story. It wasn't not that Sheila didn't love him, because he knew she did. But she was so controlling and demanding, it was tiring just being around her. She was like a drill sergeant sometimes, telling him what to do and how to do it. After a while he would just turn on the TV and tune her out. He didn't even want to have sex with her anymore—she wasn't much softer between the sheets. Brent found himself preferring to log on to the Internet at night and masturbate to the soft, sensual images on his computer screen.

While people and animals automatically create hierarchies, they also naturally fight them. A constant challenge of the hierarchy is actually a positive and productive phenomenon. That's because it ensures that the best-equipped leader remains in charge. Chimps enact this process with the most powerful skill available to them—physical strength. People try to bring down the dominant in more humane (that is, human) ways, such as with ridicule, ostracism, or brute force.[11] We see this dynamic play out daily in our obsession with critiquing the personal lives of famous people. We also experience it regularly in families. For example, growing adolescents will commonly challenge their parents for power and authority in the household. Adolescents are testing their parents to see how powerful their mothers and fathers really are. They explore the extent of their own authority in the family system, which teaches them about their power in the world. While these moments are uncomfortable for parents, they are also an important part of their offspring's maturing process. Giving adolescents too little power as they mature will backfire in their adult life. Giving an adolescent too much power before he or she is ready can also result in difficulties in adulthood. In a healthy family, the dominance hierarchy adapts and shifts to encompass the growing power of the child as he or she ages. When the dominance hierarchy does not accommodate the increasing power of its younger members in a healthy way, the younger members tend to react in one of two ways. Sometimes they assert themselves with increased acting out and challenging of the hierarchy. Alternately, some young people become passive and surrender completely to the family power structure. While this approach may be a relief to all family members as it results in less tension, an unfortunate situation can result. These individuals can become so passive as to be unable to claim their dominant status even when appropriate while interacting in the world. Thus, emotionally healthy assertive behavior can be destroyed in children when their families are extremely intolerant of such behavior.

Remarriage introduces unique challenges to the dominance hierarchy of a family. When two families blend, it is not uncommon for some children to refuse to acknowledge a new adult in the dominant role. Oftentimes a parent plays the dominant authority only for their genetic children in the household. Families attempting to contain two dominant members in one pack often struggle with ongoing tension and turmoil amongst its members, just as in a primate pack with two chimps vying for leadership.

Family hierarchies have other levels of complexity. The natural challenge of the family hierarchy is not limited to growing children and their parents. It is evident between adults as well. That is, spouses can test each other just as younger generations test older ones. Interestingly, in my practice I see this much more often in women challenging men, rather than the opposite of men challenging women. When women challenge the marital hierarchy, it can sometimes be perceived by men as nagging or controlling. This testing of the marital hierarchy is a relatively new dynamic in Western culture. Prior to the women's movement, wives typically followed husband's authority with minimal direct resistance (though perhaps with significant indirect resistance, such as via the use of guilt or more subtle forms of manipulation). Today, women have come into their own power and carry family authority just as their husbands do. This power that women enjoy can be understood as her feeling and expressing her masculine energy. The women's movement has supported women in finding this wholeness and growth by living both their feminine natures as well as their masculine sides. But this expansion for women is having interesting sexual fallout for both men and women in marriages today.

As is natural in any pack, dominance hierarchies are challenged by masculine energy. Because women are now expressing their masculine sides, they are in a position to dispute the masculine hierarchy in their own household. A woman may exert control over her partner in a way that he finds disrespectful. But from her perspective, she acts that way because he's not figuratively stepping up to the plate and earning his authority in the household pack. Such conflicts are common in my therapy room. Couples engaged in these struggles are at odds with each other, and their emotional and sexual intimacy takes a toll. Men lose interest in coming on to wives they perceive as hostile or aggressive. Women lose interest in softening to husbands they perceive as weak. Thus, this natural and healthy tendency to challenge the dominance hierarchy creates negative fallout for modern-day monogamous relationships.

FREUD WOULD AGREE

Dominance theories are not new to psychology. In fact, these concepts were evident even to the father of psychoanalysis, Sigmund Freud. Freud's theory of castration anxiety is a perfect explanation of a child's attempt to negotiate the family dominance hierarchy. Freud described that boys experience castration anxiety beginning around age three through approximately age six or seven. During this time, the boy fears that his longing for his mother will anger his father, thus inducing his father to cut off his penis (the center of his masculine power). This unconscious fear represents a child's awareness of his father's dominant role in the family. Interestingly enough, research indicates that around age six children become accurate judges of the dominance hierarchy within a group. Thus it is around these same ages that a boy would become aware of the father's power over him in the family dominance hierarchy. Obviously Freud's theory is much more complex than is presented here. However, the basic parallel is clear. Interestingly, Freud acknowledged that his personality theory was influenced by evolutionary theory. It is fascinating that he believed dominance hierarchies played a significant role in personality formation.

DOMINANCE HIERARCHIES AND 21ST-CENTURY SEX

Tricia couldn't understand the change in their sexual relationship. How could it have been so exciting when they were first together, and now it was so boring? Phil just wasn't attracting her anymore. He was a wonderful man, a smart and respected lawyer, and a terrific father—how could she be so uninterested in him? He was almost too easygoing. He was so accommodating, even in bed. His polite "Can we make love tonight?" always turned her off. How was this gesture supposed to arouse her? And he touched her so carefully, so gingerly. She didn't understand why he liked sex so much, it was so uneventful. The same thing every time.

Dominance hierarchy dynamics play out in interesting ways for modern-day couples. In an attempt to avoid the power differentials in their relationship, most couples share a very appropriate and healthy relationship goal of fairness and equality. This goal is a fitting response to the unhealthy aspects of life in a patriarchy. In such a system, feminine traits—including feminine sexual traits— have unfortunately been deemed inferior to men's. Years ago this resulted in feminine passivity, both socially and in the bedroom—a negative and disempowered version of feminine surrender. Today, this sexism is still visible in our cultural disregard for feminine characteristics in favor of masculine ones. For example, the masculine goal of achieving success is respected and admired more than the feminine goal of nurturing. One unfortunate result of life in a patriarchy is that feminine sexual potential is difficult to achieve as women do not feel safe in expressing themselves from their core essence. If a woman does not feel supported in experiencing her emotional and sexual core, sex will probably remain relatively superficial for her and her partner.

The reality that modern couples share authority doesn't mean dominance issues are bypassed. In fact, this equality often entails a constant negotiation of authority. This ongoing challenge of the dominance hierarchy in romantic relationships often appears more like war than peace, resulting in significant challenges in couples' emotional and sexual relationships. For example, it has been suggested that the dominance-related behaviors of assertiveness and territoriality are expressed by both husbands and wives in a wide variety of ways; from control over one's body, to control of privacy, and control of material goods.[12] The variety of power plays used by both men and women include aggression, hostility, guilt-induction, helplessness, and seduction. Thus, plays for power can be direct or indirect, subtle or obvious. Traditionally, women have used more indirect and subtle means of control, while men's efforts have been more direct and obvious. We see similar dynamics in the animal kingdom—those with more alpha status use more direct power plays, while others use more indirect management tactics. Regardless, these less open and loving efforts to control typically result in dissatisfaction with the relationship. Ultimately, this negatively impacts the couple's sexual experience. Thus, the sharing of authority is a very appropriate goal that unfortunately can be easily mishandled.

This situation becomes even more complex when modern and healthy relationship goals clash with evolutionary instincts. For example, while women enjoy the concept of sharing authority, many still feel the evolutionary pull to open sexually to a powerful man. They long for their man to demonstrate his strength in their relationship. When men become too flexible and accommodating in the marital pack, their partners may lose respect for them in the hierarchy. This automatically results in decreased sexual interest, as women typically do not naturally open and respond sexually to more passive males. Men in these marriages become confused because they think they are being the man their wife wants—accommodating and flexible. Of course, this assumption is true in general. But when it comes to sex, instincts still prevail. It is easy to see how men find this sexual preference confusing and counter-intuitive, as it feels different from the equal partnership she desires outside of the bedroom.

This confusion is evident in women as well. On one hand, they desire a strong masculine presence in their bedroom. On the other hand, women are often ambivalent about instinctual feminine sexual surrender. This confusion is partly the outgrowth of our cultural custom of valuing masculine traits over feminine ones. Women have learned that feminine traits, such as vulnerability and surrender, prohibit their success in a patriarchy. As a result, women commonly resist the same sexual behavior that is fulfilling for them. Women's ambivalence, coupled with men's confusion, may prevent men and women from fully exploring their sexual potential. In reality, masculine and feminine traits are equally important and equally vital and powerful; just very different. Different should not equate with superior and inferior, although this has been the unfortunate connotation in our patriarchy. Sadly, the concepts of sexual dominance and surrender have been equally misunderstood, and they too have negative connotations. In the past, this has resulted in women not manifesting their sexual potential out of shame and fear. Today, it results in women not manifesting their sexual potential because they disregard their feminine core—they literally disdain their essence! We will explore this dynamic further, and its implications, in the next chapter.

SEXUAL FANTASIES, SEX PLAY, AND DOMINANCE HIERARCHIES

Dominance hierarchies are not just evident in sexual behavior, but are a popular theme in sexual fantasies as well. We can gain further clues about masculine and feminine sexual instincts by exploring sexual fantasies involving dominance and submission. Fantasies involving submission to a dominant male have traditionally been considered very popular among women, though recent research suggests that men, too, enjoy the fantasy of being submissive to their sexual partner.[13] At one time these fantasies were considered masochistic and neurotic for women. Most recent research suggests that these fantasies are in fact healthy sexual representations of instinctual feminine energy.[14]

The study cited above revealed that men and women may enjoy fantasies of submission to a dominant partner for a variety reasons. More socially dominant women seem to enjoy the fantasy of being experienced as irresistible to an alpha male, and thus taken by a man more dominant than she. These women seem to feel even more empowered and sexy when a powerful man is so desirous of her. Less socially dominant women still enjoy these fantasies, but prefer to experience the alpha male as more sensitive and protective, and thus more of a rescuer than a powerful warrior. Interestingly, submissive fantasies seemed to be at least as popular among the men in the study as they were among the women. It was suggested that men enjoy these fantasies for different reasons than women do. A man feels great relief, excitement, and acceptance when making love with a dominant woman who is sexually engaged and excited by him. In these situations, the man may be more able to relax and enjoy himself without the pressure of having to please his partner. Thus, while submissive fantasies appear to be representative of feminine sexual instinct, for men they may be more in response to easing the pressure of having to dominate in sexual relationships.

Other researchers have suggested that some sexual role play scenarios are also related to instinctual masculine and feminine sex roles. That is, dominance and submissive sexual behaviors can be acted out in bondage and dominance sex play between two partners.[15] Such sex play can involve blindfolds, restraints, or sex toys. While years ago these sexual behaviors were considered more fringe and potentially pathological, resent research again suggests that this can be a healthy offshoot of traditional masculine and feminine sexual behaviors.[16]

MODERN MATING ADAPTATIONS

Not all women relate to the traditionally feminine desire to mate with a dominant male. That is because a fascinating social shift is rapidly taking place which has tremendous implications for human mating behavior. More recently, some women are finding the established evolutionary mating plan less tolerable. As women have developed their masculine social presence, their sexual needs have evolved in kind. Within just a few decades—surely a brief nanosecond from the perspective of an evolutionary timetable—women are now entering and competing within the male-dominated social hierarchy scene. This shift has resulted in exciting opportunities for women, as well as required huge adaptations for both men and women in many aspects of social order—not the least of which is sex! Some women particularly enjoy experiencing their masculine sides in more directly sexual ways. They get pleasure from being assertive, in control, and managing situations—including sexual exchanges. These women prefer to play a primarily dominant role in the bedroom, or a more identical role with their partner, rather than surrender to a masculine force. Instead of occasionally enjoying the experience of manifesting more aggressive or dominant sexual energy, such women prefer to maintain that stance more regularly. For them, fabulous sex may be less about sexual chemistry and more about adventure, physical sensation, or relaxation.

Similarly, some men are rather tired of carrying the dominant role in their romantic relationship. Men can find the experience of playing their traditional masculine role to be tedious and burdensome. Thus, some men enjoy a reversal of the evolutionary mating plan. We see this dynamic acted out in several recent trends. The advent of a "house husband" is one such example. Men and women are increasingly enjoying the role reversal of a man maintaining the primary caretaking role for the children. Modern men are wonderfully equipped for the challenging task of childrearing. And in many ways, this plan works tremendously well for the entire family. However, because it opposes natural mating instincts, it can backfire in the bedroom. Women in these partnerships can have difficulty surrendering sexually to a man who is mani-festing increased feminine, nurturing energy in their family pack. Thus, in spite of both partners wanting an enjoyable sex life, many couples in this situation struggle. Unfortunately, it seems very difficult for a woman to quickly move in and out of a dominance position at will in her marriage. This is a politically incorrect truth. Most of us wish only to support this flexible approach to chil-drearing and we applaud those who chose innovative household arrangements. We want to believe that it won't backfire for a couple's intimate relationship. But if we continue to avoid such uncomfortable realities, men and women will have a much more difficult time finding workable solutions to the challenges inherent in their mating adaptations. It is my hope that such couples will take their sex-ual struggles less personally when they understand the instinctual dynamics at play underneath the surface—and between the sheets.

A different example of a mating adaptation occurs when younger men are ro-mantically involved with older women. This is again a response to women hav-ing and enjoying more dominant roles in the culture. Some younger men are thrilled by the experience of loving and being made love to by a more dominant older woman. They admire their woman's strength, wisdom, awareness of her body and sensuality, and free sexual nature. But this type of sexual relationship can backfire if a woman decides (consciously or unconsciously) that she wants to return to a feminine surrender position in bed. Again, it appears tricky for women to maintain a socially dominant role combined with a sexually receptive role within one romantic relationship. This same woman would probably find it much easier to continue the dominant role in her primary relationship yet sexually surrender to a different man she perceives as more socially dominant than herself.

MONOGAMOUS SEX IS COMPLICATED

Why has sex become so complicated? It seems that something as natural as making love shouldn't require self-help books to do well. But this is be-cause our goals and Mother Nature's goals are so different. People wonder why Mother Nature isn't partial to long-term intimacy. Wouldn't it just make sense that romantic love lasting a lifetime would be best for all individuals involved? Sadly for us, the answer is no. There is in fact little good evolutionary reason for romantic love to last a lifetime. That is because our gene pool, and thus our immune system, is severely truncated by this model. And the less varied the gene pool, the less opportunity there is for growth and development of the species. In this scenario, genetic adaptations to the environment evolve more slowly. Humans are less responsive and adaptive to the changes in our surroundings if we have less opportunity for our DNA to react to these constant changes. This scenario creates vulnerability for each family and for the society at large. That is because upmatings (when a woman mates with sperm from a male she believes is more dominant than her current partner) can produce offspring with enhanced genetic capacity, including genes that encode for improved immune function. Genetic variety means stronger immune systems and better chances to fight off new varieties of pathogens. Otherwise, viruses and germs have a better chance to injure the human race. And in spite of our modern technology, advanced medical knowledge, and powerful antibiotics, lack of genetic variation remains a very real and even rising concern today.[17] Upmatings offer the society at large more opportunities to intermingle male and female genetics to strengthen resistances to epidemics and disease. The world is a living, changing entity. Humans must do the same at their most basic cellular level in order to function optimally in our milieu.

But there are additional questions about nature's lack of support for long-term romantic love. Children have a much better quality of life when they are reared by two parents. Doesn't that fact alone serve evolution? The unfortunate answer is not necessarily. From Mother Nature's perspective, childrearing offers a point of diminishing returns. The older a child grows, the more able he or she is to function independently. While older children, adolescents, and young adults are clearly given more advantages when reared in two-parent homes, two parents are no longer necessary for their survival. After an infant matures past toddlerhood, a mother can more effectively care for her child's needs without the presence of the father. Plus, if a couple separates, the vast majority of women do not desert their children. But if a mother does abandon her offspring, most fathers take over the childrearing responsibilities. Thus, the majority of children continue to be gifted with one parent's care, which is essentially all they need to grow up and reach sexual maturity themselves, after which the cycle continues and it becomes their turn to reproduce. Of course, simply surviving to adulthood may be Mother Nature's goal, but most of us want much more for our children. Thus, most mothers and fathers still strive for a two-parent household.

Evolutionary theories pertaining to attachment may also have relevance here. The parent-offspring conflict theory, developed by Robert Trivers, is one such hypothesis worth mentioning. This theory suggests that parental investment in an offspring is evolutionarily designed to be less over time than a child's investment in his parents.[18] That is, when a child is helpless and dependent on parents, parental caretaking is at its peak. As the child ages and becomes able to amble on his own, parents wean the child, encouraging the child's independent behavior. This enables parents to focus on other endeavors that would further support evolution, such as having another child. Thus, intensive parental attentiveness has an evolutionary timetable.

This theory seems to have an indirect implication for monogamy. That is, could there be a parallel to this theory for parents—that is, a parent-parent conflict theory? Parents readily admit that having children stresses their marriage.

Could it be the case that this marital discomfort is in part evolutionarily pre-disposed, to encourage parents to change partners and thus further mix up the gene pool? If so, evolution may not just support the end of love by putting a timetable on the experience of lust itself. Perhaps evolution actively encourages spouses to lose interest in each other over time. Similarly, it has been suggested that "Darwinism can explain the adaptive value and hence normality of puta-tively pathological phenomena such as family conflict, sexual jealousy, anger, and guilt."[19] Thus, perhaps the stresses that parents often feel in their relation-ship after the birth of children may have instinctual underpinnings. Of course, this does not mean parents must succumb to these conflicts if and when they exist. But it does give us a potentially less pathological context for understand-ing them.

HIERARCHIES IN OUR FUTURE

It is interesting to speculate about how the human race influences its own evolution. Some scientists have suggested that we are slowly self-selecting away from dominance hierarchies and aggression and thus "taming ourselves."[20] Clearly, Western culture is in the midst of an ongoing social transition. For ex-ample, serial monogamy is being increasingly acknowledged as an acceptable mating strategy. Decades ago, divorce was much less tolerated than it is today. In addition, the remaining gender gap is slowly being chipped away. Both men and women appear to be evolving toward a more androgynous style—that is, men are accessing more of their feminine skills while women are accessing more of their masculine skills. The new term *metrosexual* could be considered another example of this phenomenon. In addition, many modern women have learned to be really great men. As women have developed their masculine traits in their daily life, it may be at the price of their more sensitive, emotional, and vulner-able feminine selves. Similarly, as men develop their sensitive sides, it may be at the price of comfort with their masculine strength and presence.

Today, less feminine women and less masculine men may be at an advantage. Androgynous characteristics are often taken more seriously in the workplace. Less feminine women appear less emotional and less sensual, and more able to achieve work tasks. They are considered assertive and direct. Less masculine men enjoy the benefit of being more sensitive than their more traditional peers, and they are often considered better and more creative leaders. However, these strategies of relating may backfire romantically, especially in long-term mo-nogamous relationships where lust is no longer an automatic reaction to a very familiar sexual partner. In these relationships, sexual tension and attraction can easily get lost in a sea of androgyny. When women are more like men and men are more like women in the bedroom, no one feels the instinctual tension of a vulnerable and soft woman opening sexually to a strong and loving man. Many couples feel this loss acutely, although they cannot articulate why sex has become so much less exciting as the years pass.

This transition toward androgyny could offer men and women many advantages with regard to social equality. It seems likely that an increase in peacefulness and harmony between the sexes would result. However, if the trend toward androgyny continues, the disadvantage of such a social shift could be a reduction in the exquisite feeling of male/female sexual chemistry. There would also be a loss in sexual intensity when each person offers more wide-ranging but less deeply expressed sexual gifts. We explore these concepts more in depth in the next chapter.

Chapter Five

SOCIAL EVOLUTION MEANS SEXUAL REVOLUTION

OUR SOCIAL EVOLUTION

To understand how we can make monogamy more sexually exciting and satis-fying in the future, we first have to take a look at where we've been. As we've discussed, our culture has experienced a tremendous emotional and sexual growth spurt these last few decades. Prior to the feminist movement, sex roles for men and women were extremely well defined. The man was an alpha male in his household; the woman nurtured and maintained the home nest. When the feminist movement took hold, these roles were challenged and expanded for the first time in history. Women were invited to engage their previously unex-pressed masculine sides. Men were encouraged to demonstrate their more lov-ing, heart-opened selves. Everyone took a step toward wholeness, and as a result, both men and women learned to access more of themselves and offer more to the world. With this increasing broadmindedness and less rigidity of sex roles, our sex lives were sure to evolve in kind. At least that's what everyone thought was happening.

The sexually permissive atmosphere of the 1960s played a part in these changes as well. In the bedroom, women were encouraged to be more assertive so that they could increase their sexual satisfaction. The pill and other birth con-trol methods enabled sex to become much more than just about procreation. Couples were encouraged to "make love" to their partner rather than simply "have sex." Suddenly men and women had more opportunities for a variety of sexual partners and experiences. The potential for more exciting, satisfying sex became increasingly real in everyone's mind.

And then there was the downside.

For many women, increased assertiveness in the world translated into a more bold sexual style. Their expectations for great sex grew as they discovered more of their sexual potential as active, engaged lovers. Women were giving more sexually, and they wanted to receive more in return. Men responded by attempting to offer what women were asking for. They felt pressure to become better lovers, and they reached within themselves to find the emotional side women wanted. Making love required them to be more sensitive, not the emotionally cold men of the 1950s. But a strange thing happed as these transformations occurred. The sexes became more androgynous as they lost connection with their instinctual energy. And in this process, sex never actually became more satisfying for men and women in long-term relationships. While these transformations improved the sex lives of single people and couples in short-term relationships, they did little to enhance the quality of sex in long-term committed relationships.

The good news was that monogamous men were no longer experiencing their wives as sexually passive or selfless. However, men were now finding their women to be demanding and controlling in bed. Monogamous women were no longer finding their men to be cold and insensitive between the sheets. Instead, women felt their men were becoming weak and unassertive sexually. The politically correct evolution of everyone's masculine and feminine energy was backfiring in the bedroom.

And it still is. This remains a struggle for much of Western culture today. It may present as low libido in one partner, or sexual boredom. Patients often seek sex therapy after medical issues have been ruled out by a physician, and couples psychotherapy has failed to help them resurrect the intimate connection they once enjoyed and long to experience again. Androgyny, it seems, makes for a more evolved society by day, but a much less exciting sex life by night. America is experiencing a midlife crisis with regard to sex. Men and women are thinking, "Is this all there is?"

But here's the good news. This is not all there is. And amazingly enough, we live during a time when we can truly achieve so much more sexually. *For the first time in history,* men and women actually have the tools to take their sexual experience to new levels. Women are no longer passively submissive sexually. They have developed their power and can use this strength to actively open to their partner and deepen their sexual experience. Men are no longer sexually cold—they have developed their sensitivity, which will support their partners and facilitate their trust. Both sexes are acquiring the very skills needed to reach new depths in the bedroom. And in Western culture, we have the exquisite luxury of cultivating our innate sexual selves. Unlike other parts of the world, we do not have to worry about the basics of living, such as food or shelter. Instead, we can choose to expend energy cultivating our intimate connections, taking our love lives to new levels. What an opportunity for us all!

A CULTURAL MIDLIFE CRISIS

The sexual expectations and potential that evolved from the feminist movement are all too frequently not being realized. Men and women often report that a satisfying intimate life is very important to a happy marriage, yet they find it extremely difficult to achieve.[1] This is not just because monogamy isn't natural for many primates. Although monogamy isn't natural, it still can be exciting if you know what to do. Our cultural midlife sex crisis is the result of our disconnection from our instincts.

First, let's consider how out of touch we are with our primal nature. Sex is one of the few primal acts we engage in. Just like other primates, our bodies eat, sleep, defecate, and procreate. These behaviors are part of life for all mammals. In fact, they are among the few behaviors we share with nonhuman animals. And in each of these categories, when we are cut off from our body's natural flow, dysfunctions develop. Many people are cut off from their body's natural rhythms of hunger and sleep. Folks with irritable bowel are out of sync with their body's elimination rhythm. The same can be true for sex. When people lose their sensual connection, the impact is felt in their sex life. That is because sex without a sensual connection is robotic at best. Fantastic sex is really about letting go into the moment, feeling more than thinking, allowing our primal sensuality to burst forth. When we are not comfortable connecting with our more animalistic self, it's very difficult to feel sensual when making love.

This disconnection from the body's instinctual, sensual rhythm doesn't impact new romances to the same degree as it does longer-term ones. This is largely due to the hormones released when a relationship is new. The natural neurochemicals of lust are so powerful that they take up the slack, and trump deficits in instinctual connection for a while. It's just when a relationship ages that these dynamics become more acutely felt. That is why I continually make the distinction of long-term monogamy versus short-term monogamy. And there are other reasons as well that passion flows more freely in short-term relationships. Couples are not yet stuck in sexual ruts. They haven't created bad habits and negative expectations that can sabotage a sex life over time. Plus they haven't had the opportunity to hurt each other which is unavoidable in intimate relationships as time passes. For all of these reasons, long-term monogamy is the most challenging mating style for most people.

A second force behind our culture-wide disconnection with our primal nature is our focus on thinking. Most of us spend a majority of our day planning, analyzing, organizing, tabulating, and critiquing. We are constantly bombarded with information—data on the computer, the mobile phone, the TV, and in print. Our minds are sifting through countless sound bites almost every waking moment. As a result, we spend less time relating to our bodies, feeling our bodies, and connecting to our bodies. And it is the body that is our primary link to our primal, instinctual self. To make matters worse, the common ways we still do engage our bodies do not help us connect to our sensuality. That is, our typical physical activities are less about feeling our body and more about pushing ourselves and accomplishing goals. For example, fast-paced aerobic activity does little to promote a mind/body connection for most people. Instead, people use this occasion to think more—read a magazine or catch up on the news. We actually try to dissociate from our bodies during this time because we are straining ourselves and we are thus physically uncomfortable. Rarely do we take a break from our hectic schedules for gentle yoga, meditation, or massage—activities that help us feel pleasure in our bodies. As a result, we become less in tune with our physical selves over time. Our connection to our sensual selves—a woman's primal femininity and a man's primal masculinity—is therefore diminished.

WOMEN'S SEXUAL EVOLUTION

Moving through a midlife crisis is always challenging. It requires soul searching, feelings that are often uncomfortable, and confronting the choice between passivity and change. Initiating change is never easy, even under the best of circumstances. Women have accomplished tremendous change in the past few decades. They have taken themselves from a weak, passive place in our society to one of assertiveness and strength. The women who did this work fought hard for themselves and for those of us who are now clearly benefiting from their efforts. But the work of evolving as women is not over. In fact, it's only *half* finished. It's time again for a feminine revolution. And this time, it is about finding balance as women: balance between our feminine sides and our masculine sides. I believe that it is only in finding this balance that long-term monogamous relationships can survive and thrive in the 21st century. And I also believe there are three reasons why women are in the best position to lead the way.

First, in comparison to men, women are more relationship oriented. They are more aware of what feels good and what feels bad about interacting. They are the first to spot interpersonal trouble and the first to try and find solutions. Men, in general, are often less concerned about their relationship challenges—at least, until the difficulties become glaring and they can no longer be overlooked. At this point, it can be too late to fix the damage that has been done. Thus, it is women who are more likely to nip a problem in the bud, or at least grasp it before it gets too hot to handle.

Second, women are tremendously affected by the lack of sensuality in their relationships. When women feel disconnected from their own sensuality, it is often they who don't want to make love. Such women have difficulty feeling pleasure in their bodies. They have lost touch with how to use their bodies to generate satisfaction for themselves and their partners. Similarly, when a woman feels disconnected from her partner emotionally, she avoids making love. While men become concerned when their sex lives aren't satisfying, they are sometimes more tolerant of such issues and more likely to continue to have sex any way. Although this is a stereotype, I've found it to be true to some degree— women more than men avoid sex when things aren't feeling interpersonally right to them.

Third, women tend to be more interested in commitment. It is more often women who lobby for marriage, encouraging their lovers to take the plunge and commit with them. Interestingly, in Western culture, more assertive, educated women will also initiate relationships ending. These women expect a lot from their marriages and their husbands. When a relationship isn't feeling good to a woman, and she does not feel dependent on her husband, she may prefer to terminate it. Men, once again, seem more able to tolerate problems in a marriage and they may not be as likely to ask for a divorce.[2]

There are evolutionary reasons for these tendencies. The innate sexual styles of men and women are the likely cause. Women are more organized around relationships in general because they give birth and are the primary nurturers of the young. This huge task requires that women are supremely sensitive to their children. It would make sense that women use these skills in their romantic relationships as well as with their offspring. Second, women are the more finicky sex when it comes to mating behavior. As we discussed, Mother Nature chose women to be more selective in her mating habits. This helps to ensure a continued improvement in the gene pool. Plus, it is women who shoulder most of the responsibility if intercourse leads to pregnancy. Thus, women are going to be choosier than men about when and with whom they have sex. In my practice, I encourage women to use these evolutionary trends as motivation to initiate positive change in their relationship.

THE NEW FEMINISM

The challenge for women in the 21st century involves yet another transformation of feminine energy. As we have explored, the feminist movement brought women out of a passive, dependent state and into one of power and confidence. Now, for woman to translate her gains into the bedroom, she actually must return to her innate feminine nature. But rather than experience it as passive and helpless as our sisters did decades ago, women have a new opportunity to create a sexual state of active, open, and engaged surrender. Thus, women can use their newfound strength to fall deeper into their feminine selves, into that place within them where passion lies. Only a strong woman is willing to let go into the depths of her passion. Otherwise, this state feels too vulnerable to her, and she will avoid it. As women grow yet again, further into their power, they can use this energy to make monogamy more of what they want it to be.

It is not just women who will benefit from this transformation. As women grow individually, all will benefit from their efforts. Of course, woman will experience her sensuality in a much more satisfying way. She will feel more deeply what it means to be a woman. Her heart will open further, and she'll feel the world from a more sensitive, loving perspective. She'll find herself wanting to make love because the feeling of surrendering into her partner's strength is exquisite. Her softness will accelerate her husband's growth into manhood. He'll more quickly be the yang to her yin, the masculine to her feminine, the strong presence to her emotional flow.

But the benefits of woman's sexual evolution can extend far beyond the bedroom. Our society will benefit from this increase in feminine energy as well. That's because American culture, and the world at large, is currently out of balance. Masculine energy runs rampant in politics, technology, and finance. That is not to say that women are not involved in these aspects of life. Instead, it means that it is the masculine energy in all of us that motivates these systems forward. And without a softer feminine energy readily available to balance the more harsh masculine energy, our culture loses a certain flow, sensitivity, and open heart that helps to make life a more tender experience. As women cultivate this within themselves, they can offer more of this energy in all of their activities, potentially making the world a kinder, gentler place.

WHY SEX IS MORE CHALLENGING FOR WOMEN

Transformation is never easy. Change is frightening, even when we chose it. The task for women is formidable—becoming soft in a patriarchy is not a small feat, even if it is relegated only to the bedroom. Women already experience many unique sexual challenges as compared to men. Being the receptive aspect in a sexual dynamic requires that a woman open to a more assertive male. This is true for all mammals and primates. For even small creatures like mice, the female must be receptive and cooperate for sex to be successful. The male is the more active and assertive partner during copulation. For many women, this receptivity feels uncomfortably vulnerable. It requires a level of trust in her partner that he won't use his strength and force to hurt her. This age-old dynamic may leave a woman feeling overexposed or unprotected, two adjectives I rarely hear a man use to explain his feelings during sex. Thus, the task of sexual evolution requires women to go even further into this already vulnerable place where her primal energies reside.

As a woman becomes more aware of her instinctual self, she will see a pleasing shift in her man while lovemaking. Men long to feel the instinctual side of women's sexual energy. A man loves to experience his partner open to him, responsive and enjoying her body and their lovemaking. I have never heard a man say his partner was too primal or too out of control when she made love, too responsive to him, or too vulnerable. I have never heard a man say he longed for his partner to be more controlled in bed, or that she think more rather than feel, or to tune out of her body. Instead, men frequently say they want their partners to let go more during sex, be more responsive to touch, and allow themselves to open more. Thus, women's transformation will be enthusiastically received by most men.

Of course, men do enjoy sexually confident and assertive women. Men also say they long for their women to be more aggressive sexually and more directive at times. There are several reasons for this. First, everyone likes to play with a variety of sexual energy in bed. No matter how exciting it is, any single sexual dynamic will get boring if played out repeatedly. Variety remains the spice of a sex life. Furthermore, men experience assertiveness in a woman as an indication that she is enjoying herself. Men also like the sexual break that a sexually assertive woman offers him. When his woman is assertive, he can relax and enjoy himself. He doesn't have to worry as much whether she is being satisfied since she is in charge. So, as long as receptive and assertive sexual energies are accounted for, sexual tension can thrive. Many women are delighted to play with their masculine sexual energy periodically—it feels empowering and exciting to them. In this way, they very powerfully create sexual chemistry by flipping instinct inside out.

MEN'S SEXUAL EVOLUTION

Change in one partner invites change in the other. Women's growth will encourage men to access more of their primal essence. Men's growth will help women reach even deeper into their feminine core. Therefore, each spouse influences the other in a beautiful circular dance of give and take. Men's contribution to this exchange is obviously as critical to the outcome as women's. The more a man allows himself to access his more primal alpha energy, the more his woman will instinctually surrender into her feminine energy. Men have evolved tremendously in the last few decades. They are no longer cold and insensitive in their intimate relationships. Now man must return to his primal masculine self in a way that enhances intimate connection, allows his partner to trust him more, and directs both of them on a path to more succulent monogamy.

And women are longing for this transformation. I have never worked with a woman who said she wanted a weaker man, or a more passive man, or a less sensitive man. After the excitement of a new relationship wears off, women long for what is instinctual for them—to be taken and opened by a strong man. But men's next step in their sexual evolution will not be an easy one. Few men today have experienced a masculine role model with the strong yet open-hearted energy he is working to cultivate. In fact, many men today have grown up without a masculine presence in their household. These boys learn about masculinity from the media and from their peers. Unhealthy examples of passive men or overly aggressive men are primarily what he is exposed to. How sad that boys are shown two polar opposites of what it is to be a man—neither of which works well in a monogamous relationship. Sexually passive men are not strong enough to develop and maintain an exciting sexual relationship over time. They depend on the sexual energy of their partner to make sex fulfilling. This means that a man must rely on his partner's sexually masculine side to spark the fire of passion. Such an approach tends to work fine at the beginning of a relationship, because today's women easily and comfortably access their more masculine sexual energy when falling in love. However, this dynamic cannot offer enough sexual spark to keep a monogamous sex life thriving over time. Eventually this woman will want to experiment with her more feminine, vulnerable side. And she will avoid doing this if she doesn't feel her partner's masculine strength at home, in the bedroom. It is not enough that he is strong and accomplished in the world. That is, sometimes men are strong in the workplace, but they become more lazy and passive at home. Knowing that her man has the capacity for strength is not enough for her to surrender. She must feel it at home, and particularly in her bedroom, for her to let go sexually. This can be its own challenge for men who engage their alpha energy at work and want to come home and relax. But in terms of instinct, home is still a den, and he is still a member of the pack. His partner still needs to feel his instinctual energy for her to more naturally engage her own instinctual feminine side.

Men who exude too much aggressive, controlling energy at home fare no better in their long-term intimate relationship. Forceful men overpower the sweetness of their partner's feminine energy, shutting her down and making her too fearful to open emotionally and sexually. Aggressive masculine energy is what the feminist movement helped to transform decades ago. While women want strong men, in touch with their masculine essence, women have little patience for men who are heartless and who use brute force to accomplish their goals.

For a woman to offer her best, she wants the best from her partner. Men can only find what women want by looking within. The man of the 21st century, the man who can make sexual monogamy exciting by tapping into his instinctual core, will have to do the hard work of self-growth and soul searching. This man must be comfortable in his heart as well as his body. He must know himself on both these levels so that he can continue to offer new depth to his long-term relationship. Sometimes my male patients believe that this is too much work, and their lives are already filled. Cultivating their alpha energy at home requires more effort than they feel they can give to a relationship. I sympathize. Accessing primal energy requires effort on everyone's part. This process does not come easily because it is far from the way we are used to living our lives. Plus, it is hard to put effort into our home life when we expend so much energy and effort on our daytime responsibilities. However, in truth, all intimate relationships require effort, and they all entail some amount of discomfort. When couples disconnect emotionally, the result is a high degree of pain for everyone. Sometimes couples separate or divorce, which results in significant stress for extended periods of time. Thus, intimate relationships bring effort and stress, regardless of the path they take. So why not expend your energy and effort in a way that offers you the best chance of enhancing your relationship?

WHY SEX IS MORE CHALLENGING FOR MEN

Sex presents distinct challenges for men that make sexual change and transformation more difficult. Our culture expects a tremendous amount from men sexually, often leading them to feel pressure and anxiety. These expectations are frequently unspoken, but nonetheless very real. For example, men are expected to always want sex. In addition, a man is supposed to sexually satisfy his partner, and make sure she has an orgasm and a fulfilling experience. Men should control their erection long enough to have an exciting sexual experience, but not too long as to draw it out. Men must stay excited throughout foreplay and intercourse, and not lose their erection. Yes, it's very easy to see how men become burdened by expectations and pressures in the bedroom.

In addition to controlling their erection, men are expected to control their emotions, leaving them at a disadvantage sexually. If a man is not used to tuning into and feeling his emotions more generally, he will have a very hard time being present with his passion while making love. And if he's not in touch with his own feelings, he won't be as aware of his lover's feelings. This makes her less willing to be open, because women must feel seen and understood to open sexually in a long-term relationship. Men can experience their sexual anxiety in a variety of ways, including low libido, rapid ejaculation, and erectile dysfunction. (Of course, anxiety is not the only reason men have these issues.) And now, in addition to all these pressures, men are being asked to tap their instincts and tune into their primal selves. Quite simply, it's a lot to handle. It certainly has been a lot for many of my male patients to cope with. But as they understand how the dynamics of instinct play out in their sexual relationship, it is also a relief.

Many men are deeply troubled by their unsatisfying sex life. Men are discouraged by their partner's lack of enthusiasm, and they often interpret this as a deficiency in themselves. When they learn that this is actually a culture-wide problem that is the result of a variety of social changes, many men actually relax. They take their struggles less personally when they understand the vastness of the issues. And they feel liberated when they learn there is something they can do about it. Accessing primal instincts, and activating them in their partner, makes logical sense to people. Even before they learn how to make use of the information while making love, people develop increased compassion for themselves and their partners. Understanding these dynamics will help everyone make sense of their sexual struggles and decrease anger and confusion.

WHEN COUPLES NEGLECT THIS WORK

Not all couples feel compelled to work with their instincts in the bedroom. Some couples find it too intense, too emotional, or feel that it requires just too much effort. Sometimes women find that accessing their more feminine selves feels degrading. Sadly, they have learned from the patriarchy to demean their primal selves. And men have their own struggles with this work. Men may feel that a more masculine approach to life and relationships does not fit their personality. These concerns are real and true for some men and women. However, when couples in long-term monogamous relationships avoid this work, some typical sexual problems often result. As the years pass, their sex becomes much more monotonous and boring. That is because they are not reaching deep within themselves to offer something new and fresh to their sexual experience. When couples stay on a more superficial level sexually, sex simply becomes less exciting over time. Women then find themselves closing down physically and emotionally. They feel less pleasure in their bodies when their body isn't open, so touch isn't that erotic. They feel less love and reduced emotional intensity as their hearts close. At this point, sex may not be worth wanting. As one of my teachers once said, "In the long run, you get no more than you are willing to risk giving."

Men have a parallel experience. After a while, when his partner isn't enjoying herself, it becomes harder for a man to enjoy himself. He may go through the motions but feel that sex becomes more of a physical release than a shared sensual experience. He may become anxious in bed, finding his partner impossible to please and feeling afraid to touch her for fear he'll upset her. He may be tired of initiating sex, dreading more rejection. These difficulties are common reactions to a sex life that has gone stale. And as a couple's sex life becomes less satisfying, everyone becomes more vulnerable to having an affair. Some men and women do find it easier to respond with their innate sexual energy when making love with a new or different partner—especially one who is more connected to their own primal energy.

On the bright side, when couples find themselves in these struggles, they both have work to do. Rarely can they realistically point the finger at one partner as the problem. That is because we tend to become intimate with people who function at the level of connection we are comfortable with. Otherwise, sex would have either felt too boring or too vulnerable—and making love would be so uncomfortable that an intimate relationship probably wouldn't have developed in the first place. Typically, that means when one partner can benefit from this work, so can the other. This sets the tone for an even playing field, when everyone has something to learn and no one person is at fault.

BALANCE IS KEY

As men and women learn to tap their instinctual sexual nature, they need not become extreme in their behavior. All of us carry both masculine and feminine aspects within our personalities. This complexity makes us feel whole and complete. Learning to access our primal nature does not mean that women discard their masculine traits or men let go of their feminine traits. In fact, it is the *opposite*. For women to let go into their primal feminine, they must have a strong masculine base in their personality to allow for this level of vulnerability. This was one of the gifts of the feminist movement that we can now utilize in our sex lives. And men must maintain contact with their feminine side, because sensitivity and the ability to feel their own emotions, as well as those of their partner's, is essential for exciting sex. For all of us, if one essence strongly overwhelms the other, the imbalance will be felt in our intimate relationships. Thus, cultivating our primal nature in the bedroom requires that we nurture our wholeness as well as our instincts. For everyone, this nurturing promotes psychological growth and maturity. In this way, what is good for a monogamous sex life is also fabulous for personal growth and evolution as human beings more generally. Thus, making love becomes an exquisite stage for everyone's growth and maturity. In reality, tuning into your primal nature benefits you first, even before it benefits your sex life.

It is also important to remember that balance is helpful not only within each person but also in every monogamous couple's sex life. This means that lovers benefit from engaging their opposite sexual energy, with each partner offering both periodically. Sometimes women enjoy being more assertive and in control of the sexual experience, and men enjoy being receptive and gifted by a more sexually directive woman. Most couples find it very exciting to vary their sex play in this way. And of course, some sex is just fun and does not require access to instinct at all. In my practice, I have found that when a woman periodically feels her man's strength and primal masculine energy, she feels much more open and interested in participating in a variety of sexual experiences with him. That is because she feels sexually safe with him at a very basic level, and she doesn't necessarily need to be assured of this every time they make love. Men, as a result, often find that sex becomes less pressure-filled as their partners free up and relax into a variety of sexual experiences. When each partner knows the other can go deep into a primal place, there is a level of trust that carries through to all of their sexual experiences—whether they be creative, playful, dark, emotional, or instinctual.

HOW OUR CULTURE WORKS AGAINST US

While monogamy is held as the sexual ideal for couples, we are inundated with information that makes monogamy an imposing challenge for most couples. It is helpful to be aware of these messages as you embark on your path to more exciting monogamous sex. We live in a very sexualized culture. We are exposed to sexual images on a regular basis, and we place a lot of importance on a satisfying sex life. However, we are also living in a culture that isn't teaching us how to make love well and that offers little support in achieving a satisfying monogamous sexual relationship. Our minds are filled with faulty information about normal sexuality and intimacy. Understanding these cultural myths and faulty messages will help them have less impact on you.

Perhaps one of the most damaging messages for couples is that monogamy should be easy if you marry the right person. Many people still believe this, even though it doesn't play out for them in their own relationships. This expectation leads to shame, blame, and sexual acting out. Monogamy is a fabulous idea for a multitude of reasons, but it doesn't happen naturally for many human primates.

Second, many people carry the expectation that they should just know how to be a great lover—as if making love is an innate skill. While it is true that having sex is innate, making love is a learned skill that requires time and effort to master. Sadly, the vast majority of us are not born with this ability. Like any creative act, learning to give and receive love well is an art form, and art takes time to master. Most of us don't pick up a paint brush and create a masterpiece. With time and patience, we learn what we like, our particular style, and how best to manifest it on the canvas. This truth is confusing to people because most of us have had the experience of fabulous sex being effortless in a new relationship. Because it feels so good at that time, and our partners are clearly enjoying themselves, we assume we've got the skill. But in reality, great sex at the beginning of a relationship is all about the chemicals in our brain, not about our innate ability as lovers. This sets us up to believe that we, and our lovers, have talents that are actually not yet developed.

Third, our cultural striving for political correctness has done our sex lives a significant disservice. While political correctness is critical in the boardroom, it backfires in the bedroom. We view the distinctions between the sexes as crass, and for decades now we've attempted to neutralize them. But as a result, sexual tension is diminishing. In this scenario, everyone loses. A woman is not encouraged to offer her partner what he longs for and cannot get from his male friends—sensuality. A man is not supported in offering his partner what she longs for and cannot get from her female friends—masculine strength and presence. Our obsession with political correctness teaches us to minimize our differences and withhold our innate gifts. What a pity. Our differences are gifts to be celebrated—relish them!

Fourth, the cultural ideal of female thinness interferes with women's sexual self-esteem. This low self-esteem negatively impacts how vulnerable and open women are willing to be in bed. The ideal of an unrealistically thin figure creates tremendous shame and results in many women resisting being seen naked. If a woman cannot allow herself to be seen physically, it will probably interfere with her willingness to show herself emotionally. This truncates what a couple can create together sexually.

Fifth, the way we eat as a society is a great disservice Western culture has inflicted on its people. Most of what is in our typical grocery stores today did not exist 100 years ago. In truth, the ingredients for common items in the grocery store are chemicals that do not qualify as food. As a result, children and adults struggle with obesity, diabetes, and many more ailments that directly impact sex. Low libido, erectile dysfunction, and depression are just a few of the ways our food selections result in sexual issues and concerns.

Sixth, our cultural overdependence on thinking sabotages our sex lives. Brain power is encouraged to the neglect of connection with our physical selves. But without balance of brain and body, it becomes very easy for us to ignore our body and its needs. The less relationship people have with their bodies, the less sensual they are generally, and the less aware they are of their primal instincts. Plus, the more time we spend thinking rather than feeling, focusing on our brains rather than our bodies, the more difficult it becomes to feel and enjoy physical pleasure. When we are not used to feeling pleasure in our bodies, the subtleties of sexual pleasure become more elusive. This, in turn, makes monogamy more challenging because sex in a long-term monogamous relationship becomes less sensual and pleasurable. These trends only appear to be intensifying as technology plays an increasingly pivotal role in all of our lives. To me, this sets the stage for making pornography, one-night stands, and other faster and more superficial means of sexual excitement that much more enticing—because these experiences can offer a faster sexual fix than finding your way back into a body that you have neglected and disconnected from.

Finally, the message that if a couple's sex life is suffering, then someone must be diagnosed and treated, is a dangerous message that needs to be dispelled. As we have explored, not all sexual problems are the result of medical or psychiatric pathology. One such example I work with regularly is women with low libido. Sometimes not wanting sex or resisting opening to her man is a healthy and appropriate response for a woman. Women naturally surrender when they feel loved and protected. If a woman does not feel comfortable with a partner or in a particular situation, opening could lead her into dangerous territory. A woman should always trust her judgment and not be critical of her instincts to close. Instead, she can use her reactions to learn and grow. The same is true for a man with low libido—his libido may be a healthy response to an unhealthy situation.

MONOGAMY: THE UNTOLD STORY

In sum, monogamy is a complicated but valuable goal for intimate relationships. It is *essential* to remember that monogamy isn't natural, but this is only one aspect of many couple's sexual struggles. Our current understanding of sexuality is valid and accurate, even though it is incomplete. That is, men and women bring many variables into their sexual experience that can impact intimacy in positive or negative ways—intimacy issues are not just about the fact that monogamy isn't natural. In reality, all of these influences are important to recognize in keeping a sexual relationship alive and well over time. However, when advising other therapists on their work with patients having sexual issues, I remind them that working from the instinct paradigm actually subsumes much of these other variables, addressing them all simultaneously. That is because for a person to be in touch with the instinctual nature, all other sexual issues become apparent and require attention. For example, being vulnerable enough to express one's deep sexual core means working through trust issues, couples communication, past sexual trauma, body image issues, low self-esteem, and negative belief systems about sexuality. Thus, working toward connecting with primal instincts is curative for people in a multitude of very important ways. In healing sexually, people heal emotionally. For this reason, the instinct paradigm is helpful for therapists and patients alike.

MOVING FORWARD

I have spent thousands of hours helping couples find ways to create more exciting monogamous connections. I enjoy this work as I have the pleasure of watching clients evolve more than their sexual relationship. As men and women access their own depth, their strengths unfold in kind. Men and women become more confident, loving, strong, and compassionate human beings. As both partners learn to highlight their particular brand of power, they develop more self-respect and respect for their partner's unique gifts. In this process, everyone has something to learn. Men who tend toward passivity learn to access their masculine strength. Men who are aggressive develop their sensitivity. Women who are passive or shut down from their bodies learn to feel sensual and strong. Women who have developed their masculine traits at the expense of their feminine gifts acquire the exquisite sensation of vulnerability in a trusting environment. We can all continue to evolve our skills of loving and being loved.

I have never met another who has accomplished complete personal and sexual evolution, nor have I done so myself. It is the challenging path of human nature that we can always mature in our loving.

Making monogamy exciting is not a path for everyone. Monogamy seems to bring out both the best and the worst in us. It calls us to search within ourselves for more to offer our partner. But it can also tempt us to back away from the person we know most intimately in the world. That is because, for some people, sex is just not that important. Others find the discomfort of vulnerability outweighs the benefits of this level of intimacy. Plus, some men and women find passionate connection through physical sensation alone as opposed to instinct. However, many people I've worked with have found the concepts in this book quite helpful in creating a more exciting monogamous relationship. Couples may find this information more helpful at some stages of their relationship than at others. Intimate relationships are fluid, and what connects us at one point may be different than what bonds us as our relationship matures. That is the natural flow of love and self-growth.

The second part of this book is devoted to helping you connect with your primal instincts. It has a more personal tone and includes multiple homework suggestions. These assignments are essential exercises in reconnecting to your instinctual core—simply knowing this information intellectually without experiencing it more deeply in your body is not enough. May this book serve you well on your quest to evolve your sexual experience, as well as your life experience.

Part II
PASSIONATE MONOGAMY

Chapter Six

UNLEASHING APHRODITE: FEMALE ECSTASY VIA HER PRIMAL NATURE

Seductive. . . . Flowing. . . . Juicy. . . . Alive. . . . Succulent. . . . Mysterious. The beauty of the feminine. The glory of woman. We admire her grace, her sensuality, and her ability to transform a moment into something magical. However, woman's evolution has temporarily led her away from this part of herself, that is, her luscious, and more primal core. This chapter assists women in reconnecting with their feminine instinct. For a woman, finding this part of herself cannot be done by thinking alone. Instead, it is realized through homework practices that open her up to her body and her sensuality. Women often find many of these exercises vulnerable-making and uncomfortable. They find that talking about connecting to their core is easier than actually doing it. That is because experiences that push us further into ourselves often provoke anxiety. First, we're not sure we will like what we find there. Sometimes women feel like their feminine core is a bottomless pit of emotions, or a needy, empty space inside them. Plus, emotional experiences that involve our bodies *and* our sexuality can be that much more challenging. On the positive side, however, I have not met a woman who was sorry she did this work. As you learn to connect further to your feminine core, you'll be better able to access sexual pleasure. Many women find that it makes monogamy more interesting again, because they can bring so much more to the experience. And when they give more sexually, they get more for themselves in return. The bottom line, however, is that there is no right way to be a woman. Some women will feel more drawn to cultivating these aspects of themselves than others. That is perfect, because it makes for the beautiful variety and uniqueness within our species. However, it is also true that for those women who want more from their sexual experience, capitalizing on their feminine instincts is a powerful path to their goal.

STEP ONE

Growing is hard work. Allowing our deeper, instinctual selves the opportunity to unfold is no exception. This chapter details the same path I use to guide many of my therapy patients. It's a terrain I know well, and I honor the journey every time I have the opportunity to walk it with another woman seeking fuller expression of herself. I often suggest to women that they think in terms of finding the Aphrodite inside her. Aphrodite is the Greek goddess that governs enjoyment of love and beauty, sensuality and sexuality. She is a part of each woman, and can be cultivated and felt more intensively if desired. When women feel connected to the Aphrodite in them, they usually feel more connected to their instinctual feminine selves.

Unveiling your feminine spirit will take courage, strength, and a strong, solid will to care for yourself. In fact, approaching this path from any other place may take you to feminine energy, but not necessarily the kind you are seeking. Becoming passive, helpless, emotionally volatile—these are the dark aspects of woman. They are born not from strength but from fear. But we are reaching for a different feminine. The feminine we seek is not manipulative, helpless, or fragile. She is a strong, beautiful creature that is balanced in herself and confident in her radiance. So paradoxically, it will be the strength you derive from your masculine self that will enable you to find your shining and radiant feminine!

If You Don't Have a Partner

Sometimes women think they can only explore their feminine core if they have a romantic partner. But that's not the case at all. This chapter teaches a woman to connect with a deeper place within herself—partners are not required. In fact, a lover could even distract you as you learn to access and enjoy your own sensual, feminine gifts.

Why Are You Here?

Let's take an honest look at what we can accomplish. And let's consider what we aren't going to do. What we are not looking to do is bring back old sexual patterns. We aren't going to try and recreate a sexual connection you had with your lover in the past. Instead, we are seeking to explore the sexual woman you are now. We will work to develop your sensual capacities further, and ultimately increase your ability to give and receive love—emotional and sexual. We will find your juice—that luscious feminine life force that chaotic daily life, stress, and fear can suck out of you.

What we aren't going to do is make you feel infatuated with your partner. Deep, meaningful love is not about infatuation. Instead, real love is about seeing your partner for the human he is, and loving him through that. It's about presenting yourself fully to your man, in spite of the fact that you know he is like all of us—chock full of imperfections.

What we aren't going to do is turn you into a sex machine. Female sex machines exist only in porn movies. What most women with healthy connections to their feminine core report is that they are receptive to their partner, though not necessarily always spontaneously lustful. Woman's sexuality is very different from her partner's. His isn't a better version of sexuality, it's just a different flavor of loving. Woman manifests the capacity to love profoundly—and when tapped, she allows herself to open deeply, taking her lover with her into the mysterious feminine realms. This is the place where the goddess Aphrodite lives and thrives. In learning to gift others with your grace, you will come to receive so much in return.

Bring Your Journal

Daily writing will aid your process of self-discovery. In fact, I ask all of my clients to journal every day. That is because, to grow and change a pattern that has probably been a part of your psyche for a while, you'll need to focus on the issues daily. This is true for everyone. Women who journal get to know themselves faster and more deeply. It speeds up the process of self-discovery by leaps and bounds. Reading books can certainly help you understand issues, but reading alone will not change your behavior. The only way to change your behavior is to put the effort into doing things rather than just thinking things. Journaling is one fabulous way to begin the process of doing.

Your first journal assignment is a long one—perhaps the longest entry you will make. Write your life story from the perspective of your own feminine essence. This task may feel strange and unstructured. But relax your brain and your analytical thinking for a moment. Your feminine side is a part of you, and has been with you all of your life. The fact that you may not feel her presence very strongly at the moment is not a problem. Just imagine.

Imagine what she felt as a young girl. What was it like growing up in your household as a girl? What did your mother teach you about being a woman? What sort of womanly traits did she role model for you? How about your father—how did he react to your feminine side? Did that change at all as you matured into puberty? What did he "teach" you about yourself by the way he reacted to you then? And what about your siblings? Your friends? Your religion? The culture in which you lived? What feedback did you get from boyfriends about your femininity? What was your first sexual experience like? How have these influences shaped who you are now as a woman, and what you feel about your feminine self? Guide yourself through your sexual life story and explore your history. Most women learn so much about themselves this way. Often, women learn why they first put their Aphrodite selves into hiding.

Your experience of your sexuality as a young girl and as you matured is pivotal to the woman you are now. We can actually make that statement about all aspects of you. For example, consider your relationship with money. Your experience with it as a child directly impacts your experience with it now. If you didn't have enough money, or if you had more than enough money, or whether or not you had to work hard to earn money—all of this affects your current experience of money on both a conscious and unconscious level. Your sexual self is no different.

FINDING YOUR STARTING POINT

If you are like most women, you have become so disconnected from your feminine core that you've lost touch with your current location on the path. So let's continue by getting your bearings. The quickest way to do this is to journal your answers to a series of questions.

Question 1: What do you like about yourself sexually? What do you not like?

In my therapy room, it's not unusual for a woman to report that she doesn't like her current sexual self very much. But because she is so uncomfortable about her sexual concerns, for a while she may just ignore the problems. With time, her issues gain in momentum and she becomes even less likely to desire intimate connection with her partner. Rather than ignoring the issues, let's take an honest look.

Question 2: Would you enjoy making love to yourself? Why are you an enjoyable lover? Where is there room for improvement?

Question 3: If you were a man, what sort of woman would feel good to be around? What sexual style would you enjoy in a woman? Is this something you'd like to cultivate in yourself?

These are tough questions. If you are like most women, it's easy to critique your partner's lovemaking skill and focus on his approach rather than your own. It's oh so easy to see where he isn't giving enough, or where he is rote and repetitive. What about your own bad habits? Rest assured that everyone has them. Where do you withdraw? Withhold? Close down and resist him? Imagine what it feels like to make love to you. And then imagine how you could be different. Everyone can work to love better. Even if you aren't ready to enact any changes, thinking about these issues is an important step in identifying where you'd like to grow.

Question 4: What side(s) of your sexual identity are you not currently expressing?

We express many different identities throughout our lives. Major life experiences and transitions engage different sides of ourselves—such as wife, mother, and business woman. We go through shifts in our sexual identities over time as well. Rather than wait for a new and improved sexual identity to find its way to you, you can make the conscious choice to bring on an identity shift. Imagine the sexual identity you want to experience. What does she look like? Feel like? Set the intention to welcome her in all aspects of your life, not just in your bedroom. The more welcome she feels, the more accessible she'll be to you, and the greater will be her gifts.

Dialogue with Your Body

When I ask women to do this exercise, I get every reaction from amazement to disgust to curiosity. It is one of the more unusual exercises I will have you do. But, time and time again, women find it extremely helpful. What better way to get to know your deepest femininity than to actually talk directly with her? Silly as this may seem to you, your next exercise is to talk with your pelvis. Specifically, write her a letter, and have her write back.

This is not nonsense. This experience will actually help to create a link between your conscious and unconscious minds with regard to your sexuality. Our unconscious minds don't speak with us directly. But the unconscious holds all kinds of juicy information about us. In fact, it is estimated that over 95 percent of our behavior is motivated by our unconscious minds.[1] What this means to you is that over 95 percent of your behavior is not necessarily under your conscious control! Not such great news, I know. But, there are definite ways for you to improve the communication between your conscious and unconscious minds. And doing so only increases your self-awareness, and thus your power. Dream interpretation, hypnosis, drawing, and creative writing are all possible ways of exploring the unconscious realm. But, since you may not know how to interpret your dreams, and you probably don't have access to a hypnotist (at least not in this immediate moment), creative writing is your next best alternative. So, relax and break open your journal. Know that you may feel silly at first, but go for it anyway.

If you're still saying, "No way, I'll just skip this weird little exercise and keep on reading," I urge you to think again. When you opt out of any exercise in this book, you are saying, "I want some help, but not this kind of help." This attitude is a mistake, because picking only those exercises that make sense to you will drastically limit your self-discovery. In fact, it is the exercises you innately resist that have the potential to offer you the most new and helpful information. That's because these are the exercises that require you to step out of your comfort zone.

So, ask your pelvis some questions, like, "How are you? What do you need from me? How has your life been so far? What is making love like for you?" Then switch gears, and come back to your journal with the intention of expressing your pelvis's perspective. Let her write back to you—in fact, start an ongoing dialogue with her. I'm sure she'll have many interesting reactions as you read this book.

Find the Yes and the No in Your Body

Learning to tune into your body will help you become more sensual in every moment—erotic or not. This will translate into a deeper and more profound sense of who you are and what you are feeling, moment by moment. And this increases your power in the world. It just makes sense—more information about yourself can only serve you well. So, it's worth the time to get to know your body better. This is a body meditation that will help you understand your desire to experience your soft feminine center, *and* clarify any resistance you have toward her:

> Breathe slowly and deeply while relaxing your body. If you are anxious or pre-occupied, you won't get much information from a meditation. So, allow your body and mind to let go. Think first about your desire to uncover your sensual self. Feel that softness in your body. If Aphrodite had an inner sanctum in your body, where would it be located? Imagine it. And then feel her presence there. Feel your body's yes in response to her. What does it feel like to have her there? Focus in on that space. What color would she be? What temperature? Imagining her in this concrete way will help you to call her out at other times. Just take a few moments to be with your yes to her. Now, seek out the no in your body. Where would your epicenter of no be located? What part of you resists knowing yourself more deeply, and resists showing yourself more intimately to your lover? What color would this part of yourself be? And what temperature? Getting to know your no as a more real entity will help you soften your resistance over time.

Before you finish this exercise, take out your journal and write about what happened. Or, make a drawing of your yes and no. The more familiar you become with these parts of you, the more available they are to conscious manipulation in the future. Thus, if your no shows up in a sexual situation and you'd rather feel your yes, you will learn how to make that transition in the moment. Consider your yes that part of you that wants to grow and feel more sensual pleasure. Your no is that part of yourself that is frightened or overwhelmed by this mysterious part of you. Both of these aspects of you deserve your honor and respect. There is wisdom in both voices, and important information. Let them speak to you. If you are like most women, they have a lot to say.

REDISCOVER YOUR JUICY SENSUALITY

An important part of connecting with your feminine depth involves feeling, appreciating, and honoring your physical form. Your body provides a home to your identity, and all that you associate with who you are. It contains your heart and soul, your emotions, your brain, and your womb. In fact, everything that is of value to you, about you, rests inside its confines. Whether you know it or not, if you are like most adults, you have probably developed some level of disconnection from your physical self. And as a result, you have lost contact with your emotional depth and your feminine juice, which is where your passion resides. When this happens, a woman feels less alive. A woman may find that certain experiences help her counteract this process for a period of time. For example, taking a ski vacation, where she is feeling in tune with her body as she glides down the slopes, may wake her up momentarily to her body and thus her emotions; or she may enjoy the feeling of being pregnant, which tunes her back into her body for nine months—or longer, if she breast feeds. However, neither of these offers long term solutions for a woman being plugged in to herself.

The process of disconnection can unfold insidiously, without your even realizing it. Often, when a woman does become aware, she feels like the path back home, back to feeling her body, is just too difficult or complicated a task. Over time, her body feels less and less available to her. Psychologists call the end result of this disconnection *dissociation*. When we dissociate in the extreme form, we lose all contact with our emotions and physical sensations. But most of us experience it in a less intense way—such as when we tune out mild hunger pangs, or ignore our body's need for sleep. Dissociation comes in handy when we want to disengage from physical or emotional pain. However, women pay a huge price for the luxury of not feeling. That price, as you can well imagine, includes the price of your passion.

Dissociation and Its Effect on Feminine Sexual Experience

Women who feel void of sexual passion tend not to feel much sexual pleasure. Such women may describe their genitals as numb or nonresponsive. In sexual relationships, physically disconnected women struggle because the partner's touch doesn't feel pleasurable. They don't know what to ask for sexually, because nothing provides the pleasure they seek. Sex becomes a frustrating experience for both a woman and her partner. For her, it seems the harder she tries to feel, the more upset she becomes. For him, it seems the more he tries to please her, the more tension is generated between them. They both feel the loss of an enjoyable and rewarding part of life.

Why Do We Disconnect?

Dissociation from our bodies occurs for a variety of reasons. It is a defense mechanism that allows us to tolerate uncomfortable feelings or sensations by disconnecting from them. For example, physical pain can result in a disconnection from our bodies. Painful emotions can cause a similar reaction. We experience emotions through our bodies as well as our thoughts (imagine for example how fear feels in your gut, or sadness feels in your chest and heart, or anger feels in your throat). Thus, as we encounter painful emotions repeatedly, we are motivated to flee our physical sensations and find refuge in our thoughts and our heads. But physical and emotional pain is not the only reason this dynamic occurs.

Many of us live overly full, stressful lives. We spend much time thinking and planning and running from place to place. We are primarily inhabiting our thoughts rather than our bodies. In this way, stress results in disconnection from our physical self.

Interestingly, a woman who is dissociated from her pelvis typically also describes a general lack of physical pleasure in her life. While she may be well aware of a lack of sexual passion, she is less aware that her life is void of passion and pleasure in other forms. And it just makes sense that in order to feel sexual pleasure, one must be tuned into physical pleasure more generally first.

To complicate matters further, women often turn to behaviors or substances that further numb their bodies, rather than wake their bodies up to sensation. For pleasure, many women who report numb genitals choose such activities as overeating, television, or sleep. These are all pastimes that further disconnect her from her body. Rarely will she enjoy yoga, massage, hot baths, or dancing—activities that enhance her connection to her physical self.

SO NOW WHAT?

The good news is that you can guide yourself back into your physical self. You were born tuned into your body. This is your natural state. Consider an infant's relationship to her body. She certainly alerts us in a very clear way that she knows when something is physically wrong. As an adult, the process of tuning back in requires several steps. To feel sexual passion, you must first be tuned into physical sensations, pleasurable feelings, and passion in a general, nonsexual sense.

The Truth about Pleasure

It seems that, for most adults, feeling pleasure is a learned skill. That is, it must be relearned because our innate ability to feel pleasure somehow gets warped on the path from babyhood into adulthood. To feel pleasure, we must be open to feeling. But when we are open to feeling, we are in a vulnerable state. So the intensity of sexual pleasure you feel is directly related to the level of vulnerability you allow yourself. And we all resist feeling vulnerable—we tend to associate that state with being hurt.

The Pleasure of Reconnecting

There are many wonderful, luscious ways you can reconnect with your body. Just about any activity that helps you notice and feel your physical self will do the trick. For most women, repetition is the key. That is, bringing yourself back to your body on a daily basis is required. Just one or two reconnection sessions won't counteract years of paying less attention to sensation and physical pleasure. Remember that this is a process. Begin by tuning into your body generally, then feeling pleasure in your body, then tuning into your pelvis, and finally feeling sexual pleasure in your pelvis. And after you've made contact with pleasure in your body, you'll feel more comfortable bringing your partner into the experience.

Sometimes women tell me that they don't want to bother with feeling pleasure generally. They feel they don't have the time, or the inclination, to wake their bodies up fully. They simply want to feel sexual pleasure. I do not think this is possible—at least, I've never seen this approach succeed. It seems a bit like attempting to feel only one emotion and tune out the others, or taste only one flavor and not notice others. Our bodies don't make deals like this.

CONNECTING YOUR MIND WITH YOUR BODY

Begin a Regular Practice

I am a huge fan of therapy homework assignments. Reconnecting with instincts is definitely not an intellectual exercise, successfully accomplished by talking alone. Typically I recommend that women begin a regular body practice, like yoga, stretching, or dance. Yoga is particularly well suited for your goals because some of the poses are specifically intended to connect you to your pelvis. If you choose dance, consider belly dancing, because of the focus on your pelvis. In contrast, more controlled dancing, like tap or ballroom, will be less helpful in this regard.

Whichever practice you choose, be sure that it is physically enjoyable for you, and that it offers the opportunity to regularly check in and feel your body. Gentle body practices allow you to become more acquainted with the feelings of relaxation and pleasure. Lifting weights, aerobics, or power yoga usually don't offer this experience. While they may be healthy for you, they are not geared to tuning in. In fact, intensive exercises can have the effect of teaching us to tune out in our attempt to avoid feeling the discomfort they may generate. An added benefit from tuning in to your body is that you will naturally start eating more healthfully and taking better care of your physical self. That's because it becomes very difficult to overeat, neglect sleep, or avoid exercise when you feel your body so acutely. The discomfort you feel in these situations outweighs the pleasure of eating too much or not caring for yourself. Thus, regular body practices inherently support a more natural, healthful way of life.

The Sensory Awareness Experience

Becoming more aware of your body's five senses will result in increased body awareness. Focusing your attention on touch, smell, taste, sound, and sight will help you notice more subtle pleasurable sensations in every moment. And anything that helps you experience the subtleties of pleasure will benefit your sexual experience.

Take a five–week sensing tour. Each week, focus on a different sense. For example, let's start with taste—a favorite sense for women, to be sure! Focusing on taste means being extra aware of the experience of eating, and how taste creates sensations in your body. Eating slowly will be a crucial part of your experiment. The slower we do something, whether it be eating or making love, the more aware we are of our sensory experience. Which flavors and textures leave your body feeling more open, engaged, juicy, or wanting more? How does your body experience a succulent, ripe peach, versus sashimi, or fine aged camembert accompanied by a fabulous wine? Identify the foods that make your body say, "Yes! I want more."

In contrast, which tastes close you, lose your interest, bring you out of your body and into your head? Lima beans, cold coffee, or calves' liver may have this effect. Notice the foods that leave your body saying, "No! I don't want this!" How does your body communicate no to you?

The following week, tune into touch, and be aware of the different sensations between touching and being touched. Notice how fabrics feel on your body—the variations of silk, velvet, and polyester. Experience a hot bath, wind in your hair, gravel under your feet. Treat yourself to a massage, and notice how certain types of touch open your body, while others make you want to constrict and pull away. Avoiding conversation with the masseuse will help you focus.

Repeat this exercise with vision, sound, and smell. You are learning about the many ways you can offer your body pleasure, just by being more aware of your senses and the activities of daily life. Aphrodite reminds us that we all become so easily consumed with thinking, analyzing, and doing, that we lose sight of the many ways we can feel sensual pleasure in almost any moment. Plus, it is all too easy to focus on what feels uncomfortable. This tendency is actually evolutionarily adaptive, so you can be immediately aware of discomfort and keep yourself out of harm's way. But try shifting your focus to what feels good in any particular moment. Subtle as it may seem, highlighting these sensations will support the unfolding of your feminine essence.

Connecting Your Mind and Your Pelvis

The following exercises bring your focused attention to your pelvis. I've listed other sample exercises in chapter 10. The more you do, the more connected you'll feel to your body and your sensuality. That is because we know from neuropsychiatric research that where attention goes, neural firing goes. That is, there are neurons in your brain that are the communication channels between different parts of your mind and body. Whenever you use a particular channel, you strengthen it by repeatedly firing those neurons. It's sort of like forming a path in the snow. The more you walk the path, the more clearly defined it becomes. And the more clearly defined the path, the greater the chances that you will find that path again in the future.

So remember, the more you attend to your pelvis with exercises such as these, the more energy your brain invests in building neural connections between your pelvis and your mind. The stronger you make these connections, the easier it will be to experience the gifts of sensual pleasure.

Kegel Exercises

Kegel exercises involve repeatedly contracting the muscles of your pelvic floor. To do a kegel, simply tighten the muscles you would use to stop the flow of your urine stream. When this muscle tightening is done repeatedly, it strengthens your pelvic floor.

Kegel exercises were developed by a physician to assist his female patients in improving their bladder control. Regular kegel exercises keep your pelvic floor strong so that as you age, you'll have fewer problems with unexpected urine discharge—like when you cough or laugh. However, sex therapists prescribe kegels, because strengthening the muscles of your pelvic floor will make your pelvis more sensitive. It also enhances blood flow to your pelvis, which will make your orgasms more intense. Doing kegels on a regular basis brings your attention back to your pelvis in a repetitive way. The beauty of this exercise is that no one will know you are doing it! Pairing kegels with a daily activity, such as brushing your teeth, or stopping at traffic lights, will help you remember.

Pelvic Movements

Another reconnection exercise many women find helpful involves imperceptibly moving your pelvis in a circular fashion. These movements should be so small that no one will know you are doing them. You can literally stand in a grocery line while tuning into your pelvis this way, or do them while sitting in a meeting. And you will be amazed at how sensual you will feel, secretly moving your body slowly and deliberately in this age-old movement of love. You will quickly learn that such movements grab Aphrodite's attention almost like magic!

Read Erotica while Focusing on Your Pelvis

You can learn a lot about yourself from reading erotica. Women who feel disconnected from their bodies and their sensuality can get glimpses of what can help to wake them up by reading erotic stories describing what turns other women on. Think of reading erotica as an educational experience. Women are often surprised to learn that most bookstores actually have an impressive variety of erotic books written by women, for women. Reading erotica while focusing on the feelings generated in your pelvis can help you reconnect with your sensual self.

A word of warning is in order, however. Don't be surprised if many of the stories you read are actually not pleasing to you. This doesn't mean there is something wrong with you. In fact, if anything, it means you are normal. Many if not most women are very specific about what pleases them sexually. Each woman's association to what is sexy is very complex—based on her unique sexual history, her first sensual experiences, and her personality. So don't expect that you'll be reacting positively to most stories, because what turns you on may be very specific. Do your best to make this homework fun for yourself—enjoy your book while taking a bubble bath, or with sensual music as your backdrop. Set the intention to reconnect with your sensual side in a gentle, loving way.

Masturbate

What could possibly be a better way for you to connect with your pelvis, and thus your sensual core, than massaging your body? Masturbation is actually a common practice among women (and men, but you probably knew that already). And it doesn't have to lead to orgasm. You can simply massage yourself as a way to relax, release tension, or feel pleasure. Masturbation is also a fabulous way for you to learn how you like to be touched. You'll need to know this information when it comes time to teach your partner what you like.

When you masturbate as homework, take great care to create a warm, sensual, and inviting environment for yourself. What would you like to surround yourself with to help your body feel welcome? Soft blankets, incense, or candles? In our hurried lives, we rarely take the time to appreciate ourselves, and our bodies, the way we deserve. (This is ironic because it's so easy to get mad at others when *they* don't appreciate us, but that's another story). Take responsibility now for caring for yourself well. Acknowledge the wonder of your feminine form. This is the part of you that can actually create other human beings! It is also the part of you that has the capacity to literally join with another and connect so deeply that you can become one in body and spirit. This part of your body is, indeed, a sacred place. Hold this truth while you reconnect with yourself anew.

Moving: Feeling the Flow

Stretching. Pulsating. Slithering. Rocking. Hugging. Flowing. Dancing. Swaying. Undulating. Gliding.

Nothing brings us into our bodies like movement. Little may please Aphrodite as much as allowing her expression through creatively and sensually moving your body. Women's bodies were born to move. Unlike men's relatively strait, rigid forms, women have curves, softness, and suppleness. While men's movement tends toward the choppy and stiff, women's movement is naturally more flowing and graceful. Most men and many women will tell you that a woman's body in motion is almost impossible to ignore. The magic of her moving form is captivating. Generating such motion calls a woman into her depth. Feminine motion radiates from her creative core, her womb, her mystery.

Taking a few minutes every day to express yourself and your emotions through your body via movement and dance will catapult you into sensual awareness. Be forewarned that initially you will probably feel self-conscious— even with just yourself present. But don't let that stop you. Before you begin, breath into your body and learn to feel yourself from the inside. Determine what emotions you are feeling and/or what you want your movement to express. Choose music that will support this emotional experience. Sometimes you'll want to start moving slowly and deliberately, focusing on one part of your body and allowing all of your feeling to flow through that part. Other times you'll begin by taking up as much space as you can—swirling or pounding your body around the room, surrounding the space with your energy and emotion. Some days your eyes will be closed or downcast. Other days they will be glaring and intense. Using your voice by singing, yelling, moaning, or laughing will only facilitate your expressive experience.

The more you let go and let your body move as she wishes, the more connected you'll feel to your feminine core. Remember that Aphrodite experiences all emotions, not just those we typically think of as pleasurable. Holding her back while you are dancing means that you will be more apt to hold her back while you are making love. So let her flow—release her, enjoy her, and most of all, appreciate all of her expressions.

Eventually you will find it helpful to become comfortable dancing with your partner present. This will be an important step in allowing your feminine core freedom while you are making love. However, women are often self-conscious moving and dancing in front of their lover. To encourage yourself along these lines, you can first *imagine* dancing for him, or even dance for a picture of him. Get used to having someone's eyes on you while you express yourself in this way, and get used to looking into his eyes while you are expressing yourself. So, while you allow your eyes to meet his (even if it's just in your imagination), also allow your face to show whatever emotions you are feeling, and allow your body to move in whatever ways feel true for you. As you become more comfortable with these exercises, you will feel more and more comfortable feeling your depth in even the most intimate situations.

For Extra Help

Some women have a particularly difficult time connecting with their bodies. This can be because of past traumatic experiences, negative beliefs about their bodies or their femininity formed in childhood, or for reasons they don't understand. If this is the case for you, it can be helpful to get assistance from a professional. Talking to a therapists can be helpful. In addition, I frequently recommend several types of body-oriented therapists to my patients

Pelvic Floor Physical Therapy

Most of us are familiar with physical therapists, but few women know that there are physical therapists that have a specialization in working with the pelvic floor. That is, they have special training in helping women work through muscle tension and discomfort in the pelvic region. Pelvic floor physical therapists can help you to heal tissue strained or damaged during childbirth. They can teach you how to do kegel exercises in a way that is best for your body. They can prescribe homework for you to do alone, or with your partner, to improve the suppleness of your pelvic floor, thus making intercourse more pleasurable. You can look for an appropriately qualified physical therapist in your area by contacting your gynecologist, or by looking on the website www.APTA.org (the American Physical Therapy Association). As with any therapist you choose, take your time and be sure you feel comfortable with her before embarking on a treatment relationship.

Body Work

Good body work can be extremely healing for women. There are many different varieties, but all high-quality body work has something in common: it will bring you into your body in a way you probably won't do on your own, and wouldn't even accomplish in talking therapy. In fact, I encourage many of my patients to participate in body work while they are in therapy with me. It typically speeds up the process of therapy. High-quality body work assists women in getting to know their physical selves, and thus their emotional selves, in a deep and lovely way. Some types of body work include Reiki, massage, Rolfing, cranial-sacral therapy, chiropractic, acupuncture, and reflexology. Most body therapies work well for some folks but not for others. Be prepared to shop around until you find both a therapy method and a therapist you are comfortable with.

DECORATING: YOUR HOME AS APHRODITE'S TEMPLE

Your home can truly be Aphrodite's lair—her temple, her sacred space. We all draw on our surroundings to call out parts of ourselves. And we all respond to the tone of our environments, whether or not we consciously realize it. Consider the impact of a variety of atmospheres. When we need to relax and unwind, we may go out into nature. But if we are looking to rev up and have fun, we go to a bar or nightclub. If we want to connect spiritually, we attend a church, temple, or other religious site. In this way, we allow our surroundings to carry us to the emotional state we seek. Similarly, you can create a home environment that calls to your femininity.

Creating Aphrodite's lair may require some serious redecorating. Consider colors and types of fabrics that Aphrodite most resonates with—maybe velvet, or silk, or gold lamé. She might like fabrics available to drape over herself, to dance with, or to lie on, as well as special material on the furniture and pillows. Pay attention to the lighting in the room—is she drawn to candlelight or soft mood lighting? Aphrodite might also enjoy incense, photos of loved ones, or objects from her childhood. She might respond well to bringing aspects of nature into the room, such as plants, furs, or objects from the earth such as stones or wood. Allow time for this space to evolve in a soulful way. Use the surroundings to generate feelings of love, sacredness, and peace. The more attention you devote to creating her space, the more it will protect and nourish your unfolding.

USING TRANSITION TIMES: MAKING THE MOST OF YOUR MOMENTS

If you are like most women, you spend more of your days immersed more deeply in your masculine energies than your feminine selves. Unless you teach yoga or belly dancing every day, you are probably suffering from this imbalance. Many women find it helpful after a full day of living in their masculine energies to identify a time specifically dedicated to reconnecting with their feminine depth again. Thus, look for times every day to use your environment to support going within. For example, carefully choose the music you listen to while driving home from work. Select music that helps you feel more connected to your heart and body. Moving to music for a few minutes after you change out of work clothes also helps to let go of thoughts and find your deeper self again. Many women enjoy hot baths or stretching exercises in this same way. If you are concerned with taking time away from your family, remember that the better you feel, the more you have to give. From this perspective, creating sensually focused transition times for yourself is probably a win-win for everyone.

OPENING TO THE MANY FACETS OF THE FEMININE

Feminine essence is flowing and changing. In spite of this natural variability of feminine nature, it is easy for a woman to find herself stuck or inflexible in her feminine self-expression. That is because many women find only one aspect of feminine energy most comfortable to express. When this happens, she limits herself from experiencing her femininity more fully, and from realizing her power and creative potential. In addition, she restricts the variety of sexual experiences she may share with her partner. This is worth noting because men appreciate and enjoy the different flavors of feminine energy.

Women close themselves to aspects of their femininity for a variety of reasons. The most common reason is that some forms of feminine energy feel uncomfortable. A woman may feel exposed as these deeper parts of herself truly are tender and thus more easily wounded. Her partner, too, can become overwhelmed or frightened by the intensity and depth of Woman. If her partner is uncomfortable with an aspect of the feminine, she will likely shut that part of herself down.

Your Sensual Self

Isabelle stretched like a cat as she woke to the smell of something yummy in the oven. Neil was an expert at Sunday breakfast, and soon she would be enjoying the fruits of his labor. What would she do today? She rolled over into the patch of sunshine on her pillow, deciding not to think for just a little longer. Breathing deep into her body, she ran her hands over her breasts and her belly. She imagined the sunshine spreading down the length of her body, warming her in spite of the cool spring air outside her window pane. She sighed out loud as she snuggled further into her pillow and feather comforter. Soon she heard Neil's voice calling her to breakfast. Isabelle wrapped her soft, terry robe around her naked frame and headed downstairs. Greeting Neil with a hug and kiss, she settled in to enjoy her meal. The coffee, the grapefruit, the warm muffins—Isabelle took advantage of this moment to enjoy the scents and flavors being so lovingly offered to her.

Your sensual self offers you pleasure through your body's senses. You receive joy from physical touch, tastes, fragrances, sounds, and sight. When making love, you embrace sensual experience on all these levels, thus heightening your pleasure. But you do not limit your sensual awareness to sexual moments. You can bring your focus to your body regularly, thus turning any behavior or movement into a potential for physical awareness and pleasure. This aspect of you can experience eating, showering, and putting lotion on your body from a sensual perspective. You can, if you choose, even feel activities that wouldn't be considered sensual in this same way. Anything as mundane as doing the dishes can become a meditation for your sensual self. The feeling of the water, the soap, the physical movement—all this can bring you into your body and heighten your sensual experience.

Making love is the ultimate buffet for your sensual enjoyment. As you learn to think less and feel more, your sexual pleasure will heighten dramatically. You'll be more aware of the sensual aspects of various parts of your body—no longer will your pleasure be limited to your genitals and your breasts. Your sensual self is all about feeling pleasure via touch, taste, smell, vision, and hearing.

Your Nurturing Self

Faith heard his little footsteps in the hall even before he gloriously announced that the morning had, in fact, arrived. "Mommy!" he delightedly exclaimed, "it snowed last night!" "Really, honey?" Faith tried to muster as much enthusiasm as her just-wakened brain could summon. As Faith watched her sweet boy run to the window, she felt her heart open wider than wide, filling with love for this darling creature she and David had created. Faith threw on some sweats and followed him downstairs to start some oatmeal. The dogs jumped up to greet her as she entered the kitchen. Faith somehow managed to pet them and get Sam's breakfast all while downing the first of several cups of strong coffee. She left a good morning message on David's voice mail. Then she sat for a second to enjoy the moment. Faith loved it when her small but mighty kingdom was peaceful.

Your nurturing self is that part of you that receives pleasure through giving and caring for those you love. This is a creative aspect of Woman—she creates babies and art, and nurtures plants, animals, and people. This aspect of you is fed through the satisfaction and delight of feeding others, literally and figuratively. You receive nurturance by cultivating life force in others. Your love and your energy expand as you support and encourage the growth of those around you. This motherly aspect within you cares for you as well. It is that voice inside you that encourages you to slow down and rest when life has become too hectic. It is your internal mother, reminding you to get what you need for yourself. This part of you innately knows that the more you give to yourself, the more you will have to offer others.

When making love, this flavor of femininity flows from your womb, which is your creative center, as well as your heart, which is the core of your love. She brings with her the essence of love, the gift of caring for and giving to another body and soul. While making love, you can feel her power to manifest and nurture life force in yourself, your man, and your offspring.

The Instinctual, Animalistic Goddess

Sabrina was determined to stay in bed that Saturday morning. Jim was out of town, presenting her with a perfect opportunity for some R&R. When her hunger pangs got the best of her, she brought some finger food back to bed with her. Eating with her fingers was a pleasure she afforded herself whenever she could. Cuddled up in her fleece sheets, Sabrina thought about the night before Jim left for his business trip—how he had rocked her, made love to her in such a primal way. . . . Her hands instinctively reached for herself as she brought herself back to those delicious moments.

Your animalistic self runs on instinct. This flavor of Woman is closely connected to your primal nature. More tuned into your body's needs and desires than your intellect, you feel your physical being intensely and with clarity. This aspect of your feminine self relies on intuition as her highest form of knowing. She experiences her emotions from her core—laughing from deep in her belly, crying from deep in her heart. Relating to nature, she can fight like a tiger, cuddle like a kitten, or make love with the intense passion of a wild animal.

In sexual relationships, your instinctual essence relates to your partner first from a passionate, emotional place. She feels emotions through her body's perspective, as opposed to knowing them through her thoughts. Her expressions of love and desire are more raw than refined. This feminine energy longs to let go sexually, and seeks to create sensual and sexual exchanges that open her to deep, mysterious places within.

The Maiden Goddess

Lucille lay in bed, listening to the birds beneath her window. She loved waking early, to the sounds of the garden. She decided to watch the sunrise from the deck outside. Sneaking out of bed so that she wouldn't disturb Brad, she tiptoed down the stairs and out the screen door. Breathing in the fresh spring air, she closed her eyes so that she could listen more acutely. Lucille took in all the sounds of the morning, curious about what she'd experience, in spite of the fact that she'd started her day like this a million times before. . . . Opening to receive the world around her, Lucille delighted in the new day offered up with the dawn.

The maiden goddess is that sweet and tender part of woman that opens trustingly to the world around her. She is curious and receptive, seeing the beauty in all experiences and the freshness in every moment. The maiden is the youthful side of woman. Regardless of her chronological age, she taps into the innocence and the joy of early life.

In sexual relationships, the maiden goddess is the virgin within you. She opens with trust to her partner, allowing him to carry her to places she hasn't been before. She is that part of woman who feels the potential for newness in every sexual situation. She is also that part of you that feels curious about trying new sensual experiences, eager to explore new territory with her partner by her side. Her tender heart feels the fear inherent when we uncover ourselves to others. In spite of her vulnerability, she allows herself to open and explore. She delights in sharing beautiful, intimate moments with her beloved.

Aphrodite as You Age

Women often feel that it becomes harder to connect with feminine energy as they age. This sad truth arises from the cultural teaching that women lose their femininity over time. This superficial and misguided myth does not have to be true for you. Age can actually have the opposite effect if you wish—your maturity can bring with it greater self-knowledge and a deeper connection to your feminine heart and body. These very powerful feminine tools can actually increase with age if you allow it. An aging physical exterior—wrinkles, or sagging breasts—cannot change that. After all, we have spent this entire chapter finding your feminine core, and none of it had to do with your physical appearance! Older women can remain vital and alive with feminine energy if they so choose. Of course, time can challenge us emotionally. The longer we are on this planet, the more opportunities we have to be hurt, disappointed, and frustrated. Women naturally constrict when they encounter these emotions. So, in order to remain vital and sensual, you must develop a practice—such as a body practice that enables you to experience and release your feelings—that helps open you again to the world around you. If you don't make an active effort to open, you probably will lose your vitality and radiance. But that's not because of age per se; it's because of the toll life takes on all of us. Remember, this toll can be counteracted if you wish. I am quite sure the Aphrodite in you hopes you will make this choice.

A Final Thought

If you wish to become more acquainted with your sensual self, remember that you can use absolutely any moment in your life to do so. Any physical activity can become a meditation in connecting to Aphrodite and your feminine instincts, not just the exercises listed in this chapter. Whether you are cooking, folding laundry, or standing in line at the bank, it all can be experienced from an intentional attitude of love and sensuality. We never suffer a shortage of moments to tune into ourselves and become more acquainted with our sensual expression. One similarity you may have noticed among the different feminine energies is that to access them, your focus must be on a place inside you, deeper than your thoughts. So, tune into your feminine core, and enjoy the pleasure you find there!

Chapter Seven

BE YOUR BEST MAN: ADVICE FOR HIM (AND HER)

Masculine presence is a force like no other. Men respect it. Women crave it. Today, as well as historically, it is feared, revered, and valued in almost all cultures on the planet. The dark side of masculine energy is destructive, cruel, and cold. Alternately, men out of touch with their masculine core can be passive, emotionally shut down, and unreliable. But in its higher form, masculine essence offers tremendous gifts of strength, power, leadership, focus, and direction. In this chapter, we will explore how masculine traits are pivotal to a couple's experience of monogamy. We will look at the common mistakes men make in relationships that result in monogamy being more challenging for everyone. And we will identify ways that men can cultivate and develop their masculine core in their lives and relationships.

Remember that all people—men and women—exhibit both masculine and feminine energy. Masculine energy isn't just the purview of men, nor is feminine energy only expressed by women. All of us exhibit both forms of energy on a regular basis. But in a long-term monogamous relationship, passion can be facilitated by a tension between masculine and feminine energy in the bedroom. Typically, when a man exudes more masculine energy and a woman more feminine, sexual chemistry flows more freely.

Meet Jake, Mick, and Drew. These men work together in a large sales firm. It is Friday afternoon after a long week, and each of them has had thoughts of sex on their mind all day. Their differences in the bedroom later that evening are evident even while still at the office:

The meeting ran late and everyone was itching to start the weekend. But sales had been down again for the fifth month in a row, and upper management was nervous. Jake kindly but firmly requested that everyone stay a few more minutes to iron out the logistics of the latest guidelines. Just as the group refocused, Mick, a middle manager, directly challenged Jake by criticizing his new plan. Mick's tone was clearly angry and, as usual, it got everyone's attention. Jake was tired of Mick's tests and confrontations; he'd been acting this way since Jake got the promotion last year. He responded to Mick curtly, diffusing the situation for the moment. But the tension in the room remained palpable. Jake refocused the meeting one last time, noticing that Drew had become anxious from the brief, heated exchange and started doodling. Drew clearly wasn't listening to his final instructions for the following week. Jake made a mental note to talk with Drew about his lack of attention during meetings.

We will continue to learn from all three of these men again later in this chapter. From the brief introduction we see that Jake demonstrates solid alpha energy—his colleagues, as well as his wife, rely on him and trust his leadership and wisdom. Mick represents a more caustic version of alpha. He intimidates others, including his wife, and people often shut down around him as a result. Finally, Drew presents more passive masculine energy. His tendency is to tune out when he's uncomfortable, rather than dealing with problems more actively. As a result, the people in Drew's life have a hard time trusting him or relying on him.

WHAT WOMEN WANT

Jeannine was working late in her home office when Jake returned. He walked in as she was finishing a report on the computer. Jeannine loved how Jake greeted her—he seemed to really care when he asked how she was. He walked over to her chair and touched the back of her neck. Jeannine reached up to him, happy to find respite again in his arms.

Later that evening, Jeannine was sitting on the side of the bed putting lotion on her feet when Jake stood over her and kissed her tenderly. Jake's kisses always got her attention. As he felt her relax, he cupped the back of her head with his hand. Pulling her head back slightly by the hair, he kissed her mouth, this time with more insistence. Jeannine instinctively let her head fall back into his hand. "I love to love you, baby," Jake whispered in her ear. Jeannine forgot about her feet and her lotion as Jake looked into her eyes with love and longing. He guided her back to the bed and moved his body on top of hers. He gently caressed her cheeks, kissing her throat, her eyelids. He could feel her body relax under him and it always excited him, the way she opened to him. He knew she trusted him implicitly, she was so responsive to his touch. Jake turned down the lights and then it was Jeannine who reached for Jake. She pulled off her sweatshirt, but Jake didn't grab her. Instead, he stayed intimately connected to her, giving her the space to open even more. His "Hmmm, baby, you're so beautiful" communicated all she needed to know.

Men may read this thinking that Jake has it pretty good; he's got an open, responsive lover. But the women are probably thinking it is Jeannine who has it good. They think that Jake is a great lover and he's the one making this scene sensual. What is it that Jake is doing that invites such responsiveness in his lover?

There is a Jeannine in every woman, and she longs to be opened. But that woman is also self-conscious and she's afraid of the vulnerability inherent in openness. Thus, she'll only come out when she trusts her man completely, and she feels respected and cherished. She wants to know that as she opens, he'll catch her and lead her down an exquisite path of sensual adventure. Jake creates these feelings in Jeannine both in and out of the bedroom. Men like Brad Pitt or George Clooney create these sensations in movies, and women adore them. They are the male sex symbols of our nation.

The Top Five Things Jake Is Doing Right

1. He shows Jeannine his solidness and strength.
    Jake takes control of sexual situations. He moves with confidence. For example, his touch is not hesitant or tentative. This does not mean that he is insensitive, however. He constantly reads Jeannine's reactions to see if she likes what is happening. In this way, Jeannine feels his power and his desire for her, but she also feels very well cared for. She trusts that if Jake does something she doesn't like, he'll stop. Jake is also not hiding from his emotions. Part of his strength is his willingness to show up for her. He lets his passion for Jeannine show. In this way, he shows Jeannine that he knows what he's feeling and he's not afraid of his emotion. This makes Jeannine trust him more—his clarity within himself is alluring to her. She feels that if she lets go sexually, Jake can handle the heat.

2. Jake opens Jeannine's heart first, before he opens her pelvis.
    Jake seduces Jeannine's heart before he even attempts to touch her body. That is because if her heart is open, her pelvis more naturally responds. Sometimes a woman just wants a good physical experience of sex. But most women in long-term monogamous relationships want deeper sexual connections. So Jake waits until Jeannine is receptive before he touches her in a more directly sexual way. Plus, Jake uses so much more than his touch to open Jeannine. His eyes and his words speak directly to her heart. He creates a loving space for her that is so powerful, it's almost like an emotional blanket she can crawl into and wrap up in.

    If Jake wasn't as attentive to her sounds and movements, she'd probably start to shut down. She might close her eyes, stop moving, or stop reaching for him and touching him. When couples accumulate sexual experiences where a woman feels unseen and uncared for, this can start a negative loop. She learns to expect that her partner will ignore her needs. She then goes into the sexual situation closed and irritated, before it even begins. However, if she trusts that her partner is tuned into her, she'll go into a sexual situation open and expecting it to be pleasurable. This only increases the chances that both will enjoy themselves.

3. Jake capitalizes on Jeannine's sexual instincts by day and by night.
    Jake uses Jeannine's sexual instincts to his advantage. He creates an atmosphere both in and out of the bedroom where Jeannine feels she can relax into him. In this way, Jeannine can let go of the need to protect herself. She naturally opens and receives Jake's touch, his words, his body. But Jake makes use of Jeannine's instincts way before they make love. He uses his masculine presence to create a

home environment where Jeannine feels his strength, love, and support. In this way, Jeannine stays generally receptive to him, and he has to work less hard to generate these feelings in her when they are being sexual.

4. Jake honors her gifts.

Jake responds to Jeannine both verbally and nonverbally in a way that communicates his respect for her. He uses his words and actions to show Jeannine that he is more interested in her as a woman than he is with any particular part of her body. He's not grabbing her breasts or any other part of her body. Yet his touch is extremely sensual, so Jeannine knows exactly what he is thinking. This creates a space for Jeannine where she feels safe to offer more of herself. She feels that she won't get taken advantage of, so she doesn't have to protect herself. This is an important point because self-protection is instinctual for all of us. If Jeannine isn't feeling perfectly safe—that is, if she feels like Jake might touch her when she's not ready—she'll stay more careful and closed emotionally and physically. When this happens, she will not reach the heights of passion.

5. Jake creates a need in her.

Most couples in long-term relationships struggle with one person's sex drive being stronger than the other's. Jake and Jeannine are no exception—his libido is somewhat higher than hers. This creates problems because couples tend to get into a power struggle where the lower libido partner is either rejecting advances or engaging unenthusiastically in a sexual experience. Jake avoids this power play by staying aware of two issues. One, he takes advantage of their sexual interactions to offer Jeannine what she needs from him—such as his attention, his love, and his tenderness. Since Jeannine doesn't have the same need for sex in the same way Jake does, he identifies and offers her what she does want from him. In this way, their sexual experience becomes a feast for both of them. The second thing Jake does is he makes sure Jeannine feels like he wants her but he doesn't need her. He does this by not grasping at Jeannine, or chasing after her. If Jake presents himself as sexually grasping for Jeannine, she'll probably lose interest in sex with him. Women don't like feeling that their men are needy. This makes her feel like he's more like a boy than her partner. Jake avoids this by engaging Jeannine with something she wants (his strength and loving attention) which makes her come toward him rather than away.

ALPHA GONE WRONG

Jake is a great example of the tender, strong alpha energy that most women instinctively respond to. But not all men who are instinctually connected generate such a positive reaction in women. Sometimes men express their instinctual alpha traits without warmth and heart connection. This kind of male is attractive to a woman, but he makes her feel unsafe at the same time. In films, it is the Sean Penn or Jack Nicholson type of man. In the extreme, this version of masculinity can be violent and abusive.

Mick is an example of authoritarian masculine energy. While men like Mick often find women responsive to them, the relationship never develops into something deeper. For example:

Anna felt Mick was hard to love. She admired his determination and strength, but his intense personality made it difficult for her to feel connected to him. He was often harsh and critical of her and the kids. He sometimes made major decisions without even consulting her. Anna wasn't always sure she mattered to him that much.

When he had sex with her, Mick was passionate but aloof at the same time. He didn't make much eye contact with her, or tell her he loved her. Mick was a good lover, but still it was hard for Anna to feel safe with him. Anna never told Mick when she wanted something in particular during sex—like a certain touch or a different position—because she felt so self-conscious in bed with him. She very much appreciated the way he took care of the family, but sex wasn't all that gratifying for her. Lately she found herself just going through the motions when he came on to her. Sometimes she'd even pretend to have an orgasm just to move things along. She secretly longed for a man to make love to her, not just have sex.

Mick came on to Anna that night as they lay in the dark by stroking her back. Anna had gained a few pounds recently and even in the darkened room, she was self-conscious and embarrassed. She tried to focus on his touch but Anna wished Mick had left her nightgown on.

It is fairly obvious where Mick is going wrong. Anna feels unsafe and emotionally disconnected from him in their daily life as well as in the bedroom. Over time, it's likely that Mick will find his sex life rather tiresome. Anna does respond to his sexual overtures, but without much enthusiasm. It is clear that while Mick is making use of Anna's instincts, without her heart connected, sex is not great for either of them. In long-term relationships, when an emotional connection isn't tended to, women typically lose interest in sex because they are less willing to open at a deeper level. As this occurs, sex becomes less exciting for everyone. This problem is likely to intensify with time. Mick's sexual needs won't go away. Eventually he's at risk for having an affair. It wouldn't be that hard for him to do because women find his strength and powerful personality very alluring. In short-term love affairs, men like Mick typically do pretty well. But if Mick doesn't develop his tenderness and emotional side with women, sex will remain fairly superficial and physically focused.

If Mick wants to make some changes, a good place to start is a focus on his heart. Becoming more aware of his own deeper feelings will facilitate a sense of compassion for others. Learning more about how Anna is feeling outside of the bedroom will help him become more sensitive to her. When he is with Anna, he can focus more on her and resist distractions like the phone or TV. Eye contact, asking questions, paying closer attention to her reactions—all of this will encourage more intimate exchanges. Telling her he wants to be more loving and asking for her suggestions would be helpful as well.

SEX AND SENSITIVITY

Some men go to the other extreme in sexual situations and in life. Rather than being too authoritarian without enough heart, some men try so hard to be loving that they lose touch with their masculine strength. There are no famous actors that exude this energy, since women don't find it sexually appealing.

Unfortunately, many men today find themselves in this struggle because it's very easy to fall into. In an effort to please women, they ultimately have the opposite impact:

> As he was driving home late from work that evening, Drew decided he was done coming on to Tricia. Every time he asked her, she'd have an excuse not to have sex. She was too tired, she wasn't feeling well, her list was long and he was tired of hearing it. Tricia seemed to have a low libido and there wasn't much he could do to change that. When they did have sex, Tricia was bossy and easily upset. She'd start complaining almost as soon as he started touching her—his touch was too soft and it tickled, his beard was rough, his nails pricked her skin. . . . He would get so anxious that he would hardly enjoy himself. He loved her, but it was becoming difficult to be around her in general. At dinner, she'd nag him about the stuff he wasn't doing around the house. This just made him want to watch TV all night and vegetate. Unfortunately, it was hard for him to discuss it because he was afraid to hurt her feelings. He never thought marriage would feel this lonely.
>
> When Drew got home Tricia was already involved in a movie. Drew sat with her on the couch. He put his arm around her, but his touch remained platonic. He didn't let her know he'd been thinking about making love all day. Anyway, Tricia was preoccupied and upset about an issue that had happened with her parents. After the movie was over, Drew listened and tried to be supportive but he didn't think there was much he could say. They were pleasant to each other when they went to bed, but each felt more like siblings than lovers.

Drew is struggling in the same way so many great men in our culture are struggling today. His sensitivity and concern for Tricia have overshadowed his masculine strength. She isn't feeling his power at home, or in the bedroom. As a result, Tricia is testing Drew's alpha against her own masculine energy. Unfortunately for Drew, Tricia is winning. It is likely that neither of them understands how their sexual relationship went so wrong. If Drew doesn't take action, they are at risk for either having a sexless marriage, or one of them having an affair. It would be easy for Drew to have an affair because there are many women at work who find him attractive. Just because he's lost his alpha status at home doesn't mean the same thing has happened in his office. It's likely that he remains respected there by many people. On the other hand, Tricia might be the one to have an affair. She may meet a man who feels more masculine to her than Drew, and this would probably be exciting to her. Since her instinctual desire to surrender isn't being met at home, it makes her vulnerable to such situations.

There is a lot Drew can do to improve his situation. For example:

1. Reconnect with his masculine core.
   Drew can use his energy to focus on himself. This doesn't mean that he ignores Tricia. It means that he identifies activities that get him more in touch with his body to reconnect with his masculine instincts. Sports with other men—especially competitive sports—are a good way to start. Body disciplines such as Thai-Chi or yoga can also help a man become more in touch with his body. Going camp-

ing alone, or simply spending time in nature, offers the opportunity to go within. Meditation is a great centering practice that can bring men more fully into their bodies. The more Drew tunes into his body, the more solid he will feel. Many of the exercises in chapter 10 can assist in this process. Tricia will sense his increasing solidness as well, and this will be attractive to her.

This process of reconnection takes time. One camping session or playing basketball on the weekends in an adult league won't be enough. That makes sense when you think about how long Drew has probably been out of touch with his core. In fact, many men have never had the experience of feeling connected to their masculinity in a significant way. For example, some boys are discouraged from expressing their more masculine traits. If this was the case for Drew, then it may be years before he feels more in tune with his masculine presence. (It is no different for women connecting to their core—the process takes time and effort.) It requires slowly peeling back layers upon layers of emotional defenses to get to the core of the man (or woman, as the case may be). But as men and women begin to feel the difference in their relationships, it motivates them to continue. The metamorphosis can be felt even before the transformation is complete. And in a sense, it is never complete as we are always given opportunities to grow and mature in our masculine (or feminine) presence.

2. Stop the discomfort at home.

   Drew can set limits with Tricia when she's nagging him. The more he allows her to disrespect him, the worse their relationship will feel to both of them. When Tricia voices a concern, Drew can listen carefully and decide if it's reasonable. If it is, he can act on it rather than procrastinate. If he thinks it's unreasonable, he can respectfully explain why he's not going to do it. Either way, this approach will calm Tricia down because he'll be responding to her requests in a respectful manner.

3. Stay strong when she's upset.

   Drew can respond to Tricia's emotions with strength and presence. When Tricia is upset, Drew tends to tune her out. But this communicates to Tricia that he can't handle her emotion. In the bedroom, this backfires because Tricia will be less likely to let go sexually if she believes, consciously or unconsciously, that Drew can't handle emotion. She won't feel safe with him and sex will become boring. So, Drew can build her trust by making good eye contact with her when she's upset. He can listen attentively and calmly to her. This will probably result in Tricia calming down more quickly in the moment. If she feels like he can handle her emotional storm, she'll be more apt to open sexually to the instinctual passion within her.

NOT EVERYONE WANTS TO BE KING

There are many men who understand the concepts of hierarchy and sexual instincts, but who aren't feeling drawn to cultivating that in their own lives. In fact, research shows that men rate attributes as "being seen as a man of honor" and "being in control of your own life" as more important measures of masculinity than sexual prowess.[1] Some men put their energy into other very important pursuits, such as work, family, recreation, or hobbies. Few men are complete alphas, and not everyone wants to be king. That's just natural—few women feel

called to live completely in feminine energy as well. Passionate sex isn't important to everyone, nor should it be. Everyone is different. It is no problem if passionate sex with the same person over time isn't that important to you. People
have numerous priorities in life, and there are many satisfying, useful ways to
spend your time. Nonetheless, many men still find it helpful to understand the
dynamics of sexual energy. Knowledge is power, whether or not you choose to act
on it in any particular way.

SOME TYPICAL QUESTIONS MEN AND WOMEN
ASK WHEN DOING THIS WORK IN THERAPY:

What If Her Libido Is Higher?

Phil could see that Sandy was angry. It didn't take a rocket scientist to figure that out.
They hadn't had sex in about 6 weeks—maybe more. It was so easy for him to ignore
the situation but Sandy's behavior made it abundantly clear; he should just suck it
up and get it over with. Sandy was always so much nicer, sometimes for days after
having sex. But he hated trying to get an erection for her. It was pressure he didn't
need, he had enough on his mind. And after almost 20 years of marriage, what did
she expect anyway? He did everything else she wanted and needed—he worked hard
and took awesome care of the kids when he was home. He loved Sandy, but wanting
to have sex with her was a different story. In bed that night Phil reached out to her.
He tried his best to summon up a fantasy that might arouse him.

Low libido in men is becoming more and more common. Some of this is due
to the fact that libido is increasingly understood, so clinicians are better able to
diagnose problems with it. In addition, libido is now being talked about in our
culture, and thus men are more apt to ask for help with it. But it seems likely that
some of the increase in men's libido issues is due to an increasing disconnection
from masculine sexual instincts.

Libido issues in men can be the result of many things, such as stress, anxiety,
or medication side effects. However, low libido in men is also easily related to
life or relationship problems that leave a man feeling less strong in his masculinity. When a man feels emotionally or physically weak, he feels a loss of alpha
status. He feels less powerful in his world, and his libido may suffer. Depression
can have this effect, as can financial stress, or repressed emotions like anger. A
man may be at a particular risk for such an outcome if he feels disrespected or
unappreciated at home. Thus, many men with a decreased sex drive are well
served by focusing on a reconnection with their masculine core.

When a man wants to raise his libido, he must do it for himself. If he is only
trying to please his partner, it will probably not work. For people to increase
their libido—man or woman—they must want it for themselves. Otherwise it
will feel like pressure and it probably won't be effective. Sometimes men in this
situation believe their partners expect too much from them. If this is the case

for you, then start by working on these more general relationship issues. If your sexual concerns are a result of what isn't feeling good in your relationship, addressing your relationship issues more directly should help the situation.

What If He Doesn't Want to Be Alpha?

When Brenda first came on to him, John had no idea how much he would enjoy their relationship. He'd never even entertained the thought of dating an older woman. But Brenda was a fabulous lover, and so easy to be around. Unlike John's ex-wife, who was always irritable, life with Brenda was much less complicated. She loved his cooking, and she traveled for work so he had ample time to himself. Brenda knew what she wanted sexually and she certainly knew how to make John feel good. She was happy to take John out to dinner and he enjoyed not having to plan everything. Yes, John wondered how he hadn't figured this out sooner. Older women had so much more to offer!

Some men and women find the whole hierarchy dynamic to be tiresome and outdated. From a social perspective, this is certainly true. And the recent social trend of older, more established women on the singles scene offers new opportunities for folks seeking something different in their romantic relationship. For the first time in history, it is becoming more acceptable for younger men to date older women. Oftentimes this creates an excellent sexual match, at least for a period of time. Older women who enjoy these relationships are often less sexually needy and self-conscious, and are more interested in helping to co-create a satisfying sexual relationship. This dynamic can be great for an older women's ego. Women who have experienced a more traditional marriage and found it lacking may feel empowered by this arrangement. Younger men can enjoy the ease and comfort that an older woman can provide. Some men feel they are working so hard at the office that they don't want to work equally hard at their intimate relationship. Other men simply enjoy the feeling of being well cared for.

However, for most people in long-term relationships, and particularly those people attempting to make monogamy exciting, traditional masculine and feminine sexual instincts remain supremely important. Instincts are less important to couples who do not put as much emphasis on a passionate sex life. And they may not be as central to couples who are focused on physical sensations alone rather than the sexual dynamic in the relationship. Otherwise, after a while, capitalizing on traditional sexual instincts becomes almost imperative to keeping a sexual relationship functioning well in a monogamous long-term relationship.

It is true that a focus on instincts requires much effort on everyone's part. Relationships take energy whether they succeed or fail. So, it's probably wise to channel your efforts into behavior that will likely enhance your sexual and emotional relationship. And remember, if he doesn't take the alpha role, then she will. This dynamic is almost impossible to avoid, because the formation of hierarchies is natural. In a monogamous long-term relationship, it is usually the case that if someone doesn't claim alpha status, the relationship will feel more like siblings than lovers, and sex suffers.

What If He Does the Suggestions in This Chapter and She Still Doesn't Respond?

Couples can get into behavioral ruts and patterns that are hard to break. Once they are regularly responding to each other in a particular way, it's very difficult to change the course of the relationship. But it's not impossible. Be patient and keep working at it. I tell my patients that either way, this is a good training period for them. Hopefully in time they learn how to improve their sexual relationship and create a more intimate and satisfying union. But if this effort fails, they are developing new skills they can bring to a future relationship so that they don't repeat the same mistakes.

Communication is always a good place to start. Try drawing her out with questions, such as:

- What would you like to try in bed that we've never done?
- What can I do to make your experience better?
- How do you like me to come on to you?
- What is your best sexual memory of us?

If she is withholding emotionally or physically, talk to her about it. Tell her the impact that it is having on you. Be sure she is aware of how destructive her behavior feels to you. If you are afraid you are going to have an affair, let her know that. Sometimes people keep fears like that secret which prevents conversation, communication, and healing. Most importantly, if you aren't talking about it, you can't resolve it.

If you are unable to progress with the issues alone, then consulting a therapist may be helpful. Most marriages seem to require therapeutic help at some point. Remember that long-term monogamy isn't necessarily natural, so you will both have struggles periodically. These struggles can become huge rifts if they aren't addressed in a timely way, and they certainly can make monogamy more challenging over time.

What If She Is More Interested in the Kids than in Him?

If your partner is more interested in spending time with the children than with you, of course your first step is to talk with her about it. It may be that one or both of you have emotions that need to be expressed and resolved in order to set your relationship back on track. Some women tone themselves down sexually after they've fulfilled their goal of having children, so now is probably the time to pay more attention to capitalizing on sexual instincts—hers and yours.

Reading this book together may provide an opportunity to start some important dialogue about making positive changes in your relationship. Neither of you is getting what you need from the other, so there should be room for growth on everyone's part. It is very important work because this situation is a set-up for one or both of you to have an affair. Anytime partners' needs aren't getting addressed in their intimate relationship, it can make them vulnerable for extracurricular sexual activities.

What If She Has Gained Lots of Weight and He Isn't Attracted to Her Anymore?

Overweight is a tricky issue in Western cultures. Women receive pressure to maintain an impossibly thin physique. But thin is the cultural ideal of female beauty, and the majority of Westerners endorse it, if only in the privacy of their own minds. We are sort of brainwashed that way. Obviously, this is a delicate issue. Some weight gain is practically inevitable as women age. When a man has this concern, I suggest that he first consult someone he trusts who knows his wife to see if his issue is reasonable. Sometimes men are overly critical, and another person's opinion may add a dose of reality. Keep in mind that every magazine ad you have seen is a touched-up photograph. And women feel harassed by these images just as you are enamored by them. While men struggle with weight issues too, women are particularly burdened by them because of cultural stereotypes of female beauty.

If you still feel that her weight is an issue, then addressing it in a supportive way is your best option. The bottom line is that weight gain is a significant health problem. It will most likely benefit her if she is able to feel more fit and comfortable in her own body. Suggest that the two of you begin a healthy eating plan together. Approach this as a team effort rather than as her problem. Do what you can to help her find time in her schedule for enjoyable exercise—like dance classes, or walking in the evening. Criticizing her weight directly will backfire. Remember that women's bodies are evolutionarily designed to retain more body fat than men, and there is more social pressure on women to look attractive. Both of these issues probably add to her secret desires for food—we always want what we can't have, whether it be chocolate, sex, or whatever. So your compassion and support is extremely important.

Finally, keep in mind that most men do not leave marriages because of their wife's weight. Nor do most men have affairs because they find their wife physically unattractive. So, try and keep this issue in perspective. If you are upset with her, it is likely that you are angry about issues other than her weight. See if you can get to the bottom of your concerns so that you can address outstanding relationship issues as directly as possible.

What If He Thinks He Might Have an Affair?

Affairs rarely end well. More often than not, affairs result in serious pain for all involved. That does not mean that couples cannot heal from affairs, because many do. Some marriages use them to grow and strengthen, while others fall apart in their wake. But all create immense emotional pain that must be worked through. If you fear you are at risk for an affair, talk about it with your partner. Try and find compromises and creative solutions for your concerns. Sometimes a sex therapist or a couples therapist can be a helpful mediator in this regard.

Try to think realistically about what an affair can really offer you. Affairs are tricky for several reasons. First, they represent a fantasy relationship that appears more passionate than is realistic. Love affairs have the luxury of not revolving around the mundane aspects of life. You don't have to deal with children's needs, cleaning the bathrooms, overdue credit cards, or grocery shopping. Second, remember that sex at the beginning of a relationship is when it's most exciting. So you are experiencing the icing on the sexual cake in the first few years of a love affair. Don't be fooled into thinking that great sex will always feel that easy without effort. Finally, there are reasons why you are seeking an affair, and reasons why your monogamous relationship isn't faring well. Obviously, both you and your long-term partner are contributing to the current state of the relationship. Taking the time now to clean up your part of the relationship struggles will at most save your marriage, and at the very least it will prevent you from making the same mistakes in a new romance down the road. The statistics on remarriage are not impressive, as these marriages often fail. Learn about your role in the relationship problems before you make the same mistake again. People feel so miserable when after the stress, financial destruction, and emotional challenges of a divorce, they receive the same criticism about their behavior from a new partner.

What If She Is Reading This Chapter and Her Man Is Too Authoritarian?

If your man is too authoritarian, talk with him about it. Make sure he is aware of the impact this has on you. Sometimes we assume our needs are obvious in a relationship when in fact they are not. Obvious or not, if you don't communicate, your chances of getting your needs met are greatly diminished. Take a look at yourself and see why you have settled for this type of romance. You probably found his masculine presence attractive at first, but without a softer side, it stops feeling good after a while. You may have a tendency to become passive, which is a version of feminine energy that serves no one. Weak, passive feminine traits can be complimentary sexual energy to a man's authoritarian masculine energy in intimate relationships. So start talking with him, and expect to repeat yourself. Don't say something once and assume that's enough. These dialogues require much repetition in order to have an impact. Remember that when a couple has been relating a certain way for a while, patterns are difficult to change and will require effort on both of your parts. But not dealing with it creates more problems for both of you emotionally and sexually down the road. If he's not willing to work with you, it's unlikely that you will relax into him and enjoy your sexual relationship. Remind him that sex will be less satisfying for him as a result. Obviously, this cycle makes monogamy more challenging for everyone.

What If She Is Reading This Chapter and Her Man Is Too Passive?

Oftentimes a woman is afraid to give her partner feedback for fear of hurting his feelings. This is commendable, but it is rarely a workable solution. When problems aren't addressed they often intensify with time, and they only become more challenging to discuss. Keep in mind that the impact of your words may be more related to how you say them than what you actually say. If you speak lovingly and without anger, your partner will perceive what you say much differently than if you wait until you are fed up and berate or patronize him. Plan what you are going to say and how you are going to say it, and then stick to your plan.

The good news is that there is much you can do to support your man's growth. It is a fact that the more feminine energy you offer, the more masculine energy you will get from him. It may take a little time for this energetic shift to occur in your relationship, but it happens. Try to be less controlling and directive. See if you can soften your eyes, your heart, and your body around him. Be less constricted physically and he'll feel the shift. If need be, take yoga classes or some activity that helps you find a more tender place to relate from. You may do just fine interacting this way outside of your relationship. But just like your man can be assertive and in control at work but passive at home, so too can you be soft in your day-to-day life but tight and constricted with him.

When you do want to step in with criticism or direction, pick your battles wisely. Ask yourself how important the issue really is. If it's just about how he loads the dishwasher, that's a statement that is probably better left unsaid. It will likely have the effect of irritating you both while not resolving anything substantial. Of course, if you are irritated with how he loads the dishwasher, that probably means you have deeper concerns with him that aren't being addressed. Try to get to the root of the issues and discuss them in a cooperative manner. In this way you have a chance at resolution, rather than just feeding the negativity in your relationship. When tension builds it makes sex less appealing for everyone. If your sex life suffers, your emotional intimacy probably will too. This cycle makes monogamy that much more challenging.

This process of shifting your relationship will take effort on both of your parts, and it takes time. Remember that you are changing a dynamic that probably took years for the two of you to create. Ask your friends for help. A support system is always a good idea when attempting to make significant changes in any aspect of behavior.

IN CONCLUSION

When a man connects to his masculine instinct, he grows in confidence, emotional strength, and presence. Men report feeling an increased sense of purpose and self-direction. As with women connecting to their feminine core, this work results in deep benefits for men that extend far beyond the bedroom. In fact, the transformation is evident to others in the way a man carries himself and interacts with those around him.

Thus far we have explored the role of instincts in a traditional monogamous relationship. As intimate relationships become less traditional, the role of sexual instincts may be altered. That is because more unique sexual bonds entail more complex dynamics, which are influenced by a greater variety of factors. In the next chapter we will explore some of these more creative alternatives to a traditional monogamous bond.

Chapter Eight

RETHINKING CULTURAL NORMS: CREATIVE ALTERNATIVES TO ENHANCING SEXUAL CHEMISTRY

Some couples seeking more passionate connections find creative adaptations of monogamy to be helpful. These alternatives are considered unusual from the perspective of the general culture. However, couples who practice them believe they are key components for keeping their marriages alive and vital. In seeking more passion, some couples choose creating physical distance, controlled intercourse, Tantra, swinging, or polyamory. Of course, these options are not without challenges, as we will discuss. But proponents find the difficulties inherent in such romantic connections to be well worth the benefits.

OPTION #1: CAPITALIZING ON AGE DIFFERENCES

What It Is

Among the most sensual and erotically charged relationships I have seen, many consist of a younger woman and an older man. At first, I thought this was coincidence. However, I realize now that this dynamic makes complete sense. These couples share some fascinating common characteristics that seem to capitalize on human's innate sexual instincts. That is, many women love to be opened and cared for by a strong, powerful man. Many men love to open softer, more vulnerable women. Does the opposite hold true? Of course—men receive pleasure in being opened, and women are gratified by opening and taking their man. But many people find sex *most* ecstatic when they are true to their natural and innate sexual inclinations as female and male.

Capitalizing on age differences means that there is a significant age discrepancy between partners—maybe six to eight years - and that the man is older. It seems that less than that may not allow enough time for the couple to experience the benefits of the age difference, and significantly more than that may create an age gap that may not necessarily support sexual chemistry.

Politically correct? Not really. Usually when younger women marry older men, psychological issues are believed to motivate their union. Specifically, younger women are perceived to be longing for the paternal care and attention they did not receive in childhood. And the older men are understood as lewd and crude, seeking to take advantage of a younger, more vulnerable, and less mature partner. A more developed man would prefer a more mature woman. A healthy woman would prefer a partner more her equal than her father. And of course, this is sometimes the case.

However, it is also true that no marriage begins from purely healthy motivations. All unions support healthy drives *and* unhealthy ones; loving impulses *and* selfish ones. A marriage is only as strong as its participants. And being human, every participant is flawed, and these flaws contribute to their mate choice. As a result, all loving unions are naturally flawed in some ways. Blemished but beautiful; perfect in their imperfection. Such is life. Thus, we could (and often do) dissect any union for potential flaws.

Why It Works

This arrangement works because it capitalizes on humanity's natural instincts as pack animals. In any pack, problems arise. As we discussed in chapter 4, the masculine energy inherent in every pack member naturally competes for power and control. Traditionally, this competition was primarily felt between adolescent boys and their fathers—the pack members with the most masculine energy.

These family dynamics have become even more complex as women evolve. As women have developed their masculine sides in these last decades, their masculinity now enters the family mix. Mothers now compete with fathers, consciously and unconsciously, for who is the most powerful dog in the pack. But women who feel confident in their man's strength seem less irritable and testy with their man. This is the dynamic that an older man more effortlessly creates in a household pack.

When a family has a clear *loving* masculine influence, infighting is limited. This is not the old fashioned Archie Bunker type of alpha authority. A great leader is one who leads with strength *and* compassion. Compassion requires maturity and a loving, open heart. Superior leaders exhibit both of these traits—examples might be Martin Luther King, or John F. Kennedy. When a mature man marries a balanced and strong younger woman, both enjoy the peaceful kingdom that results. The man feels safer in their alpha status and can more comfortably express their loving and tender feelings toward their partner. The woman feels secure in knowing there is a strong man supporting her, thus promoting both her assertiveness and self-expansion, while at the same time enabling her to let go and sexually open to her lover. All members of this pack are supported in living at their highest potential; women can be strong yet feminine; men can be tender yet masculine. From an evolutionary perspective, everyone wins.

It is possible that this dynamic works for an additional reason as well. It is natural for humans to desire what others covet. In Western culture, power is most coveted in men, while youth and beauty is most coveted in women. In these relationships, women are aware that their man's power is a desirable commodity in the world; men are aware of their partner's relative youth in that same way. Plus, the social exchange theory posits that marriage involves an exchange of assets. In romantic relationships, assets are anything from power to beauty to intelligence to health. It seems plausible that spouses will automatically take their partners less for granted when they exhibit traits highly valued in the culture.

What the Critics Say

From the feminist perspective, this is a politically incorrect alternative for several reasons. First, some might perceive this system as promoting a power dynamic that is unfair to women. Instead of recognizing this arrangement as freeing up a woman to experience all sides of herself and thus more of her potential, some may view this as women regressing in the social order. This criticism *can* hold true if partners are not mature, that is, if the woman is passive in the relationship, or if the man is authoritarian. Second, men typically die younger than women. Elderly women already spend a significant portion of their lives without a partner. Women choosing to marry older men will obviously exacerbate this problem for themselves. Third, for the first time in history, it is more socially acceptable for an older woman to marry a younger man. This is clearly a victory for all women, an open acknowledgement of women's continued vitality and sensuality over time. It would appear that countering this trend would support the longstanding cultural myth that women lose their sensuality as they age. Such a notion is false and detrimental to women.

Good Candidates for Trying It

For most women to feel deep bliss and passion, they must allow themselves to let go fully while making love. It is typically women who are strong in their masculine personality traits, but balanced in both their masculine and feminine energies, that can allow themselves this luxury of letting go sexually. Such women are great candidates for this intimate arrangement. They enjoy the emotional and sexual art of letting go and releasing into a stronger, masculine energy. They take pleasure in immersing themselves in the feeling of being sexually ravished. Men who prosper in this relationship dynamic feel comfortable in a strong, alpha role. They feel confident and purposeful in their lives, and self-assured in their masculinity.

On the other hand, women who tend to be less comfortable in their masculine energy—such as women who are more innately passive—may not benefit from this arrangement because the power dynamic with their man would be unequal. This would be especially the case for a woman paired with a man who was not compassionate and loving. Also, women who enjoy spending more time in their masculine energy at home would probably not enjoy this arrangement because they would feel compelled to regularly compete with their man for alpha status. This competition could easily ensue in frequent power struggles even over the minutiae of life. Similarly, men who do not enjoy manifesting their deeper masculine selves would feel burdened or pressured by this arrangement.

Benefits to You

A strong, balanced woman in a relationship with an older man will find herself less tempted to engage her man in power struggles. She will find it easier to relax into his strength and trust his ability to care for her. As a result, she will feel less innate resistance to surrender sexually. However, the benefits to her are not limited to the bedroom. An older man may be more likely to express his love more openly and freely. Because he is likely to be more confident in his masculinity, he may be less apt to hide his desires for his wife. This overt expression of longing from a man can translate into a woman feeling cherished and loved.

Men innately recognize the multiple benefits of this intimate arrangement. Evolutionary psychologists explain that men are drawn to younger women. This theory holds true in that most men acknowledge they would automatically choose a sexual partner younger than themselves. This preference is evident in real life, as most men do marry younger women. A man's instinctive alpha tendencies flow more freely when he is the oldest member of his figurative pack. As with women, men enjoy multiple benefits outside of the bedroom from this age discrepant arrangement. He may enjoy his time at home more because he struggles less with his wife—she challenges his alpha status less because his age alone provides for a natural, comfortable sexual hierarchy.

OPTION #2: CREATING PHYSICAL DISTANCE

What It Is

Creating physical distance in a marriage means that both partners capitalize on ways they can create physical, *but not emotional,* space in their union. The adage "absence makes the heart grow fonder" is applicable here. There are many ways to create healthy physical distance in an intimate partnership. Separate bedrooms are one way to create such breathing space. Sometimes professional couples live in separate cities, reconnecting on weekends. Other people make personal hobbies and alone time with friends a priority—as much of a priority as time with their partner. In this way, romantic time together is cherished, partners look forward to seeing each other, and lovers do not take each other for granted. I have recommended this option to many couples, even though they are often reluctant to experiment with it. It flies in the face of our cultural beliefs about intimacy. However, as time passes, these same couples feel the deterioration in their desire to be together. The right amount of physical distance cultivates healthy longing. And healthy longing is an essential ingredient to sexual chemistry.

This simple fact is apparent with young lovers—the longing they feel for each other can even be described as painful at times. But the bliss they feel when reuniting is palpable. Such couples plan and prepare for their time together. They put effort into their appearance, and they plan their evenings. These behaviors only fuel sexual interest and spark, even in long-term relationships.

Why It Works

Physical distance supports sexual chemistry for several reasons. First and foremost, the majority of marriages experience detrimental effects from being too close, or what therapists refer to as enmeshed or undifferentiated. Enmeshed couples don't have clear identities and boundaries. Their lives are bound together so tightly that they don't function independently. Examples of enmeshment might be when a spouse regularly avoids discussing important issues because of fear of hurting or enraging their partner, or couples who spend all their free time together yet don't find this time pleasurable. Some degree of enmeshment is typical in marriages. More enmeshed couples find themselves avoiding deeper intimate contact on one hand, but afraid of healthy distance on the other. Great sex and enmeshment are the poorest of bedfellows.

Of course, creating physical distance isn't a cure-all for emotional enmeshment. Couples can use physical distance to avoid each other, yet remain in an unhealthy dependency at the same time. However, physical distance does assist individuals in supporting their own identities apart from the couple, which in turn supports the health of their intimate connection.

Some couples find that physical distance helps to ease habituation, which is the natural decline in response to being repeatedly exposed to a sexual stimulus (including a sex partner). In intimate relationships, couples naturally become less eager to see each other, less excited by the other's touch, less enamored by the one they love. It just makes sense that limiting intimate time together causes private time to feel more valuable and cherished, promoting a sense of newness and freshness.

It is also the case that when we have limited access to something we value, we tend to want it more. Simply put, we want what we cannot have. This applies to cars, alone time, and food, as well as people. In fact, one theory suggests that this explains the decline in attraction many couples report after getting married. Perhaps the simple fact that we finally have our partners makes them less desirable. When couples have less access to each other, they naturally place more significance on the time they do have, and take better care of each other during those hours.

What the Critics Say

Critics of this option question whether it is indeed possible to allow for physical distance while avoiding emotional distance. However, it is the case that many marriages have little to no physical distance but much emotional distance and/or disharmony. And where there is emotional dysfunction, there is probably no sexual tension. In fact, many marriages use a variety of unhealthy techniques to literally create emotional distance between spouses. There are a multitude of ways men and women accomplish this—watching TV, caring for children, drinking alcohol, working long hours, talking on the phone . . . the list is endless. However, it is likely that if time together was a limited commodity, it would be considered more precious and much of this avoidance behavior would diminish.

Another very valid criticism is that for some couples, this option would be a cop-out. That is, they would use this physical distance to support further emotional disengagement. Sleeping in separate bedrooms would only offer them yet another way to disconnect. For these couples, physical distance supports detachment and unhealthy relating. This outcome occurs when partners are not truly motivated to enhance their sexual connection. Physical distance only augments a love affair when both partners really do want to improve their connection.

Good Candidates for Trying It

I promote physical space for couples who feel passion slipping away but who are committed to keeping their marriage together. I encourage them to consider how much space they need to facilitate their sexual connection while protecting and even facilitating their emotional connection. For each couple, the answer is different.

Most couples prefer to start creating personal space by pursuing personal hobbies and time with friends. Often couples are initially committed to this plan, but then life gets the best of them and the relationship quickly returns to unhealthy habits. As a result, a more drastic change, such as separate bedrooms, may have a more positive and lasting impact. Some couples literally schedule their "sleepover" nights, such as every Wednesday, Saturday, and Monday. Other couples prefer to invite each other more spontaneously for sleepover dates. For couples living in separate cities, regular weekend contact becomes critical to maintaining their intimate bond. For them, sleeping in the same room when they are together is essential.

Benefits to You

Creating physical distance is a fabulous option for couples seeking a more secure but flexible approach to facilitating passionate connection. That is because each couple can tailor this option to meet their individual needs. Couples with children find this option quite workable as it can allow for continued, uninterrupted family time. For example, some couples choose to reside in separate bedrooms, others regularly engage in a hobby outside of the home, while others simply vacation without their partner several times a year. You'll know you have found the right balance when you find yourself longing for your partner's attention when you aren't together, and putting more effort into cherishing the time you do spend together.

OPTION #3: LIMITING ORGASM
What It Is

The practice of limiting orgasm is also referred to as controlled intercourse and the Karezza Method. Initially inspired by sacred Hindu and Tantric writings, these techniques are considered an expression of sacred sexuality by Western practitioners. Though never widely practiced, the concept of men retaining their semen has had support in various spiritual communities and cultures for centuries. Today's Western practitioners advocate that women limit orgasms as well as men, and it is often suggested that sex be scheduled or structured so that the heart dictates lovemaking practices rather than bodily desires. With this practice, cravings for orgasm are said to diminish over time. Ironically, it is in this control of bodily desires that practitioners find freedom, release, and sexual bliss that they believe exceeds the pleasures inherent in more natural sexual expression.

Couples who practice limiting or controlling orgasm engage in unlimited sensual time together. Tender, loving physical connections are highlighted and encouraged. Making love is a priority and considered a sacred and essential vehicle for cultivating their intimate connection. In fact, it is by making love that individuals nourish and heal their partners. Sexual healing and growth is the primary goal of this intimate practice. As a lifestyle, couples are loving and connected emotionally as well as sensually. Sex is considered the elixir of life.

Why It Works

Proponents of controlled, nonorgasmic or at least limited-orgasm intercourse believe that it works because it balances the brain's neurochemistry.[1] Specifically, orgasm results in a neurochemical high in the brain, primarily because of dopamine release. However, with every action there is an equal and opposite reaction. Thus, following the dopamine release, there is a dopamine crash that results in a person ultimately seeking another orgasm. This cycle of stimulation seeking is believed to eventually result in lovers becoming satiated with each other. The brain's natural inclination over time would be to then seek stimulation from a new lover, or perhaps, to stop seeking sex altogether. In addition, there is a prolactin increase following orgasm, which may be related to a desire for emotional distance rather than connection. Theoretically, controlled intercourse thus works by preventing this cycle of neurochemical changes that may alter people's perceptions and support sexual satiation. As a result, lovers maintain themselves in a state of open-hearted longing for each other, rather than a feeling of closed-hearted withdrawal.

In addition to avoiding a dopamine crash, proponents of controlled orgasm suggest that the focus on cuddling and nonorgasmic intercourse causes the release of oxytocin in the brain, a hormone that promotes attachment and tenderness. It is also a hormone believed to be associated with monogamous behavior. Because nonorgasmic intercourse is encouraged, individuals theoretically maintain higher baseline plasma oxytocin levels and thus feel loving feelings more continuously.

What the Critics Say

Critics say that orgasm during sex is natural and healthy, and that orgasm should not be avoided. They say that when not having orgasms, men become physically uncomfortable and women can develop a variety of physical neuroses. Critics also believe it is unrealistic to take the spontaneity out of sex. In fact, most people simply state that they are not willing to live without orgasms and spontaneous intercourse. Finally, lack of orgasm alone is not what results in a loving, sensual, and erotic connection. Couples must be willing to commit significant amounts of time to nurture and cultivate their relationship.

Thus, regular, loving, intimate contact is required for this method to be of benefit. Otherwise, lack of orgasm can become an additional point of separation between lovers, and their connection and romantic attachment may dissolve. Controlled orgasm is thus a lifestyle as much as it is an approach to lovemaking.

Good Candidates for Trying It

Couples must commit to a loving and tender lifestyle involving much mutual attention and physical focus to be good candidates for controlled intercourse. Each individual must take responsibility for his or her body and maintain control of sexual reactions. Couples must be willing to experience a challenging learning phase in which they sustain intimate contact without the typical release of orgasm. Individuals must be open-hearted, as this method is akin to a spiritual discipline in its spiritual, physical, and emotional demands. Relatedly, couples must be eager to continuously practice cultivating their emotional and sensual relationship so that they may support each other's growth in this lifestyle.

Benefits to You

Practitioners of controlled intercourse suggest that many of the emotional challenges inherent in intimate relationships are avoided by this lifestyle. They propose that loving and tenderness flow naturally from the state of longing induced by controlled intercourse. They describe feeling an ongoing deep state of love akin to the feelings associated with the beginning of a love affair. In fact, practitioners suggest that they can more regularly reach levels of sexual ecstasy that are superior (more open-hearted, loving, and longer lasting) than with body orgasm.

OPTION #4: TANTRA

What It Is

Tantra is an ancient Eastern path of spiritual enlightenment. It began in India, perhaps around 5000 B.C. In its truest form, Tantra is a spiritual philosophy entailing a complex and precise mixture of body practices and written scriptures. Sexual ecstasy may be attained after many years of disciplined practice involving meditation, chanting, worship of the sacred masculine and feminine energies, ritualized breathing, and heart-centered lovemaking. In Tantra, lovemaking becomes a divine act, and lovers experience each other as sacred. Tantric lovemaking encourages the appreciation of masculine and feminine sexual energies inherent in each individual. Lovers learn to weave these energies with their partner, ultimately transcending their humanness. The body is honored as a vehicle for giving and receiving pleasure. Sensuality is cultivated and celebrated. In Tantra, making love leaves the realm of mundane human activity and becomes an ecstatic art form.

Those who practice Tantra experience it as a discipline and a way of life. Tantra is generally learned under the supervision of a guru or spiritual guide. There are a variety of Tantric spiritual traditions, including Buddhist and Hindu. To most Westerners, these distinctions are not significant. Most Westerners learn Tantra from weekend and week-long workshops. While the basic breath and body practices can be introduced in this relatively short period of time, students must practice regularly, perhaps daily, to become skillful with the work. Beginning practices might include controlled breathing, ritualized honoring of one's own body and one's sexual partner, and open-heart meditations. Students learn to manage their orgasms with their breath. By using their breath to carry sexual energy throughout the body, men learn how to delay orgasms, and both men and women learn to enhance their orgasms by spreading the impact throughout their bodies.

Beginning Tantrikas may practice breathing exercises together. For example, sitting cross-legged in front of each other, one partner's breath is brought down the body from the nose to the genitals, and out into the other lover's body where the breath is received in the pelvis. This person then cycles the breath up the body and out the nose so that a circular breathing pattern is maintained. Couples hold hands and maintain loving eye contact and heart focus during the practice. Disciplined breath practices such as these are intense and highly stimulating for both partners. Couples are guided in learning new ways of making love that may or may not involve genital contact or orgasm, but always result in a deeper spiritual connection. *The Complete Idiots Guide to Tantric Sex* by Dr. Judy Kuriansky offers more complete information.

Why It Works

The spiritual aspects of Tantra involve worship and prayer. Such practices seem to bring healing to people for reasons which science does not fully understand. Tantra's sexual healing potentials appear to tap these same curative elements.

Practitioners of Tantra learn to make love from an extremely open and vulnerable place. Reaching this level of vulnerability with a partner means that individuals show themselves at profoundly intimate, personal levels. When this experience is done with sensitivity and love, it can be transformational. Sex can reach levels of ecstasy, and lovers can fall in love more deeply than they had previously dreamed possible. This is because in a mature relationship, the more we show ourselves, the more deeply we are capable of loving and being loved.

What the Critics Say

As tantric practices become more popular in the West, more practitioners are considering themselves expert and offering workshops. These workshops are extremely personal in that they teach men and woman how to feel and manage their sexual energies. When teachers are not the utmost of professionals, the workshops can decompensate into orgies. For this reason, readers interested in pursuing Tantra are advised to thoroughly investigate the workshop and the presenter. You may find it helpful to speak with others who have completed the training to be sure it will be a comfortable and safe experience for you.

Tantric workshops are intense and they are very opening experiences. Because they encourage openness and self-exposure, they can be titillating as well as disturbing. As a result, they can bring up challenges and traumas from the past. For this reason, individuals should be prepared for emotional growth work as well as sexual growth work when embarking on this path. Should you choose to learn Tantra in a workshop format, you may find it helpful to have already identified a therapeutic professional who can help you assimilate what you learn once the workshop is complete.

Tantra is a commitment of the heart, body, and spirit. It is a powerful practice with many very real benefits. However, it is not an activity that can be engaged in lightly. Individuals who are not able to devote considerable time and effort to the practice will find it minimally helpful in making a significant change to their sex lives.

Good Candidates for Trying It

If you wish to engage your partner in a spiritual ride of a lifetime, Tantra may be for you. Couples who are spiritually open, liberal-minded, and seeking more heart-centered, tender lovemaking are good candidates for Tantra. Both partners must be willing and enthusiastic about committing to regular practice time together. Both must also seek to heighten their sexual experience not simply via their bodies, but by connecting their bodies *and* their spirits. As with any spiritual discipline, Tantrikas are determined to engage in their devotional practice even when they do not feel like connecting or making love. That is, making love becomes a way of devotional worship that includes but surpasses sexual contact.

Benefits to You

Tantric practices teach the art of making sex magical. Women learn how to open their hearts and bodies to deep levels of sexual bliss. Men learn how to please women sexually on a spiritual level and how to control their orgasms.

Both men and women develop a greater understanding of the sacred in themselves and in their partner. In this atmosphere, sexual healing can be the result.

OPTION #5: SWINGING

What It Is

Swinging is an alternative lifestyle in which committed couples engage in sexual play with other individuals or couples. Swingers connect in designated nightclubs, at beach resorts, and on Internet Web sites. They tend to be highly sociable individuals who enjoy sex as fun, recreational play. Societal stereotypes portray swingers as employing an "anything goes" mentality. However, in reality most swingers attempt to adhere to strict boundaries and guidelines in their sexual practices. Swingers consider themselves emotionally monogamous. That is to say, they engage in sex play with others, but they make every effort to limit emotionally intimate contact with their lovers. Commitment to one's life partner remains the primary focus. Sex play tends to happen in the presence of one's spouse, with everyone in agreement. In this way, swingers attempt to remove the secrecy and dishonesty inherent in extramarital sex.

It is estimated that approximately 2 percent of couples have engaged in swinging at least once.[2] However, it is difficult to gather research following swingers over the course of their relationship. As a result, we know relatively little about how many swingers remain in the lifestyle over time, and how swinger's sexual relationships ultimately fare. One recent survey of over 1,000 swingers found them to be generally mainstream in their political beliefs, middle-class with several years of college education, and predominantly white. In addition, they endorsed less racist, less sexist, and less conventional attitudes than the general population.[3]

Swinging couples set their own boundaries, which may or may not include intercourse. Some couples agree to oral sex or foreplay only; others require the partner's presence so that no sex play occurs in private. Amongst swingers, female-with-female sex play is common, and swingers acknowledge that the women usually set the rules for the couple.

Why It Works

Swingers identify a multitude of reasons for engaging in sexual nonmonogamy. Many report that it enhances their emotional and sexual connection by counteracting boredom and creating a mutual sense of adventure and excitement. Some say they take their partners less for granted because they see their loved ones being desired and appreciated by others. Others say swinging enables them to engage in sexual behavior that otherwise would occur in secret, which would ultimately harm their intimate bond. Couples who swing find such sex play arousing; they feel that they are able to bring back this excitement to make their private sexual relationship more exhilarating.

What the Critics Say

Swinging is a very controversial lifestyle choice. There are many more critics of this approach than there are proponents. Obviously, folks who consider monogamy a requirement to marriage believe that this choice is morally wrong. Spread of venereal disease is a concern. Swingers acknowledge that jealousy can be a problem, as well as maintaining the social secrecy many couples feel is necessary as this option is so actively discouraged in our culture. Some individuals struggle with guilty feelings, as even consensual sex may counter moral or ethical social customs. Contrary to societal stereotypes viewing swingers as sex machines, sexual dysfunction is not uncommon in swinging circles. That is probably because of several reasons. Men are likely to feel additional pressure to perform when sex becomes so public. A woman may have difficulty climaxing when she is with a partner whom she does not trust and who does not know her body explicitly.

Swinging is clearly a risky move in a marriage—it is impossible to know how nonmonogamy will impact an intimate union until the couple experiences it firsthand. Even couples who feel totally committed to emotional monogamy may not be able to control their tender and loving feelings with others once sex is involved. This may be particularly true for women, who more typically require some level of heart connection to enjoy sexual intercourse. By its very nature, intercourse probably makes matters emotionally complicated, because the oxytocin released in the brain at that time promotes loving feelings and the desire to bond.

Good Candidates for Trying It

Swingers tend to be adventurous folks who enjoy sex. They are typically outgoing and playful. People who find swinging rewarding have learned to control their jealous and guilty feelings. Swingers find sex fun, and they typically enjoy parties and nightlife. However, some couples do swing outside of the party scene. That is, some swingers play with the same couple repeatedly, or the same couple can have a single woman they play with regularly. Thus, not all swingers are exceptionally social people.

Benefits to You

Swingers identify the primary benefit of swinging as a more exciting sex life than traditional sexual monogamy can offer. They believe that they enjoy the best of both worlds—emotional monogamy and sexual nonmonogamy.

Most swingers feel that swinging actually enhances their marriage and their sex life with their partners, thus supporting them in maintaining a loving intimate bond. Research supports this notion as increases in attachment anxiety have been shown to increase passion.[4] Many swingers have extensive, close, and rewarding social networks.

OPTION #6: POLYAMORY

What It Is

Polyamory, or polyfidelity as it once was called, is the practice of openly maintaining several loving, intimate relationships at one time. The polyamorous consider themselves as having multipartner relationships and families. All partners agree on this arrangement, and honesty amongst partners is a priority. Polyamorous folks acknowledge that humans are capable of intimately loving more than one person at a time. They do not engage in casual sex, as they form loving intimate partnerships. However, it is possible for a person to practice a polyamorous lifestyle while swinging simultaneously. Polyamory differs from polygamy, in which a man has multiple wives. A polygamous man does not necessarily profess to love his wives, nor do his wives have other sexual partners.

Polyamorous individuals may maintain a hierarchy in their intimate relationships. For example, they may refer to their legal partner as their primary, and all other partners as secondary. Obviously, being legally married to more than one person is not done because it is against the law in Western societies. Other polyamorous practices include three-way partnerships, or group love relationships. Polyamory differs from swinging in that swingers attempt to maintain emotional monogamy. In polyamory, couples are emotionally and sexually nonmonogamous.

The polyamory lifestyle involves many challenges. As with swinging, couples struggle with jealousies and issues of trust. Time is a practical and very real concern, as individuals attempt to share quality romantic time with more than one lover. Couples must be willing to communicate about difficult matters and engage in nonpossessive loving. People are expected to be loyal to their word rather than to a single partner. Another significant challenge unique to polyamory is rearing children in a lifestyle that can be quite confusing. Legal issues can also be complex, such as resolving wills or health care benefits.

Why It Works

Advocates of polyamory state that it works because they want it to work, because living any other way wouldn't work for them. They believe monogamy is not natural, and loving more than one person at a time feels good and right to them. They believe that practicing polyamory keeps their hearts open to life and the world around them, which enables them to love everyone better—including their intimate partner, and most importantly, themselves. Polyamorous people say their goals are loving more and living more vitally, not simply more sex.

What the Critics Say

There are multiple religious and moral objections to this alternative lifestyle. Many find it blatantly shameful and unethical. Some feel that the potency of love is lessened when it is shared or divided among different partners. Thus, rather than loving one person well, it is suggested that polyamorous people love several people half-heartedly. Family life is also a significant challenge, and critics are quick to point out the potential dangers in rearing children in such a confusing atmosphere.

It is difficult to calculate how many polyamorous relationships actually stand the test of time. While we know that approximately 50 percent of monogamous marriages end in divorce, we do not have reliable statistics for polyamorous couples at this time.

Good Candidates for Trying It

Candidates for this lifestyle are honest, secure, autonomous individuals who enjoy deep intimate relationships but who feel naturally capable and eager to love more than one person well. These individuals find freedom and openness to be more valuable than the security of a single, monogamous intimate connection. Sharing one's loved one means that there is little room for insecurity or unhealthy dependency. They take responsibility for feelings of jealousy and are willing to share a loved one in the most intimate of ways. Polyamorous people experience their most important love relationship to be with themselves. They believe they can love others best when their primary concern is knowing and caring for themselves well. Thus, independence and a strong sense of self is required.

Benefits to You

Practitioners of polyamory believe that their lifestyle opens their minds and hearts, and encourages a less judgmental approach to life. They experience their lifestyles as more free and supportive of their natural inclinations to love. They may feel less pressure in intimate relationships because they don't have to meet all of their loved one's needs. The polyamorous have an extended support network, sexual variety, and multiple partners for enjoying the simple daily aspects of living. Polyamorous people say the point is having multiple *loving* partners, not just multiple sex partners. Some believe that they learn and grow more because they are emotionally, intellectually, and sexually stimulated by multiple people.

SUMMING UP

In this chapter we explored a variety of practices intended to create more ecstatic sexual experiences for committed couples. We examined two practical options—capitalizing on age differences and maintaining physical space; two spiritual approaches—Tantra and controlled orgasm; and two multiple-partner lifestyle choices—swinging and polyamory. Of course, none of these options will prove beneficial unless both partners are fully committed to their manifestation. If you are like most couples, you want very much to improve your sex life, yet you found none of these options particularly appealing. Why? All of these options are extreme in their own way. Couples must devote significant effort and time to each of these alternatives, as these lifestyle choices aren't easily achieved. In addition, none of them is openly supported in our culture.

Sadly, it is likely that couples choosing to practice any of these alternatives will feel themselves criticized by friends and family. That is because others naturally feel threatened when people make choices that fly in the face of prevailing culture wisdom. We all feel much safer when we, and everyone around us, behave as our culture dictates. But for most people, the cultural wisdom of how to be married does not work well from a sexual perspective. It results in too much safety, too much boredom, and not enough tenderness and sensuality. When a couple I'm seeing wishes to explore the boundaries of their love life in one of the ways described here, I prepare them for the backlash they will feel from others. Keeping in mind that this is an issue for the criticizer, not the criticized, can be helpful.

Finally, it may be useful to consider these options as just that—options, not *solutions,* to the challenges inherent in monogamy. An individual or couple may experiment with different options at different points in their relationship. Thus, expecting to follow the flow of love in the course of a committed relationship with an attitude of openness and creativity may be the most realistic solution of all.

Chapter Nine

MAKING LOVE: SUCCULENT MONOGAMY

Would you enjoy making love to yourself?

For most of us, this is a challenging question. And one that we tend not to think too much about.

Who are you are as a lover? How do you imagine your partner experiences you sexually? How do you give to your partner sexually? What do you want in return?

We all have both positive and negative aspects to our sexual style. Most of us mean well—we try hard to be a good partner, emotionally and sexually. But intimacy is a challenging playing field. Without ongoing attention, we all fall short in our game. We get lazy, smug, or overly focused on our partner's behavior rather than our own. But passion is like any enjoyable emotion—you have to work at it to make it happen. Just like joy, peace, and contentment, sexual ecstasy is actively created in a long-term relationship. Committed relationships really are the ultimate training ground for giving and receiving love. And the better you can love, the better monogamy will feel to you and your partner.

TO HAVE SEX OR TO MAKE LOVE—THAT IS THE *REAL* QUESTION

Sex may be an innate act—one that we are instinctually programmed for. But making love is a different story. Making love is a learned skill—a skill taught by no one. You can't go for lessons, there's not much in the way of teaching videos, and the Learning Channel just hasn't caught up with our need for good lovemaking education as of yet. Other than a few lucky souls who have an innate knowledge of what making love is really all about, most of us are just flying by the seat of our pants. Literally. Making love is like any other skill—a few lucky people are born great at it, but most others need practice and guidance to get the hang of it.

What makes a fabulous lover isn't something external to you. Our culture is very confused by this. It's got nothing to do with your appearance, the size of your breasts or penis, or how many orgasms you can have. What makes you a great lover is mostly your willingness to open your heart and body and go somewhere—somewhere mysterious, intimate, and deep—and share the adventure with another human being. It's not so much what you do in bed, but the spirit in which you do it, that makes a great lover.

All of us can improve our skills as lovers. Learning to make love better means learning to give and receive more, emotionally and sexually. The more you hone these skills, the more evolved your intimate connection will become, and the more you'll cherish each other. If there is a better goal for living than loving each other well, I certainly don't know what that could be. And making love is a profound and perhaps the most intimate way we can express love for our partner.

AT FIRST IT'S A BREEZE

Physical intimacy is paradoxical. At first, it's oh so easy. It literally comes naturally for most couples who are falling in love. That is because the hormonal balance you enjoy at that time makes sex with your partner outstanding. In addition, your heart is open automatically. Falling in love causes our emotions to expand and flow freely, without conscious effort. Finally, at the beginning of a relationship, your partner hasn't disappointed you yet. As a result, you are much more willing to make yourself vulnerable emotionally and physically.

Over time, however, couples must actually learn how to create great sex by making love. Herein lies the challenge—lusty interchanges no longer happen automatically. Instead, they must be generated with ample amounts of determination and tenderness.

MAKE IT A DANCE OF THE HEART
AND SENSES, NOT THE BRAIN

Making love is a dance because it involves being in sync with each other, seeing and feeling where your partner is at, and responding in a way that promotes each of you traveling further into the depths of intimacy. Just as when partner dancing, you don't take a random step without being aware of where your partner is, and how they will likely be impacted by your movement. But you do this as far outside of your thinking sense as you can. This means that you stay alert with your feeling sense, and literally intuit your way through it. Practicing the following techniques will help you bring it all together.

Making Love with Your Intention

Take a moment and consider what typically is your intention when making love. Is it your intention to have an orgasm? To connect with your partner? To get it over with? Setting your intention means determining in advance what sort of ambiance you want to create with, and for, your lover. Whether or not you are aware of it, you already do set an intention *and* communicate it nonverbally, every time you make love. So, rather than leaving this very important aspect of lovemaking up to your unconscious mind to determine, I suggest that you take this matter up consciously and use it to create better sexual experiences for you and your partner.

For her: Try experimenting with a variety of intentions to see what feels most helpful. If you set an intention hours before you make love, you can remind yourself repeatedly of your goal. This will reinforce your statement and help to make it a reality. Some great places to start might include: I want to generate as much love with my partner as possible; I want to open as fully as I can with my partner; I want to surrender control to my partner; I want to show my partner my deepest self; I want to have fun with my partner; or I want to make my partner feel good. Obviously, the list is endless. Writing your intention on paper may help to solidify it in your mind.

For him: To generate as much sexual chemistry as possible, men are well served by focusing on one intention. You want to create an experience that will cause your partner to open, relax, and let go into the moment. Obviously, the more she lets go and enjoys herself, the more you will enjoy yourself. In order for her to relax into the moment, she needs to feel safe. And what she wants, but isn't telling you, is that she longs to feel cherished. This means that she wants to feel exquisitely treasured by you. You can help her feel cherished in the way you look at her, talk to her, and touch her. Sometimes men get confused and think this means sex always must be dainty and romantic. That's not the case at all— it just means that she'll need to feel cherished in order to enjoy engaging in a variety of sexual experiences. You'll find that the more you cherish her, the more wild and crazy your sex can get because she'll trust you. When she feels treasured (not needed, or lusted after), she'll feel safe enough to open more fully to you, making love in a less controlled way. Cherishing her means honoring, respecting, and appreciating her heart and her body. You can communicate this with your words, with your actions, and with the way you look at her. When she feels this, she will let you take her farther because she'll trust you more. She'll be more open to sexual experimentation because she will feel less afraid, and she'll feel more sexually confident. Thus, whenever and however you approach your partner sexually, maintain the intention of cherishing her.

Making Love with Your Heart

Making love is as much a work out for your heart as it is for your pelvis. Sex, in contrast, is merely a workout for your pelvis.

Making love with your heart means that you consciously feel your love for your partner while you are intimate. While this may sound like logical advice, it can be surprisingly difficult to achieve. *And if you are like most of us, you aren't doing this as well as you think you are.* Just because you love your partner doesn't mean you are actually feeling this love all of the time. Life has a way of closing our hearts without our awareness. The stress of our days, the challenges inherent in the inevitable pain of life, all this closes our hearts. Oftentimes we are walking around emotionally shut down without even realizing it. As a result, feeling love for our partner requires conscious intention. If we attempt to *make love* when we aren't *feeling love* for our spouse, we are playing with fire. These experiences can end up in fights, as it is easy to hurt each other during intimate moments when our hearts aren't open and full. And it can be a painfully long process to heal these wounds because they can leave an indelible mark in their wake.

The take-home message here is this—if your heart isn't open, do something about that before you begin your physical experience together. You cannot expect sex to automatically open your heart, because it probably won't. Expecting lovemaking to offer you something it cannot will only lead to emotional pain. You have to do the work of opening your heart *first*.

Remember back when your relationship was new, and you were in love? Your heart was open for your partner 24 hours a day. When you made love, your heart was already brimming over with adoration. Remember how awesome that was? Well, these last few paragraphs are as important as any in this book to help you re-create those feelings. When you've been with your partner for some time, these emotions won't just happen automatically. You have to actively find them.

Similarly, do not expect your partner to open your heart for you. Your partner is responsible for opening his or her own heart, and you are responsible for opening yours. As mature adults, that's how it is. If you get lazy with this, you both will feel it. If you put forth significant effort and you still can't feel your love for your partner, then that is clearly a bigger and more immediate problem than whatever is happening in your sex life. If this is the case for you, you may find it helpful to read a book on relationship dynamics.

I counsel many of the couples I see to deliberately do a heart-opening exercise either alone or in tandem before they come together sexually. This can be as simple as thinking about the reasons you love your partner and then deliberately feeling your heart inside your body, so that you notice the literal physical sensations of loving your partner. Sometimes people find it easier to imagine their partner as a child and love the child first, and then watch the child age in their mind's eye while they hold onto loving feelings for their partner. Or try gazing at a favorite picture of your partner, or a picture of the two of you.

If you prefer doing an exercise together to open your heart, make it a part of foreplay. Try a loving-kindness meditation inspired by Buddhist teachings. Simply gaze into your partner's eyes (or imagine doing so) and repeat the words, "May you be happy. May you be free from suffering. May you feel joy." Feel the truth of these words as you speak them silently to yourself. Invite your heart to open as you send these loving intentions to your partner. You can intensify this exercise by sitting across from your partner and gazing into your partner's eyes. For a while, focus on sending these words while your partner focuses on receiving them. Then switch roles. Many people find such exercises too "out there" to practice. However, homework like this really can single-handedly turn your sexual relationship around. So, I invite you to put your self-consciousness away, gather up your courage, and give it a try. Your only regret will be that you didn't practice this exercise sooner.

Be aware that men are often more challenged by heart meditations than women. That is because we've trained men from a young age to disengage from their hearts. The way society turns boys into men is through disconnection from their feeling selves. Ladies, have patience with him as he finds his way back into his body and his emotional self. It will be very vulnerable-making for him (much more than for you), and he may be shy and resistant to it. Remind yourself that he's lived a life where this sort of behavior and self-expression were discouraged. Now you are turning the tables on him. Give him time—like a few years! He's had a lifetime of brainwashing to work through. And while you are at it, consider the difficult task ahead of him. His job is to both open his heart *and* show his strength and power. If that's not a paradox, I don't know what is. Do give him space to learn to walk this fine line.

Making Love with Your Attention

Sex with a new lover is particularly fabulous because a new partner is a novel stimulus, and new stimuli grab our attention much better than stimuli we have grown accustomed to. And if our attention is riveted, we will feel and experience more intense sensation. The take-home message here is that the more you can focus your attention on the pleasurable aspects of your sexual experience, the more satisfaction everyone will feel.

For her: A woman gets into significant trouble when she is attending to her thoughts rather than to her body. Analyzing what he's doing that she doesn't like, thinking about how her body looks naked, even listening for the children all take her attention away from the moment. And he feels it. When she is distracted, touch isn't pleasurable, making love becomes a chore, and she's not relating intimately with her partner. Instead, making love well requires that a woman focuses her full attention on the moment—particularly on what she is feeling in her heart and body.

If you have trouble maintaining your focus sexually, a daily meditation practice will help tremendously. Research proves it. For example, paying attention to your breath can help you stay aware of your body. Or doing a relaxation exercise before making love can be helpful in slowing your thinking and tuning in to your physical self. Whatever technique you use, continue bringing your focus back to your body, relaxing *into* him, and opening to receive him even more fully.

For him: A man has almost the opposite challenge. He can easily err on focusing too much on bodies—his or hers—and not enough on the woman he's making love to. Or he may find that his quick glance at the score on the TV screen will easily bring even the most ecstatic sexual experience to a screeching halt. A woman is much more engaged with her partner when he is engaged and fully attentive to her. This means she needs to feel his attention on her heart and her emotional experience, not just her body or her pelvis. Remember, for a woman to feel sexually safe and willing to let go, she must feel that her man is completely aware of her and what she needs in any moment. His full attention will enable her to trust and surrender to him.

Making Love with Your Eyes

Eyes really are a window to the soul. To create ecstatic sexual experiences, most of the time partners must feel a deep, soulful connection. Eye contact is a powerful way to create this.

Many couples tend to close their eyes without realizing it when making love. That is because eyes-open sex is a more intimate act. Sometimes people close their eyes because they want to get lost in fantasy about another person. Or people close their eyes in an effort to concentrate more fully on physical sensations. Be aware that much of the time that your eyes are closed, your heart is probably less connected to your lover. And this will limit where the two of you can go together. For sexy, high-chemistry sex, women and men can use their eyes to create sexual tension.

For her: Practice letting your lover into your body through your eyes. This means literally letting him see deep inside of you via your eyes. This is easy to practice and feel. Look into a mirror with steely, cold eyes that shut someone out. Now look with open, receptive, soft eyes that let someone in. The more of that look you give your partner while making love, the closer he will feel to you.

Let your man love you. Allow him to emotionally feel you when he is with you. Show yourself to him through your eyes.

For him: In contrast, men, you can create sexual tension in your partner by literally entering her with your eyes. Imagine looking deep inside her, and feel into her heart and soul. Make an effort to really see her. Then try to experience in your own body what she is feeling. There is little that is more sexually exciting for a woman than to be seen, felt, and loved. If you look lovingly into her heart and soul, her body cannot help but respond to you. She will very likely have the feeling of melting when you look at her this way. I encourage my male patients to practice this type of eye contact with their partners at random times during the day. Practice while having dinner. Look deeply into her eyes and learn to feel her heart and her body. She may get nervous as you learn to read her better, because it will give her a sense of losing control. In effect, she will be right. She is losing some control because you'll learn to know what's happening with her before she tells you. But it is this same loss of control that will create fabulous sexual tension for you both.

If this exercise is a challenge for you, learn mindfulness meditation. Mindfulness meditation results in our getting much better acquainted with our own thoughts and feelings. The more we are able to understand ourselves and our own feelings, the more capable we are of understanding other people's feelings. And since men are taught from an early age to ignore their feelings, learning this skill may take some time for you. Becoming mindful of your own feelings and internal life may be the single most beneficial sexual technique available to you.

Making Love with Your Presence

Making love with your presence means making love with more than your body—it means making love with the essence of yourself that you put out into the world. You can think of it as your magnetism, your fundamental nature, or even your charisma. It's difficult to describe because you feel it more than you see it. With my patients I refer to it as their energy field. And both men and women can make use of this energy to create very powerful sexual chemistry.

Most couples find that to create great sexual chemistry, women need to offer soft, vulnerable feminine energy, and men need to generate strong, masculine open-hearted strength. In this way they create a polarity of masculine and feminine energy. For most couples to manifest high sexual tension over time, women need to express mostly feminine energy in their sexual interactions, while men express mostly masculine energy. Think of it as highlighting our true animalistic natures. It is also true that most couples also find it exciting for her to occasionally be more aggressive sexually and him to be more vulnerable. However, in a long-term monogamous relationship, the majority of the energy flow needs to be true to a person's biological nature for sexual tension to thrive. For example, imagine always balancing his softer side with her strength, or his vulnerability with her control. This dynamic will tend to be a libido killer for a woman (and often for a man) over time. For great sex, and intense sexual chemistry, everybody does best by getting back to basics.

For her: Get soft! Feel your innate feminine energy, and offer this beautiful, luscious side of yourself to your partner. Make love to him and with him from that supple, porous place. This means cultivating your openness and your vulnerability. Expose the sensual goddess in you. Finding this goddess state within yourself is not about changing who you are. It is *the exact opposite.* It is about uncovering the truth of your core. And this beautiful softness is at the core of woman. Access her, enjoy her, and then share her delightful loving essence with your man.

For him: Feel your strength and your inner masculine power. From an *open hearted and loving place,* offer her this masculine essence in yourself. Remember, if your heart isn't open, she'll contract because you will feel cold and dangerous to her. However, if your heart is open but you are not showing her your strength, she'll experience you as weak and wimpy, and she won't trust or respect you.

Men, if you are having a hard time finding a strong masculine place in yourself, imagine feeling the energy and presence of something strong and powerful—like an oak tree, or a lion. Feel the essence of that powerful energy inside you, and let it shine through. Show her that strength in your eyes, your tone of voice, the sureness of your touch, and in your longing for her. Show her you want her, as opposed to need her, which she will interpret as weak. That is, she wants to be longed for, but she doesn't want to feel that you need her to survive because then she'll feel like your mother, not your lover. When she feels your strength coupled with your longing and love for her, she'll look forward to making love to you.

Making Love with Your Voice

Whether you realize it or not, your voice is a primary vehicle for communicating to others. The tone and volume of your voice can give listeners much more information about you than your words ever could. We all interpret meaning in people's voices, whether or not we are consciously aware of it. And we will tend to trust the meaning we glean from voices more than words, because we all innately know that our voices are harder to manipulate than words. It's easier to say something we don't mean than to modify our voices to hide our emotions.

Consider, as an example, hearing your partner say, "I love you." If your partner speaks curtly while walking out the door, it won't mean nearly as much to you as when the same words are spoken softly while hugging you and kissing your cheek. And of course, they will mean something different if your partner looks deep into your eyes and whispers them after you've had an orgasm.

Here's a good rule of thumb. Talking while making love can enhance your partner's sexual experience, as long as your voice appropriately expresses the mood. That is to say, no street voices while making love. Don't use the same tone as you would use with a friend in conversation, or while talking in a public place. This will simply communicate to your partner that what you are doing is no big deal. When making love, you never want to communicate that! So, go ahead and talk, but be aware of what you are saying with your voice, not just your words. Men, deeper and softer is usually the way to go. Women, try slower and more sultry, with more hmms and sighs. Use your voice, and watch your partner's sexual excitement rise!

Making Love with Your Pelvis

I saved this one for last because, in a way, it is the least important! Paradoxical as it seems, when you engage all the other aspects of making love that we just discussed, what you do with your pelvis is just not as important. When you engage your lover's heart and body fully, the actual act of intercourse becomes a smaller piece of the fabulous sex puzzle. There is interesting research that supports this phenomenon.

Studies show that women are less aware of their level of genital arousal than are men. Instead of relying on their bodies for this information, women tune into their thoughts and feelings to determine whether or not they are sexually aroused.[1] Obviously, women are very different from men in this regard—men have a very obvious external barometer of their level of sexual excitement. And remember, her pelvis will only respond when her heart is open. So focusing less on her pelvis and more on her heart will probably serve both of you better, since this is more of how she determines her level of arousal anyway.

Nonetheless, we cannot deny that there is an art to making love with your pelvis! Once again, women and men can manifest their art very differently.

For her: A woman's pelvis, and specifically her vagina, can be either a warm and juicy ocean of exquisite delight for a man, or a cold, uninviting cavern. And you have much control over which topography you offer him. If you choose to gift him with your succulence, then relax your thighs, your vagina, and the muscles of your pelvis. Imagine your body opening for him—feel yourself spreading to receive him. Let your pelvis melt away, and imagine filling yourself with him. As he enters you, imagine taking him deep into your own body, receiving him into your sacred spaces. You can play with him by tightening and relaxing your vaginal muscles if you want to. You can also move your hips back and forth slightly, regardless of what position your body is in. These motions may cause him a great deal of pleasure, you'll know immediately based on how he reacts.

But most importantly, move in a way that you enjoy. Remember, if you are feeling pleasure, then he will, too.

For him: Remember rule number one: your woman will have the most profound sexual experience if you enter her heart as well as her vagina. That being said, you can create more ecstasy in her if you play with her a bit, rather than taking her straight to orgasm. In fact, depending on your woman, you may want to forget about the goal of orgasm altogether if this creates tension in her, and simply focus on her feeling pleasure. Either way, take her up the excitement scale and without letting her peak, linger there, and then gently and lovingly bring her back down. Foreplay with your fingers and tongue are almost always a fabulous idea. However, be aware that many women experience foreplay like this even more vulnerable-making than intercourse, so be particularly sensitive to her during this time. Vary your movements but always be aware of her reactions, so that you learn what she particularly likes. When you do enter her, be sure not to hurt her. Remember that her vagina and cervix are very delicate. In order for her to relax into you fully and let go, she must trust that you won't thrust too deeply or cause her any pain. Many women enjoy specific types of stimulation—deep thrusting is typically not what all women want *all* of the time. After all, the vast majority of nerve endings are in the lower third of her vagina. Learn to stimulate her G-spot, the entrance of her vagina, and also practice entering her in a more subtle, repetitive way. Many women find repeated subtle thrusting actually very stimulating at the right time.[2] As you practice different movements and learn to read her reactions, you'll have more control over her level of excitement, and she'll adore you for it!

SUPPORTING MONOGAMY BY CAPITALIZING ON BRAIN CHEMISTRY

Capitalizing on instincts isn't the only way to spice up a monogamous sex life. Biology can teach us other sexual lessons as well. Researchers have attempted to study how the emotional experience of passion is created and maintained in intimate relationships. It has been suggested that passion is actually the result of newness, or increases in intimacy.[3] It is these new experiences that ignite the pleasurable neurochemical changes in the brain. This explains why passion is so high at the beginning of a romance, when *everything* a couple experiences is new. It also explains why varying your lovemaking routine can result in more passion, because that makes things feel new again. Of course, a passionate romantic relationship does not guarantee a monogamous one. However, many people acknowledge that their failure at monogamy was in part due to missing the passionate spark lost from their relationship. If this is true, then an ongoing focus of intensifying your intimate bond will support a more passionate relationship over time. Continuously deepening your connection to your instinctual nature will bring a constant experience of newness to your romance, since you are always uncovering new territory within yourself. We never completely know anyone, and lovers can always offer their partners previously unseen parts of themselves. So, rather than focusing on the fact that monogamy isn't natural, pay attention to the ways you can offer something fresh to your partner, propelling your passion forward. The exercises in chapter 10 will help you achieve that.

ANOTHER WAY TO SEX UP YOUR SEX LIFE: ADVENTUROUS SEX

Like our emotional selves, our sexual selves have a deeper, mysterious side as well. This more creative sexual side involves all those sexual preferences and desires people feel hesitant to bring to their lover. It is typically a potent place for fantasy, adventure, and new experiences. It is the stuff that porn movies are made of, the secret desires that can make people sometimes feel self-conscious, awkward, or insecure. But it can also be the lifeblood of a passionate connection in a long-term relationship. Sadly, it is often when a couple has been together for a while that they become *most* inhibited about such deeper sexual longings. Strange as it may seem, increased familiarity with a lover can make it even *more* challenging to show these very personal parts of ourselves, thus making us feel even more vulnerable. It is ironic that when we need passion's creative and adventurous fire the most, we can be the most resistant to offering it.

For men or women, this adventurous side of sex may involve dirty talk, bondage, anal sex, blindfolds, angry sex, or role plays of threesomes. Sharing these sexually intense longings with a long-term intimate partner takes courage because it feels so exposing to show this side of oneself. But when we prevent ourselves from exploring this energy in an intimate relationship, it can be hurtful to the relationship in the long term. That is because long-term sex partners will engage in the same pattern of foreplay and monotonous sexual positions year after year, even decade after decade. It is astonishingly easy to get into sexual ruts, because one sexual pattern seems to work well and it then becomes safe and easy. However, sexual patterns become boring when couples stop trying to bring more of themselves into the bedroom. Remember, it is newness that makes things interesting sexually. To continue creating newness in a sexual relationship means that both partners must occasionally dig deeper inside themselves to find something novel to offer up sexually. Our deeper, sexually adventurous sides are a fertile ground to mine for this cause.

When people do not engage their more mysterious sexual sides, these aspects of the psyche don't just evaporate. They may be played out alone, such as privately in fantasy life or via online porn. Some people feel uncomfortable expressing more base sexual energy with their intimate partner, so they channel it to a less intimate experience such as an affair, prostitute, or strip club. Obviously, this energy that could mean juice for a sexual relationship is now being expended elsewhere, and in ways that can be very hurtful to a monogamous relationship. Others are so intolerant of these aspects of their sexual energy that they succeed in keeping it from everyone—including themselves. We can shut our sexual energy down so completely that even we aren't consciously aware of it.

As a culture, we do not teach people to use their creative sexual leanings to their advantage. And unfortunately, it just doesn't happen naturally. Monogamous men and women benefit from finding this energy within themselves, and then having the courage to share it in a way both partners can benefit. In fact, playing with our more adventurous sexual sides can be a significant contributor to keeping passionate sex alive, which could only support succulent monogamy over time.

FINAL WORDS OF WISDOM

Making love truly is an art form, not a science. Consider it an intimate method of self-expression via your body. Every time you make love, use your body to communicate information to your partner. When couples try and turn sex into a purely physical science, it becomes much less sexy and more rote. Here are a few final guidelines that can help take your loving to a deeper and more intimate level.

Slow Your Lovemaking Way Down

When we do things slowly, it's the opposite of doing them on automatic pilot. This means you experience heightened physical sensation, and you feel emotions more deeply. Unfortunately, we live in a culture that reinforces the exact opposite experience. When constantly trying to turn up the volume of stimulation, folks can actually become numb to sensation. Sexually speaking, this is a bad idea. We see this play out when women become reliant on high-speed vibrators to orgasm, and men need dramatic Internet porn scenes to get excited. Rather than continuously turning up the amplitude on your sexual stimulation, take your sensual experience in the other direction. Slowing things down and feeling more deeply creates fabulous erotic moments. Experiment sexually with "less is more."

Give Your Partner What You Long For

We all tend to think about sex in terms of what we can get, as opposed to what we can give our beloved. However, approaching lovemaking in this way tends to limit what you can create with your partner. Ultimately if you give freely and with a full heart, you'll find that this is actually the path to getting more for yourself. That is because, when we genuinely give to someone, our hearts open. We feel love and compassion toward them. And when our hearts open, we open ourselves to feeling more. So, not only will your partner reap the rewards of your sensual giving, you will, too. If you don't believe me, try it and see. Not only will your partner respond differently while making love, you will probably also notice a difference in the way he or she interacts with you outside the bedroom. This is because, when we give genuinely and with an open heart, we can shift a relationship's dynamic into a more loving space. So, serve yourself by focusing on loving your partner well.

Incidentally, this is actually a dynamic with which you are already familiar. Remember when your relationship was new, and the sex was extraordinary without either of you having to try? In truth, you both were focused on pleasing your partner. You wanted each other to have a great sexual experience. And so, your partner did. And so did you. Unfortunately, over time couples lose interest in serving their partners in this way. When we give with a closed heart, it does not feel good to the receiver. As a result, sex can become much less exciting in long-term relationships.

Prep Yourself

Prepping yourself means taking some responsibility for getting yourself in the mood before you connect with your partner. Rather than making it your partner's responsibility to get you there, you both will have a much better experience if you take steps to open your own heart and tune into your body. This is actually another example of something you used to do when your relationship was new that helped you feel excited. You were thinking sexual thoughts about your partner, making plans for sensual time together, and doing things that made you feel sensual, such as wearing particular clothing or cologne. All this is about deliberately prepping yourself for making love and simultaneously stoking your own arousal.

You can start your own fires burning via all of the techniques that you used when your relationship was young, such as those I just mentioned. Most likely, ladies, you will be best served by sensually tuning into your body. You can read erotica, dance sensually, or practice yoga postures that open your heart and body. You can create your own fantasy scenarios, and play them out in your mind during the day. Hot baths or other physically relaxing experiences can help. Just be sure to do *something* to open your heart and or body before you come together with your partner. You and your partner will reap the rewards when you take jump-starting your arousal into your own hands. Gentlemen, you are probably best served tuning into your heart. Remember why you love your woman. Think about what she may be feeling now, what makes her happy or sad, and what she needs. Try to quiet your mind and feel your love for her. And then try and let that show when you connect with her.

Remember that You Drive Your Partner Crazy, Too

One final word to the wise. We all drive our partners crazy. This means that you, too, can act obnoxious periodically. It is human nature. However, it is important to keep this truth in mind as you seek to further develop your sexual relationship. It is all too easy to focus on how your partner upsets you. This becomes a great reason not to love your partner well, and not to make love to your partner. However, we tend to forget that we offer our own version of the same crazy-making behavior right back at them. So, keep in mind that you both are in the same boat, as you struggle to manage in the deep and mysterious waters of physical intimacy.

Chapter Ten

HOMEWORK FOR BETTER SEX

Sensuality is a choice. So is better sex. These are not inflexible traits, like IQ or height. They are character qualities and behaviors that can be cultivated, depending on our motivation for manifesting them. Like all self-improvement choices—such as the resolve to be friendlier, more honest, or more conscientious about bodily care—they require practice, dedication, and attention to achieve. They are commitments we make to ourselves to improve our lives, and the lives of those we love.

The homework listed here will teach you what mature sensuality really feels like, as well as how to manifest it with your partner. And since our sensual experience is a key ingredient for fabulous sex, in doing these practices, you are well on your way to incredible lovemaking!

This chapter offers homework for women and men separately, as well as for couples to practice together. These are all homework exercises that I have given patients in my therapy practice, to help them become more sensitive to physical pleasure, tender emotions, and the joys of being alive. Exercises are divided into levels, offering you a general guideline of their increased intensity. Most of the practices will become more helpful with repetition.

There is no need to complete the homework in the order provided. Nor should you feel required to engage in practices that make you too uncomfortable. Whenever we are learning new skills, some discomfort is expected. But do not push yourself into situations that will overwhelm you. Nor should you engage in practices with a partner you do not feel comfortable with. Remember, they are meant to enhance your enjoyment. Only you can determine which of these exercises are right for you. And of course, have fun with them! Sexual pleasure can be a very excellent adult playground!

HOMEWORK FOR HER

Welcome, ladies, to yourselves. These homework assignments are meant to introduce you to aspects of yourself that you have lost touch with—aspects of your sensual self, your luscious juicy inner being. These exercises will teach you about pleasure—how to feel it in your body, and how to enjoy it. You will learn to feel your sensuality as originating from within your body, so that *you* benefit from it first, before sharing your pleasure with your lover. This is unlike what you may now believe—that feminine sensuality starts from the outside in, beginning with how you look and act (rather than how your body feels), and that your sensuality is for his pleasure, not yours. These practices can be enjoyable for you, or as challenging as you make them. I hope that you relax and allow your body to teach you more about who you are.

Level 1
- Questions for Your Journal:

  - What are the benefits of improving your sex life with your partner? Why does your man deserve to have great sex with you? Writing your answers is worth the time and effort because it invites you to think about them on a deeper level.
  - Every woman has motivations for wanting to make love, as well as reasons she doesn't. Frequently she will feel both of these drives simultaneously, which can be very confusing for her (and for her partner). Make two pie charts, one depicting your reasons for saying yes to sex, and the other illustrating your no. For example, on your "Yes" chart, you may feel that you want more pleasure in your life, or that you would like a more intimate connection with your partner. Your "No" chart shows how you benefit from *not* exploring your sensual self—perhaps you enjoy power in withholding your vulnerability from your partner, or you are uncomfortable with showing yourself so deeply. Learning more about your sexual yes and no enables you to make more conscious sexual choices.

- Learning How You Push Your Man Away:

  - We all have bad habits that we use to push our lovers away. Sometimes these are conscious, such as going to bed early to avoid intimate time together. At other times, they are unconscious, such as deliberately starting a fight to distract your man from getting close to you. For one week, focus on identifying all the subtle and obvious ways you push your partner away. Better yet, write them down so you can see them in black and white. This exercise will enable you to make more conscious choices concerning how you create distance with your man.

- Creating Memorable Moments:

  - Most of the moments that make up our lives are not memorable. We often cannot even recall the moments of yesterday. However, as you learn the ingredients that make moments unforgettable, you can become more skilled at creating them in your life. You can learn to manifest such moments sexually, resulting in more profound and exciting sex. Begin this exercise by reflecting on the more awesome moments of your life. Rather than focusing on an experience, such as "my wedding day" or "the birth of my baby," literally identify a particular moment that represents the meaning of the experience—for example, "the moment the nurse laid my baby on my breast." After you have identified several such moments, consider the elements that made these experiences memorable for you. These exquisite seconds probably involved powerful emotions, as well as a profound connection with another person, nature, or even God. How can your translate this information into your sex life? Use what you have learned as a beacon to guide you in creating ecstatic sexual moments for yourself and your lover.

- Opening Through Your Tightness

  - Life has a way of making our bodies tight, often without our even realizing it. When we are stiff, it becomes very difficult to feel sensual. Thus, it is helpful to practice opening your body through its tightness. Lie in bed and recall a recent sexual experience in which you felt closed. Notice how this makes your body feel— what physical constriction feels like. Feel how your muscles tense and become more rigid. Perhaps your eyes close, the muscles of your face contract, or your belly tightens. Now, practice moving your body into a more open, receptive space. Coach yourself with a mantra, such as, "Relax," or "Open." Use your breath to relax your body—starting perhaps with your belly, allow your breath to expand your muscles and tenderize you. Allow your eyes, your heart, and your pelvis to become receptive. Feel the difference in this more open state of your body. As you learn to practice freeing your body into a relaxed state, you'll be better equipped to use this mantra while making love to make this shift with your lover.

Level 2

- Connecting Your Heart and Your Pelvis:

  - For profound sex, a woman must feel a strong connection between her heart and pelvis. In other words, she will only feel love if her heart is open. She will only feel a desire for sex if her pelvis is open. An open heart without an open pelvis leaves her feeling loving, but asexual. An open pelvis without an open heart turns sex into a colder, more superficial act. It is actually quite common for women to feel that their heart and pelvis have become disconnected. If this feels true for you, you can teach yourself how to reconnect these vital aspects of your sensual experience. Take private time to lie naked on your bed. Begin by breathing deeply and allow your body to relax. Once you feel more connected to your body than to your thoughts, place one hand on your breast, and spreading your legs, cup your vagina with your other hand. Then simply breathe, and feel your body. Imagine that you are strengthening the connection between your heart and pelvis with each breath. Visualize a beautiful gold cord weaving these tender parts of your lovely feminine self together.

- Showing Him Rather Than Telling Him

  - Letting go into sexual ecstasy requires that you allow yourself to feel your feelings fully, without holding back. Most adults must relearn not only how to feel deeply, but also how to allow these feelings to show. We avoid showing deep emotions because it makes us feel vulnerable. However, without this skill, sex can never evolve beyond the ordinary. Your goal is to show the emotions of joy, pleasure, and hurt. This means that your face, your voice (via sounds rather than words), your eyes, and your body will all reflect your emotional experience. As you become more comfortable showing your deep feelings, you will then be better able to express uninhibited feelings of passion.

- Opening Your Pelvis with Your Breath

  - When you want to feel sensual, or when you wish to make love, you want to feel the pleasure of your pelvis being open and receptive. Practicing this feeling on your own will make it easier for you to achieve it whenever you choose. First, relax your body and do your best to clear your thoughts. Focus on the rhythm of your breathing, and how your breath feels in your body. Use the simple meditative technique of feeling your breath entering and exiting your nose. Notice the sensation of the air coming into your nostrils, and how your entire body feels as you expand to receive the air. After you have enjoyed this rhythm for a while, change your focus to your pelvis and imagine breathing air directly into your vagina. Feel the sensation of the air entering your feminine self, expanding you, and filling you. Relax the muscles of your pelvis to allow a fuller experience of these sensations. Enjoy the pleasurable feeling of openness that you are creating. Imagine your man lying with you, and feel your body open further to receive him. This is a fabulous, sexy meditation to do before joining your partner to make love. Also, when making love, you can use this technique to relax your pelvis further and intensify your sexual experience.

- Receiving from the Sun

  - Most women benefit from practicing the art of receiving sexual energy. That is because receiving sexually often presents a variety of conflicts for women, both conscious and unconscious. Women who practice receiving when they are alone typically find themselves more open to receiving from their beloved. Believe it or not, you can practice receiving sexually from the sun. When you are alone in your house, lie naked on a soft blanket in a patch of sunshine. Breathe in the warmth and luxuriate in the sensations generated by the sun's delightful energy. Expand your focus over your entire body, allowing every part of your physical self to engage in the experience. Slowly spread your legs, enjoying the sensation of your body opening. Let the sunshine bathe your pelvis and the exquisite interiors of your body. Stretch like a cat and accept the sun's lovely warmth, inside and out. Explore the pleasures of being open and receptive.

Level 3

- Letting Go

  - To fully enjoy making love, women must learn to let go into the experience. Holding your emotions or your body tightly is the opposite of this practice. Letting go is a learned skill—don't expect yourself to be able to let go all at once. When a woman lets go while making love, she lets go to her man. In doing so, she allows herself access to more sensation and emotion. But letting go of control can be unsettling, especially if you aren't used to it. In this exercise, practice letting go for just a moment—he doesn't even have to know you are doing it. Just feel the emotional and physical experience of giving yourself to him for just a little while. Some women feel this as a sensation of falling; others describe it as their body becoming less solid. As this becomes comfortable for you, tell him that's what you are doing so that he can receive you consciously, and you can practice sharing the experience together.

- Write a Fantasy and Give It to Your Partner

  - Sharing sexual fantasies with your partner is a fabulous way to teach your partner more about what you long for. Write a fantasy script that you would like to play out. Be sure to take into account as many details as possible—what people are saying, where they are, what they are wearing, and how they respond. Is there silence or music in the background? What sort of touch is involved? Leave your fantasy for him to read on his own time. Writing fantasies is a marvelous, sexy way to teach your partner more about what you like.

- Giving to Him but Feeding You Both

  - Each woman has her own unique sexual gifts. Perhaps you are particularly adept at massaging your partner, speaking to him in soft sexy tones, sensually dancing, or giving nurturing embraces. Whatever your particular gift, experiment with highlighting it the next time you make love. Intensify this skill, taking it to an even more powerful level. As you gift your lover in this way, notice how you impact his sexual bliss. Then tune into the feelings that *his* increased pleasure generates within *your* body. This is an exercise in learning how giving translates into receiving. When you give sexually with an open heart, the energy you generate can actually be exchanged in a feedback loop. Ultimately, what you give him will come back to you, for your own heart and body to enjoy!

- Sing to Him

  - I know, I know, you don't have a good singing voice. And you feel self-conscious when you sing. But what you don't yet realize is the amazing impact your singing will have on your man. Choose a soft love song and play it loud in the background. Lie on top of him, and softly sing into his ear. Most men will respond with gratitude and love, not critical comments about your voice. And as you open his heart, he'll give you more. This is yet another way to enhance your sexual experience. In singing to him, you gift yourself.

- Don't Play by the Rules

  - It is natural for couples to create sexual patterns when making love. We determine what we like and what we are willing to do, and then make love within those boundaries. While this is natural, this is also the recipe for boring sex in a long-term relationship. Most of us feel self-conscious when we step outside of our sexual comfort zone. However, the alternative of boring sex is equally uncomfortable, just for different reasons. Find your sense of humor and try something new. Bite your man's neck when you are on top, rip his shirt off rather than waiting for him to undress himself, or push him onto the floor rather than making love on the bed. Make your experience a little more base and primal. Expect to feel silly and self-conscious at first; most women do. But shaking up your sex life in this way paves the way for more ecstatic lovemaking.

HOMEWORK FOR HIM

Gentlemen, the fact that you are reading this chapter bodes very well for your sex life. The exercises below will help you offer what your woman needs so that she'll be comfortable gifting you more of her delectable sensual self. Be prepared for some of these exercises to seem strange to you. But they will help you bring out aspects of your masculine self and your heart that your woman is longing to feel. Most men find that they must repeat the exercises regularly in order to really learn from them. Remember, you have a tremendous impact on your woman's sensual experience, including what she offers you sexually. These exercises will teach you how to enhance your sexual relationship with your woman, so that both of you enjoy more of what you long for.

Level 1

• Show Her Full-Bodied Passion

  • Women crave men who feel passion throughout their entire body rather than just via their penis. Women are transfixed by men who show passion through their eyes, the tone of their voice, and the way they move. Passion coming just from his pelvis seems superficial to her, and she'll close her own body in response. It takes practice for most men to learn how to show excitement for their woman in an intense, full-bodied way. As with any unfamiliar emotion, men feel self-conscious as they learn to show their passionate feelings more openly. However, those few lucky men who have women falling all over them know this innately. In my therapy practice, I encourage men to use a variety of methods to cultivate full-bodied passion. For example:

    • Use Music to Feel Your Body: Music can help a man feel his body and access deeper feelings within himself. Consider the song "Mama" by Genesis. Yes, it's an old song, but it's a very powerful one from this perspective. The words and music create a powerful sense of a man's sexual longing for a woman. Play it loudly—listen to the words, and feel the intensity of this longing throughout your body. Then practice showing more of this full-bodied longing to your lover.

    • Use an Eastern Body Practice to Feel Your Body: Tai Chi, Chi Gong, Yoga, or any of the martial arts help men become more aware of their bodies and learn how to experience feelings throughout their physical selves. Men who spend most of their time thinking for a living become particularly out of touch physically. Everyone prefers a lover to access sensuality rather than just thoughts while making love. After all, sex is nothing if not a physical, sensual experience. Thus, men who are not in touch with their bodies find their women lose interest in sex. Men serve themselves and their women well by engaging in a daily body practice that brings them back into physical and intellectual balance, tuning into their bodies as well as their brains.

  • Feel a Range of Emotions

    • Men become more comfortable leading their partner in ecstatic sex when they learn to manage a variety of emotions on their own, first. One way to do this is by watching intense movies that depict men feeling a range of feelings, such as passion, anger, tenderness, and fear. As you watch an actor in a deep feeling state, try and feel those same sensations in your own body. This will help you develop familiarity with these more intense but less comfortable emotions. Remember, the greater your range of emotional expression, the more varied and intense your sex life will become.

- Spend Time in Nature

    - Your partner longs for you to connect with her on a deep level. You cannot feel your partner this way unless you have the ability to feel yourself deeply first. Spending time in nature allows a man to get away from the chaos and distractions of life and tune into his inner world. Taking extended time in nature may cause you to feel uncomfortable feelings, like grief or sadness. However, in learning to fully experience these natural emotions, you'll be much better equipped to connect to your woman on the more passionate level that she desires. Ultimately, you cannot feel in her what you do not let yourself access in yourself. And women adore the sensation of being felt at a deep level.

Level 2

- Making Her Feel Safe

    - For a woman to relax and enjoy herself sexually, she must first feel safe with her partner. Feeling safe means that she trusts him to love her, to take care not to hurt her, and to take her needs into account. It is only when she feels this level of safety that she will let herself go into more ecstatic sexual experiences with you. There are many practices you can do to encourage her feelings of safety. For example:
        - Make solid loving eye contact with her, particularly when she is upset with you. Holding her gaze in an open and loving manner (not a cold stare) enables her to feel your strength. Practice looking at her this way during the day, as well as when you are making love to her.
        - Women feel safe when their feelings are acknowledged. During the day, as well as when you want to be intimate with her, try to feel what she is feeling. Literally imagine breathing into her body and notice what it feels like to be her in that moment. Then, with compassion, let her know you are aware of what she is feeling. A woman adores it when a man knows what she is feeling without her having to tell him. These sorts of experiences will only make her want to be more intimate with you.

- Cherish Her

    - What makes you valuable to your partner is not your brain, your body, or your paycheck. What makes you valuable to your partner is actually how you make her feel. Of course, you can use your brain, body, and paycheck to impact her feelings. However, the bottom line is this: your partner will want more of you when she feels good being around you. And what women long for most is feeling cherished. Ask your partner what you can do to make her feel cherished, both inside and outside the bedroom. She might appreciate your focused attention when discussing personal matters, a phone call checking in with her during the day, or your doing the dishes. Whatever her request, if you follow through with it, your sex life will likely explode. That is because a woman who feels cherished only wants more intimacy with her man.

- Ice Cube Play

  - Any practice that helps us feel our bodies and our sensuality will support feeling more pleasure while making love. Creating more intensive sensations while making love will help your woman feel her body more. Take an ice cube from your glass and play! Starting with her neck, run the ice cube lightly over her skin. Direct her by whispering in her ear to feel the cold, the wetness, the sensual pleasure as her body tingles in response. When she seems ready, circle her breasts and then her nipples with the ice cube. Run the ice cube down her belly, circle her belly button, and then slowly spread her legs and run the ice cube over her thighs. Whisper that you want to hear her sigh or moan if she likes it. Run the ice cube over the skin around her vagina. Some women enjoy the sensation of the ice cube inside them—so experiment with tantalizing her! If you wish, ask her later to return the favor.

Level 3

- Expand Her Ability for Pleasure

  - As much as your woman desires passionate connection, she can be afraid of its intensity at the same time. Most of us have a sort of passion "brake" that automatically stops us from reaching more ecstatic heights. You can gently teach your woman how to tolerate more and more pleasure so that her brake doesn't take over and minimize her pleasure, and yours. To do this, you must learn to read your woman's sexual responses. Your cues will be the way her body moves, how the muscles of her face and body tense and relax, and the sounds she makes. If she tends to be sexually shy, she may not give you enough cues. In this case, encourage her to make her pleasure more evident to you. Tell her how much it pleases you when she shows you how she feels. Learn to take her body to her pleasure edge, slightly de-escalate her, and then cycle her back up again. As you become more adept at controlling the intensity of her sexual pleasure, you will be able to slowly increase her body's ability to tolerate more and more passion. And of course, the more pleasure she feels, the more pleasure you will feel, too. Take turns giving and receiving. This homework is definitely a win-win situation!

- Feel Your Deepest Emotions

  - What were the most challenging moments of your life? Every man has moments that make him or break him. Write about them. Better yet, talk to someone trusted about them. Men are taught to hold their feelings in and be stoic. It is this same stoic attitude that creates bad sex from a woman's perspective. She wants to feel more of you than your stoic exterior. Start to crack your stoic wall when it is appropriate to do so. Learning to be able to let down your guard in the right circumstances will enable you to let down your guard when making love—a trait your woman will adore.

- Define Your Masculine Self

  - Men learn what masculinity looks like and feels like by watching their fathers. If a man's father was angry and aggressive, his likely response is to moderate his masculinity to avoid being destructive like his father. The other probable scenario is that he internalizes his father's angry role and has become angry himself.

Alternately, if a man's father was passive, he may have internalized a passive masculine role and may find himself repeating it in his own marriage. Regardless, healthy masculine intimate connection (that same connection that is necessary for great sex in a long-term relationship) requires that a man be both strong and tender toward his woman, at the same time. Which aspect of the masculine role would you benefit from enhancing?

- If you are overly passive in your romantic relationship, then practice being sexually assertive. Come on to your woman with determination and confidence. Show her a more primal side of sex—moan, feel your body instead of thinking, and practice leading your sexual experience rather than passively letting it unfold.
- If your tendency is to be aggressive or overly assertive with your woman, then slow down and tune in to your emotions, and hers, when you are making love. Touch her face tenderly, tell her you love her and that she is beautiful, and concentrate on making love to her rather than just having sex.

COUPLES PRACTICES

These exercises are all about making love—man and woman, making love to each other's hearts and bodies; enhancing their intimate connection; creating succulent, tender moments that transport them further into the ecstasy that only sexual communion can provide. Learning to travel together in these realms takes practice, patience, and a sense of humor. It requires that both man and woman allow more of themselves to be seen. Of course, showing more of yourself usually means feeling vulnerable. But it is only at this level of surrender and exposure that deep sexual merging can occur. Relax into this experience of getting to know yourself and your lover more completely. And above all, enjoy yourselves! You are about to create what most lovers only imagine.

Level 1
- Write Your Partner's Story

  - Write an intimate portrait about your partner. Describe in several pages your partner's life, including highlights and pivotal moments, disappointments, hopes, pains, joys, and dreams. Is your partner satisfied with life? Why or why not? What do you wish for your partner and your intimate relationship? Respectfully and lovingly read your partner's story to them. This exercise can increase couple's compassion and understanding of each other.

- Fun Homework to Get Things Started

  - As you begin the couple's exercises, you may enjoy engaging in some lighter sex play. Try some of the following:

Ladies

  - Go to a restaurant without panties.
  - Have your lover shave your pubic hair or, if you prefer, go to a spa for a Brazilian wax.

- Surprise your lover with a Henna tattoo in a strategic place!
- In your most seductive voice, leave your partner a sexy phone message with a promise for something special that evening.

Gentlemen

- Rent a mutually agreeable erotic film for the evening.
- Rather than make love, gift your partner with a kissing session—leave no part of her body untouched!
- Whatever time you normally spend in foreplay, triple it!
- Read a sexual technique book offering more fabulous, fun ideas to turn up the heat.

- Learn to Meditate

  - Meditation may be one of the more powerful skills for supporting fabulous sex in a long-term relationship. This is the case for two reasons. One, folks who engage in a regular meditation practice have a superior ability to ignore the brain's incessant chatter. This is a remarkable skill when making love because brain chatter distracts us from feeling physical pleasure. Secondly, the ability to focus intensively on one's physical sensations enhances sexual pleasure. There are also many other emotional and medical reasons why meditation is good for you. So, in the interest of great sex, begin a shared, daily meditation practice.

- Conserve Your Energy for What Matters

  - To get the best from our partners, we must focus on giving our best. This is particularly difficult after a challenging day, when our energy is low. However, we cannot expect their excellence without holding ourselves accountable to offer ours. For most of us, this means literally being conscious during the day to conserve energy for the time dedicated to our loved ones. Ecstatic sex doesn't just happen. We must plan to bring our sweetest gifts to create an exquisite experience! For this practice, assess your schedules and see where you can streamline. If you want a fabulous sex life, conserving time and energy for your intimate life must become a priority.

- Share Your First Turn-On

  - What is the first time you remember being sexually excited? For most of us, these early experiences of passion leave a profound and lasting impact. Sharing such memories with your partner can be sexually exciting, plus it can also help develop mutual understanding and strengthen intimate connections.

- Sensate Focus

  - Lovers can discover much about their own bodies and a partner's body via simple touch and massage. In sensate focus, full-body massage becomes a way to learn more about the art of making love. It is a process of massage that initially entails no sexual contact, and then over a period of weeks or months, culminates in orgasm and making love. Practice taking turns giving your partner a loving, tender massage—30 minutes or more. During this time, the giver focuses on touching the partner's body in many different ways, and appreciating the partner's body; the receiver focuses on the sensations, and what it feels like to receive. With time, the women's breasts are included, and ultimately the massage becomes sexual. Sensate focus offers the opportunity to learn how to love each other's bodies more intimately, and how to receive and enjoy this loving.

- Breathing Together

  - Breathing together is a romantic way to feel your body and tune into your partner's body while sharing intimate moments. Lie together unclothed, one of you on top of the other. He then breathes with her, following her lead. To intensify the experience, gaze into each other's eyes. Feel your bodies and the heat generated from your shared breathing. Getting into each other's breath rhythm can be difficult at first—sometimes even frustrating. But this is an exercise in surrendering to your partner while developing a greater ability to focus on him or her. These skills create deeper sensual connections while making love.

- Compliment Your Partner

  - It's easy to focus on what your partner is doing sexually that turns you off. In this exercise identify what your partner does sexually that you like, and tell what it is. Did your partner once do something that you now miss? Ask for more of it. Explain how good it makes you feel. Encouraging your partner with positive words will increase your likelihood of getting more for yourself sexually.

- Romantic Homework to Set the Mood

  - As you begin the more intensive exercises below, the following romantic suggestions can help you create a safe and loving environment together:

    - Buy your lover flowers for no reason.
    - Pick a romantic hotel and spend the weekend away, sharing practices from this chapter.
    - Take a candlelight bath together.
    - Feed your partner dinner with your hands—pasta works great for this messy sexy play!
    - Get your beloved an "I love you" card. Mail it to your lover's place of work, or leave it on the front seat of the car.
    - Burn a CD or load your portable music device with the most meaningful songs you and your partner have enjoyed. Have it available in your bedroom for your next romantic encounter, and give your partner a copy to keep in the car.

Level 2

- The Total Care Game

  - Play the ultimate game of giving and receiving with your lover. For about four hours, allow your partner to do everything for you—feed you, dress you, brush your teeth, read to you, whatever you wish. You exert no effort and only receive. Then switch roles so that you both can experience what it's like to have your partner care for you so intimately.

- Expressing Passion without Words

  - Learning to express your passionate feelings without words is a fabulous sexual skill. That's because, one, your partner will greatly appreciate the feedback and will be better able to love you well upon knowing what you like; two, hearing your own excitement and your passionate expressions will intensify the heat of your encounter; and three, allowing yourself to moan and sigh may help your partner to be less self-conscious and become more comfortable letting go sexually. You'll see how sighs and moans may amplify your sexual experience.

- Almost Yoga

  - Couples can use yoga postures to explore intimate and loving connections. When a woman does a yoga pose with her man assisting her, she can feel her body and her emotions more intensively, as well as strengthen the intimate connection with her lover. The following pose should be approached in this way: First, the woman lies on her back, knees falling open, bottoms of her feet together, arms stretched above her head. She then closes her eyes, focusing on sensations in her body and her emotions. Second, her man places one hand on her heart, the other on her lower belly; she breathes in the sensations of having his hands on her body in this way. Third, she opens her eyes, allowing eye contact between them.

- Reenact a Favorite Sex Scene

  - Recall a sex scene in a movie that one of you found particularly exciting. Watch the movie again together, and then act out the scene. Each of you must play the role as exactly as possible. Remember that you are acting, so that you have poetic license to pretend as necessary to make the scene as accurate as possible. Try to let go of your own personality and feel into the role both emotionally and physically. This exercise encourages you to engage in new sexual experiences that increase your sexual repertoire and your comfort level in trying out new sexual adventures.

- Use Your Eyes

  - Learn to give your lover access to your deepest self through your eyes only. We constantly inform people of what we are thinking and feeling with our eyes. If our eyes really are windows to our soul, the more we allow our lovers to see into our eyes, the more profoundly we connect with them. Practice the following exercises sitting comfortably across from your partner. Take turns between being the one showing yourself while the other is the one seeing you.

    - Relax your eyes and imagine that they are opening to accept your lover's gaze. Soften your heart and allow your lover access to your deepest emotional self. Show your lover who you really are.
    - Now show your partner the love and longing you feel. If what you feel at that moment is the pain of rejection or the feeling of not being met by your partner, show that instead. Find the raw truth of these feelings inside yourself, and then relax your eyes and allow your lover to see them.

- The "Take My Hand" Game

  - Couples who slow their lovemaking down and feel profoundly into each moment share more ecstatic sexual experiences. Playing the "Take My Hand" game helps couples develop these skills. Start with the woman in control. Taking her man's hand, she places it wherever she chooses on her body, holding it there as long as she wishes, but without movement. Her job is to feel fully the sensation of his hand, taking in the intoxicating experience of being touched. His role in this game mimics hers—he attempts to experience what his hand feels like for her, on her body. That is, he feels his hand not only via his own body, but also via her body. In this way, he becomes more in tune with how she experiences his touch. She can move his hand as many times as she wishes. Then reverse roles and play again.

- Do a "Giving Experiment"

  - Take turns ravishing your partner sexually, your only focus being your partner's pleasure. Start by opening your heart, and set the intention of offering your lover a truly profound experience. Make love to your partner in whatever way you believe will be most pleasurable *for your partner*. Do this exercise on different days to ensure that each partner has the opportunity to feel the full impact of feeling profoundly loved and ravished.

- Demonstrating Your Love while Making Love

  - Newness fuels the fires of passion like perhaps nothing else. Couples can feel this increased excitement when making love in a hotel room, playing with a new sex toy, wearing lingerie, or having sex in a different room of the house. Newness is exceptionally easy to create when lovers first meet, as everything from kissing to having dinner together is novel territory. As years pass, these same couples must make extra efforts to create unique experiences, or their sex lives go stale. What most people don't realize is that newness can not only be created by new techniques and new environments, but also when sharing emotions. Showing more feelings during intimate moments takes lovemaking to a new and more profound level for both partners. To take your sex from ordinary to extraordinary, add elements of something new to your sexual encounters.

Level 3

- Make Love for the First Time, Again

  - For many women, the loss of virginity is a disappointing or even uncomfortable experience, emotionally and physically. Many couples find that role playing together a loving and tender first experience of making love can be very powerful both in healing old wounds, and in creating a sweeter and more profound sense of intimacy between them. In this exercise, the man takes care to make his woman feel cherished and well cared for as he gently initiates her into a beautiful experience of making love.

- Cervical Massage

  - We carry stress in our bodies. This is particularly evident when we get a massage, as most of us have certain particularly sensitive body parts like our shoulders or back. Many women seem to carry tenderness in their cervix. And without releasing this discomfort in a loving way, a woman's cervix can be uncomfortably tender when making love. A wonderful healing couples exercise is cervical massage. This exercise should not lead to making love. It involves quiet, gentle time in which her man very tenderly and delicately massages her cervix with his fingertips, allowing her to release any emotional or physical pain stored in this very sensitive part of her body.

- Masturbate in Front of Each Other

  - This is a very intimate exercise that requires much tenderness on both partner's parts. Take turns, separating the experiences by a day or more so that each practice is fully felt and appreciated by both individuals. Be sure to first create a loving and safe environment. The goal of this practice is not to turn your partner on. Rather, this is an exercise in allowing yourself to be seen more deeply by your partner. It is a gift of self-exposure. The partner receiving the gift can take special care to honor and respect the delicacy and sacredness of such an intimate offering of love.

- Take Your Partner to Sex School

  - In sex school, you teach your partner exactly how you want to be made love to. This includes how you like your partner to come on to you, talk to you, look at you, and touch you. You play the teacher while your partner plays the student. The teacher leaves no opportunity for misinterpretation. Like any type of schooling, sex school needs to last for more than one session. That's because much information is being transmitted, and students need repeated opportunities to absorb the information. After each class, teachers can talk about what they did and why. This is an extremely powerful and intimate exercise. Sometimes couples resist it initially because it makes them feel so vulnerable. However, when we hold back, or we are tentative with our approach, we teach our partners to be tentative and withhold passion. This is an extremely effective way to teach how we want to be made love to.

- Pretend to Create New Life

  - Making love with the intention of creating a baby is an incredibly sensual and emotionally powerful experience. Whether or not having a child interests you in this moment, pretend with your lover that you are going to create life together. Use your birth control! This is an emotional experience, not a literal one. Make love in a way that allows both of you to feel the power of love in bringing new life to this planet.

IN CONCLUSION

Consider yourselves armed and dangerous! You and your partner now have enough techniques in your sexual armamentarium to become true sexual superstars. If you practice even one-third of the exercises, your sex life will likely skyrocket to levels most people only dream about. Fabulous sex really is a learned skill that takes practice. And in this case, practice does make perfect!

One final word of advice. Be prepared to feel the need for alone time and a desire to pull back intermittently as you come together more intimately. This is a natural process that all couples experience as they move together. The dance of intimate connection involved pulling toward each other and then away, coming closer and then taking some time to breathe. Couples who don't give each other periodic breaks in the intensity of lovemaking find themselves suddenly angry and critical of each other. You may pick fights or otherwise shake up your intimate connection. Think of it as a law of nature—what goes up must come down; what expands must contract. If you allow this process to unfold naturally, you'll be less tempted to force distance with damaging behavior or hurtful words. So try your best to allow this push/pull dance to unfold gently, in its own time. And please remember, as you and your partner travel this adventurous and exciting path together, sexual pleasure *and* having fun is your goal. Bring your sense of humor into bed with you, and enjoy the wonderful world of ecstatic sex!

CONCLUSION

In reading these final words, I hope that you are left with questions as well as answers, new approaches to perceiving old problems, and a more compassionate understanding of your sexual self. For most of us, the realization that monogamy isn't natural is a very difficult pill to swallow. It has not been easy for me, or any of my patients. We are afraid of breaking up homes, and of the financial and emotional destruction that could result. And because of these fears, as a culture we have ignored the truth about monogamy. But one of the ironies of life is that we tend to create what we are most afraid of. And isn't this exactly what the data on divorce and affairs indicate is happening? These statistics remind us that we cannot improve the problems inherent in intimate relationships by pretending they don't exist. In fact, our head-in-the-sand approach only intensifies the issues as time passes—and it burdens coming generations with the same struggles. But there is an alternative. When we open our hearts and minds to view intimacy in a realistic way, we are able to identify unique, creative solutions that facilitate loving—rather than generate anger, shame, and closure between lovers.

It is my hope that within these pages, you have found truths to guide your personal unfolding, and the evolution of your intimate relationship. Ladies, I hope you have learned that femininity isn't about your hairstyle, or the size of your miniskirt. These superficial expressions of femininity may be important for a short-term fling, but not as the magic that enhances a long-term monogamous relationship over time. Instead, femininity is about an open and loving heart, a willingness to be vulnerable and seen by your man, a desire to receive your man and take him with you as you experience the sensual adventures of life. This openness is what a man's soul truly craves. May you open to your luscious feminine depth and enjoy your femininity, allowing her to fill your body, your life, and the lives of those you cherish. Gentlemen, I hope you have learned that masculine energy is about much more than big biceps, fat wallets, or strikingly good looks—these instinctual representations of masculinity are trumped by the more evolved masculine traits that modern women long for: your willingness to be present and intimate with her, to cherish her, and to hold a strong and loving place for her to release her heart and body to you. This willingness is what a woman's soul truly craves. I hope that the open-hearted strength you cultivate makes your life full and rich with meaning and purpose.

When we encourage men to be men and women to be women, everyone becomes an expert at something, rather than no one being an expert at anything. In this way, we offer our lovers what they cannot create for themselves—or find in superficial connections with others. These are the gifts that keep relationships exciting and rewarding over time. Together, let us work to transform what it means to be intimate into a new, more powerful light. In this way, we can carry monogamy well into the new millennium. Let us facilitate a new era of sexual understanding that may enable marriages to feel fabulous and sensual over time.

We can use the truth about monogamy to destroy intimacy, or take it to new and awesome levels. And why not the latter? Sexuality is the most awesome playground to do this work of learning to love more fully. What better way to mature into manhood or womanhood than through the delight of sexual pleasures? When we remove the dictum that great sex should just happen in monogamous relationships, we are actually freeing ourselves. We open the door to developing our skills as lovers. We offer ourselves an opportunity to approach making love as an art form rather than a science. We allow for sex to become an act of exquisite pleasure and adventure—surpassing the limits of our biology. Such are the rewards of opening to the realities of our animal nature, and then taking sex to a superhuman level—above the animal, and into the ethereal.

NOTES

CHAPTER 1

1. George P. Murdock, *Ethnographic Atlas* (Pittsburgh: University of Pittsburgh Press, 1967).

2. Helen Fisher, *Anatomy of Love: A Natural History of Mating, Marriage, and Why We Stray* (New York: Random House, 1992).

3. David Barash and Judith Lipton, *The Myth of Monogamy* (New York: W.H. Freeman and Company, 2001).

4. David Barash and Judith Lipton, *Strange Bedfellows: The Surprising Connection between Evolution, Sex, and Monogamy* (New York: Belleview Literary Press, 2009).

5. Barash and Lipton (2001).

6. Phillip E. Lampe, "Adultery and the Behavioral Sciences," in *Adultery in the United States: Close Encounters of the Sixth (or Seventh) Kind,* ed. Philip Lampe (Buffalo: Prometheus Books, 1987), pp. 165–198.

7. Michele Weiner-Davis, *The Sex-Starved Marriage: A Couple's Guide to Boosting Their Marriage Libido* (New York: Simon and Schuster, 2003).

8. Dietrich Klusmann, "Sexual Motivation and the Duration of Partnership," *Archives of Sexual Behavior* 31 (2002): 275–287.

9. Ibid.

10. Jody Van Laningham, David R. Johnson, and Paul Amato, "Marital Happiness, Marital Duration, and the U-Shaped Curve: Evidence from a Five-Wave Panel Study," *Social Forces* 78 (2001): 1313–1341.

11. Julian Savulesccu and Anders Sandberg, "Neuroenhancement of Love and Marriage," *Neuroethics* 1 (2008): 31–44.

12. Pew Social and Demographic Trends, *Modern Marriage* (Pew Research Center, 2007).

13. Murdock (1967).

14. Helen Fisher, *Why We Love: The Nature and Chemistry of Romantic Love* (New York: Henry Holt, 2004).

15. David J. Schneider, Samuel R. Carter, and Teri L. White, "Paradoxical Effects of Thought Suppression," *Journal of Personality and Social Psychology* 53 (1987): 5–13.

16. Timothy Wilson, *Strangers to Ourselves: Discovering the Adaptive Unconscious* (Cambridge: Harvard University Press, 2002).

17. Ibid.

18. Edward Laumann, Anthony Pacik, and Ramond Rosen, "Sexual Dysfunction in the United States," *Journal of the American Medical Association* 281 (1999): 537–544.

19. Wilson (2002).

20. Mark Spiering and Walter Everaerd, "The Sexual Unconscious," in *The Psychophysiology of Sex,* ed. Erick Janssen (Bloomington: Indiana University Press, 2007): pp. 166–184.

21. Steven Gamgestad, Randy Thornhill, and Christine Garver-Apgar, "Adaptations to Ovulation," in *The Handbook of Evolutionary Psychology,* ed. David Buss (Hoboken, N.J.: Wiley, 2005): pp. 344–371.

22. Ibid.

23. Cindy Meston and David Buss, *Why Women Have Sex* (New York: Times Books, 2009).

24. Wendy Maltz and Larry Maltz, *The Porn Trap: The Essential Guide to Overcoming Problems Caused by Pornography* (New York: Harper Collins, 2008).

25. Lampe (1987).

26. Paul R. Amato and Bruce Keith, "Parental Divorce and the Well-Being of Children: A Meta-Analysis," *Psychological Bulletin* 110 (2004): 26–46.

27. Ibid.

28. Linda Waite and Maggie Gallagher, *The Case for Marriage: Why Married People are Happier, Healthier, and Better Off Financially* (New York: Broadway Books, 2001).

29. Mindy Scott, Erin Schelar, Jennifer Manlove, and Carol Cui, "Child Research Brief: Young Adult Attitudes about Relationships and Marriage: Times May Have Changed, But Expectations Remain High," *Child Trends,* Publication #2009–30 (Washington, D.C.: Child Trends, 2009).

CHAPTER 2

1. Gurit E. Birnbaum, Harry T. Reis, Mario Mikulincer, Omri Gillath, and Ayala Orpaz, "When Sex Is More than Just Sex," *Journal of Personality and Social Psychology* 91 (2006): 929–943.

2. Charles G. Sibley and Jon E. Ahlquist, "The Phylogeny of the Hominoid Primates, as Indicated by DNA-DNA Hybridization," *Journal of Molecular Evolution* 20 (1984): 2–15.

3. Helen Fisher, *Why We Love: The Nature and Chemistry of Romantic Love* (New York: Henry Holt and Company, 2004).

4. David Schnarch, *Constructing the Sexual Crucible: An Integration of Sexual and Marital Therapy* (New York: W.W. Norton & Co., 1991).

5. Virginia Colin, *Human Attachment* (Philadelphia: Temple University Press, 1996).

6. Richard Dawkins, *The Extended Phenotype* (Oxford: Oxford University Press, 1992).

7. Geoffrey Miller, Joshua M. Tybur, and Brent D. Jordan, "Ovulatory Cycle Effects on Tip Earnings by Lap Dancers: Economic Evidence for Human Estrus," *Evolution and Human Behavior* 28 (2007): 375–381.

8. Randy Thornhill and Steven W. Gangestad, "The Scent of Symmetry: A Human Pheromone That Signals Fitness?" *Evolution and Human Behavior* 20 (1999): 175–201.

9. Elizabeth Pillsworth and Martie G. Haselton, "Women's Sexual Strategies: The Evolution of Long-Term Bonds and Extrapair Sex," *Annual Review of Sex Research* 17 (2006): 59–100.

10. David M. Buss, *Evolutionary Psychology: The New Science of the Mind,* 3rd ed. (Boston: Pearson, 2008).

11. Bianca P. Acevedo, Arthur Aron, Helen Fisher, and Lucy L. Brown, *Neural Correlates of Long-term Pair-bonding in a Sample of Intensely In-love Humans,* Poster Session #297, Society for Neuroscience (2008).

12. Buss (2008).

13. Fisher (2004).

14. Ibid.

15. David M. Buss, *The Evolution of Desire: Strategies of Human Mating,* 2nd ed. (New York: Basic Books, 2003).

16. Daniel G. Amen, *Sex on the Brain* (New York: Harmony Books, 2007).

17. Judith Feeney, "Adult Romantic Attachment," in *Handbook of Attachment: Theory, Research, and Clinical Applications,* 2nd ed., ed. Jude Cassidy and Phillip Shaver (New York: Guilford Press, 2008), pp. 456–481.

18. Deborah Davis, Phillip Shaver, Keither Widaman, Michael Vernon, William Follette and Kendra Beitz, "I Can't Get No Satisfaction: Insecure Attachment, Inhibited Sexual Communication, and Sexual Dissatisfaction," *Personal Relationships* 13 (2006): 465–483.

19. Birnbaum et al. (2006).

20. M. Lynne Cooper, Mark Pioli, Ash Levitt, Amelia E. Talley, Lada Micheas, and Nancy L. Collins, "Attachment Styles, Sex Motives, and Sexual Behavior," in *Dynamics of Romantic Love,* ed. Mario Mikulincer and Gail Goodman (New York: Guilford Press, 2006), pp. 243–274.

21. Deborah Davis, Phillip R. Shaver, and Michael L. Vernon, "Attachment Style and Subjective Motivations for Sex," *Personality and Social Psychology Bulletin* 76 (2004): 1076–1090.

22. Omri Gillath and Dory Schachner, "How Do Sexuality and Attachment Interrelate?" in *Dynamics of Romantic Love,* ed. Mario Mikulincer and Gail Goodman (New York: Guilford Press, 2006), pp. 337–355.

23. Feeney (2008).

24. Joseph Lichtenberg, "A Discussion of Eight Essays that Propel Attachment and Sexual Theories into the 21st Century," in *Attachment and Sexuality,* ed. Diana Diamond, Sidney Blatt, and Joseph Lichtenberg (New York: Analytic Press, 2007), pp. 237–261.

25. Gillath et al. (2008), p. 350.

26. Susan Sprecher and Kathleen McKinney, *Sexuality* (Thousand Oaks, CA: Sage, 1993).

27. Anthony Bogaert and Stan Sadava, "Adult Attachment and Sexual Behavior," *Personal Relationships* 9 (2002): 75–86.

28. R. Chris Fraley, Keith E. Davis, and Phillip R. Shaver, "Dismissing-Avoidance and the Defensive Organization of Emotion, Cognition, and Behavior," in *Attachment Theory and Close Relationships,* ed. Jeffry A. Simpson and W. Steven Rholes (New York: Guilford Press, 1998), pp. 249–279.

29. Gillath and Schachner (2006), p. 342.

CHAPTER 3

1. David Geary, *Male, Female* (Washington, D.C.: American Psychological Association, 2010).

2. Paul MacLean, *The Triune Brain in Evolution: Role in Paleocerebral Functions* (New York: Springer, 1990).

3. Louis Cozolino, "It's a Jungle in There," *Psychotherapy Networker* 32 (2008): 20–27.

4. David Schmitt, "Fundamentals of Human Mating Strategies," in *The Handbook of Evolutionary Psychology*, ed. David Buss (Hoboken, N.J.: Wiley, 2005): 258–291.

5. Jane Lancaster and Hillard Kaplan, "The Endocrinology of the Human Adaptive Complex," in *Endocrinology of Social Relationships*, ed. Peter Ellison and Peter Gray (Cambridge: Harvard University Press, 2009), pp. 95–118.

6. Schmitt (2005).

7. Ibid.

8. Geary (2010).

9. Schmitt (2005).

10. Ibid.

11. Frans De Waal, *Our Inner Ape* (New York: Riverhead Books, 2005).

12. Jeremy Taylor, *Not a Chimp* (Oxford: Oxford University Press, 2009).

13. Richard Dawkins, *The Ancestors Tale* (New York: Houghton Mifflin, 2004).

14. Taylor (2009).

15. David P. Barash and Judith E. Lipton, *The Myth of Monogamy: Fidelity and Infidelity in Animals and People* (New York: W.H. Freeman and Company, 2001).

16. Hasse Walum, Lars Westberg, Susanne Henningsson, Jenae Neiderhiser, David Reiss, Wilmar Igl, Jody Ganiban, Erica Spotts, Nancy Pedersen, Elias Eriksson, and Paul Lichtenstein, "Genetic Variation in the Vasopressin Receptor 1A Gene (AVPRIA) Associates with Pair-Bonding Behavior in Humans," *Proceedings of the National Academy of Science* 105 (2008): 14153–14156.

17. Nancy Segal, "Behavior Genetics, Human Ethology, Evolutionary Psychology, and Culture: Looking into the Future," in *Uniting Psychology and Biology*, ed. Nancy Segal, Glenn Weisfeld, and Carol Weisfeld (Washington, D.C.: American Psychological Association, 1997), pp. 483–484.

18. Steven Gangestad, Randy Thornhill, and Christine Garver-Apgar, "Adaptations to Ovulation," in *The Handbook of Evolutionary Psychology*, ed. David Buss (Hoboken, N.J.: Wiley, 2005), pp. 344–371.

19. Jared Diamond, *The Third Chimpanzee: The Evolution and Future of the Human Animal*, 2nd ed. (New York: Harper Perennial, 2006).

20. Rachel Herz, *The Scent of Desire: Discovering Our Enigmatic Sense of Smell* (New York: Harper Perennial, 2007).

21. Gordon Bermant, "Sexual Behavior: Hard Times with the Coolidge Effect," In *Psychological Research: The Inside Story*, ed. Michael H. Siegel and H. Phillip Zeigler (New York: Harper and Row, 1976), pp. 76–77.

22. Walter Everaerd, Stephanie Both, and Ellen Laan, "The Experience of Sexual Emotions," *Annual Review of Sex Research* 17 (2006): 183–199.

23. Knut K. Kampe, Chris D. Frith, Raymond J. Dolan, and Uta Frith, "Reward Value of Attractiveness and Gaze," *Nature* 416 (2001): 589.

24. Louann Brizendine, *The Female Brain* (New York: Morgan Road Books, 2006).

25. Matthew H. McIntyre and Carole K. Hooven, "Human Sex Differences in Social Relationships: Organizational and Activational Effects of Androgens," in *Endocrinology of Social Relationships*, ed. Peter Ellison and Peter Gray (Cambridge: Harvard University Press, 2009), pp. 225–245.

26. Erno J. Hermans, Peter Putman, and Jack van Honk, "Testosterone Administration Reduces Empathetic Behavior: A Facial Mimicry Study," *Psychoneuroendocrinology* 30 (2006): 859–866.

27. Peter B. Gray and Benjamin C. Campbell, "Human Male Testosterone, Pair-Bonding, and Fatherhood," in *Endocrinology of Social Relationships,* ed. Peter Ellison and Peter Gray (Cambridge: Harvard University Press, 2009), p. 291.

28. Teresa Julian and Patrick McKenry, "Relationship of Testosterone to Men's Family Functioning at Mid-Life," *Aggressive Behavior* 15 (1989): 281–289.

29. Elizabeth G. Pillsworth and Martie G. Haselton, "Women's Sexual Strategies: The Evolution of Long-Term Bonds and Extrapair Sex," *Annual Review of Sex Research* 17 (2006): 59–100.

30. Alan Booth and James M. Dabbs, "Testosterone and Men's Marriages," *Social Forces* 72 (1993): 463–477.

31. Ibid.

32. Allan Mazur and Joel Michalek, "Marriage, Divorce, and Male Testosterone," *Social Forces* 77 (1998): 315–330.

33. Sari van Anders, Lisa Dawn Hamilton, and Neil V. Watson, "Multiple Partners Are Associated with Higher Testosterone in North American Men and Women," *Hormones and Behavior* 41 (2007): 454–459.

34. John C. Wingfield, Robert E. Hegner, Alfred M. Dufty, and Gregory F. Ball, "The 'Challenge Hypothesis': Theoretical Implications for Patterns of Testosterone Secretion, Mating Systems, and Breeding Strategies," *American Naturalist* 136 (1990): 829–846.

35. Sari van Anders and Neil V. Watson, "Testosterone Levels in Men and Women Who Are Single, in Long-Distance Relationships, or Same-City Relationships," *Hormones and Behavior* 514 (2007): 286–291.

36. Sari van Anders, Lori Brotto, Janine Farrell, and Morag Yule, "Associations among Physiological and Subjective Sexual Response, Sexual Desire, and Salivary Steroid Hormones in Healthy Premenopausal Women," *Journal of Sexual Medicine* 6 (2009): 739–751.

37. Roxanne Sanchez, Jeffrey C. Parkin, Jennie Y. Chen, and Peter B. Gray, "Oxytocin, Vasopressin, and Human Social Behavior," in *Endocrinology of Social Relationships,* ed. Peter Ellison and Peter Gray (Cambridge: Harvard University Press, 2009), pp. 319–339.

38. Ibid.

39. Ibid.

40. Brizendine (2006).

41. Gerianne M. Alexander, Teresa Wilcox, and Rebecca Woods, "Sex Differences in Infants' Visual Interest in Toys," *Archives of Sexual Behavior* 38 (2009): 427–433.

42. Gerianne M. Alexander, "An Evolutionary Perspective of Sex-Typed Toy Preferences: Pink, Blue, and the Brain," *Archives of Sexual Behavior* 321 (2003): 7–14.

43. Gerianne M. Alexander and Melissa Hines, "Sex Differences in Response to Children's Toys in Nonhuman Primates," *Evolution and Human Behavior* 23 (2002): 467–479.

44. C. Robert Almli, Robert H. Ball, and Mark E. Wheeler, "Human Fetal and Neonatal Movement Patterns: Gender Differences and Fetal-to-Neonatal Continuity," *Developmental Psychobiology* 38 (2001): 252–273.

45. Martin Daly and Margo Wilson, *Homicide* (New York: Aldine de Gruyter, 1988).

46. Geary (2010).

47. Daniel G. Amen, *Sex on the Brain* (New York: Harmony Books, 2007).

48. Ibid.

49. Helen E. Fisher, *The Sex Contract: The Evolution of Human Behavior* (New York: Quill, 1983).

50. Rosemary Basson, "Human Sex-Response Cycles," *Journal of Sex & Marital Therapy* 27 (2001): 33–43.

51. Steven W. Gangestad, Randy Thornhill, and Christine E. Garver-Apgar, "Adaptations to Ovulation," in *The Handbook of Evolutionary Psychology*, ed. David Buss (Hoboken, N.J.: Wiley, 2005), pp. 344–371.

52. Gangested et al. (2005), pp. 344–345.

53. Schmitt (2005), p. 268.

CHAPTER 4

1. David C. Geary, *Male Female: The Evolution of Human Sex Differences* (Washington, D.C.: American Psychological Association, 2010).

2. Ibid.

3. Irenaus Eibl-Eibesfeldt, *Human Ethology* (New York: Aldine de Gruyter, 1989).

4. Ibid.

5. Mirra Komarovsky, *Dilemmas of Masculinity: A Study of College Youth* (New York: Norton, 1976).

6. M. Hamit Fisek and Richard Ofshe, "The Process of Status Evolution," *Sociometry* 33 (1970): 327–346.

7. Glenn Weisfeld, "Discrete Emotions Theory With Specific Reference to Pride and Shame," in *Uniting Psychology and Biology*, ed. Nancy L. Segal, Glenn E. Weisfeld, and Carol C. Weisfeld (Washington, D.C.: American Psychological Association, 1997), pp. 419–443.

8. Lee Ellis, "Dominance and Reproductive Success among Nonhuman Animals: A Cross-Species Comparison," *Ethology and Sociobiology* 16 (1995): 257–333.

9. David M. Buss, *Evolutionary Psychology: The New Science of the Mind* (Boston: Pearson, 2008).

10. Dana K. Carney, C. Randall Colvin, and Judith H. Hall, "A Thin Slice Perspective on the Accuracy of First Impressions," *Journal of Research in Personality* 41(2007): 1054–1072.

11. Christopher Boehm, *Hierarchy in the Forest: The Evolution of Egalitarian Behavior* (Cambridge: Harvard University Press, 1999).

12. Jose Orathinkal and Alfons Vansteenwegen, "Couples' Conflicts: A Territorial Perspective," *Sexual and Relationship Therapy* 21 (2006): 27–44.

13. Patricia H. Hawley and William A. Hensley IV, "Social Dominance and Forceful Submission Fantasies: Feminine Pathology or Power?" *Journal of Sex Research* 46 (2009): 568–585.

14. Ibid.

15. Eva Jozifkova and Martin Konvicka, "Sexual Arousal by Higher- and Lower-Ranking Partner: Manifestation of a Mating Strategy?" *Journal of Sexual Medicine* 6 (2009): 3327–3334.

16. Ibid.

17. Brad Spellberg, *Rising Plague: The Global Threat from Deadly Bacteria and our Dwindling Arsenal to Fight Them* (New York: Prometheus Books, 2009).

18. R.L. Trivers, "Parent-offspring Conflict Theory," *American Zoologist* 14 (1974): 249–264.

19. Glenn E. Weisfeld, Carol C. Weisfeld, and Nancy L. Segal, "Final Overview: Uniting Psychology and Biology," in *Uniting Psychology and Biology*, ed. Nancy L. Segal, Glenn E. Weisfeld, and Carol C. Weisfeld (Washington, D.C.: American Psychological Association, 1997), pp. 525–534.

20. Jeremy Taylor, *Not a Chimp* (Oxford: Oxford University Press, 2009).

CHAPTER 5

1. James K. McNulty and Terri D. Fisher, "Gender Differences in Response to Sexual Expectancies and Changes in Sexual Frequency: A Short-Term Longitudinal Study of Sexual Satisfaction in Newly Married Couples," *Archives of Sexual Behavior* 37 (2008): 229–240.

2. Helen Fisher, *The First Sex: The Natural Talents of Women and How They Are Changing the World* (New York: Ballantine Books, 1999).

CHAPTER 6

1. Timothy Wilson, *Strangers to Ourselves* (Cambridge: Harvard University Press, 2002).

CHAPTER 7

1. Michael Sand, William Fisher, Raymond Rosen, Julia Heiman, and Ian Eardley, "Erectile Dysfunction and Constructs of Masculinity and Quality of Life in the Multinational Men's Attitudes to Life Events and Sexuality (MALES) Study," *Journal of Sexual Medicine* 5 (2008): 583–594.

CHAPTER 8

1. Marnia Robinson, *Cupid's Poisoned Arrow* (Berkeley: North Atlantic Books, 2009).

2. Richard J. Jenks, "Swinging: A Review of the Literature," *Archives of Sexual Behavior* 27 (1998): 507–521.

3. Curtis R. Bergstrand and Jennifer Blevins Sinski, *Swinging in America* (Santa Barbara: Praeger, 2010).

4. Deborah Davis, Phillip Shaver, Keith Widaman, Michael Vernon, William Follette, and Kendra Beitz, "I Can't Get no Satisfaction: Insecure Attachment, Inhibited Sexual Communication, and Sexual Dissatisfaction," *Personal Relationships* 13 (2006):465–483.

CHAPTER 9

1. Meredith L. Chivers, Michael C. Seto, Martin L. Lalumiere, Ellen Laan, and Teresa Grimbos, "Agreement of Self-Reported and Genital Measures of Sexual Arousal in Men and Women: A Meta-Analysis," *Archives of Sexual Behavior* 39 (2010): 5–56.

2. Edward Eichel and Philip Nobile, *The Perfect Fit* (Essex, England: Signet, 1993).

3. Roy Baumeister and Dianne M. Tice, *The Social Dimension of Sex* (Boston: Allyn and Bacon, 2001).

INDEX

About the Author

DR. MARIANNE BRANDON, PhD, is a clinical psychologist and a Diplomat in Sex Therapy through the American Association of Sex Educators, Counselors, and Therapists (AASECT). She coauthored *Reclaiming Desire: 4 Keys for Finding Your Lost Libido* and has contributed to multiple professional publications. Dr. Brandon is president and director of Wellminds Wellbodies LLC (www.wellminds.com), a center for integrative and holistic psychological care in Annapolis, Maryland. She specializes in working with men and women struggling with low sex drive. Dr. Brandon lectures extensively to therapists, physicians, and the public on topics of sexuality. She cohosted the radio show *In Bed with Dr. B and Ted* (www.inbedwithdrbandted.com). Dr. Brandon completed her doctoral training at Ohio University and her internship at the University of Connecticut School of Medicine, and is a graduate of a postdoctoral fellowship from the Sheppard and Enoch Pratt Hospital in Baltimore. She lives in Annapolis with her husband, Steven Saltzman, MD.

About the Editor

JUDY KURIANSKY, PhD, is an internationally known licensed clinical psychologist. She is also an adjunct faculty member in the Department of Clinical Psychology at Columbia University Teachers College and in the Department of Psychiatry at Columbia University College of Physicians and Surgeons. At the United Nations, she is a nongovernmental organization representative for the International Association of Applied Psychology and for the World Council for Psychotherapy, and is an executive member of the Committee of Mental Health. She is also a visiting professor at the Peking University Health Sciences Center, a Fellow of the American Psychological Association, a cofounder of the APA Media Psychology Division, and a member of the board of the Peace Division and U.S. Doctors for Africa. A certified sex therapist by the American Association of Sex Educators and Counselors, she is a pioneer in the field of sexuality. An award-winning journalist, she hosted the popular LovePhones syndicated call-in radio show for years, was a feature reporter for WCBS-TV and CNBC, and now regularly comments on news and current events for television worldwide. Her wide-ranging expertise from interpersonal to international relations is evident in her books, with titles ranging from *The Complete Idiot's Guide to a Healthy Relationship* and *Sexuality Education: Past, Present and Future* to *Beyond Bullets and Bombs: Grassroots Peacebuilding between Israelis and Palestinians*. Her Web site is www.DrJudy.com.

Dr. Brandon's book is a gem for serious scholars exploring the psychological foundations of love and attraction as well as for lay readers who are committed to making monogamy work in their lives. A comprehensive review of theories of childhood socialization is seamlessly integrated into explanations of who we fall in love with, and why. Detailed strategies for couples to use in enhancing their relationship are provided for readers at all levels of expertise. Highly recommended for therapists, social scientists, teachers of human sexuality and marriage/family courses, and lay readers.

—**Curt R. Bergstrand,** PhD, associate professor of Sociology, Bellarmine University, and co-author of *Swinging In America: Love, Sex, and Marriage in the 21st Century*

Monogamy is far from obvious. Even most pair-bonding species regularly deviate from its unwritten rules. Marianne Brandon gives us an honest look at the pleasures and problems of an ideal that humans seem only partially hard-wired to reach.

—**Frans de Waal,** PhD, author of *The Age of Empathy*

Brandon does a masterful job taking on unsupported hypotheses, misguided ideas, and old-fashioned notions on monogamy to provide a nice reality check on where "together forever" stands today. Well-researched, intelligent, and holistic, Brandon makes a massive topic accessible and applicable to professionals and the public alike. Readers seeking to bolster their monogamous efforts will feel empowered with the easy-to-follow exercises, as well as inspired by Brandon's wisdom, thoughtfulness, and hope in making love magical over the long haul.

—**Yvonne K. Fulbright,** PhD, MSEd, sexologist, sexuality educator, author, and founder of www.sexualitysource.com and sensualfusion.com

Brandon's *Monogamy: The Untold Story* is a much needed book that addresses the realities of our biological heritage and the expectations of our culture in a refreshing and forthright manner. The seamless fusion of science and practice make for a lucid and pleasurable read. This is a book for anyone who wants a deep understanding of monogamy and sound advice on how to make it work better for them.

—**David C. Geary,** PhD, author of *Male, Female: The Evolution of Human Sex Differences*

In *Monogamy: The Untold Story,* Marianne Brandon presents complex concepts about relationships and sexuality from the fields of anthropology, sociology, and psychology, and does so in an easy to understand manner. She guides readers on a journey of reconnection with their sensory experiences and to an appreciation of the important relationship between love of oneself and love of a partner. A must-read for couples who want to attain or maintain sexual vitality.

—**Dr Susan Kellogg Spadt,** PHD CRNP, Drexel University College of Medicine and Widener University College of Human Service Professions

Dr Brandon's book on monogamy is packed with great information on how to keep a marriage or committed partnership alive. She gives direct and practical advice without talking down to her reader. She gives a fair analysis of the social limitations of marriage as it stands and then gives couples some invaluable creative alternatives to enhance their chemistry. I think the book is timely and should be read by anyone looking to make a long term partnership last.

—**Tammy Nelson,** PhD, author, *Getting the Sex You Want*

Marianne Brandon's *Monogamy: The Untold Story* shines a bright, new light on the age-old problem of how to feel sexual passion in an ongoing sexual relationship. *Monogamy* contains some startling insights and explodes the myth that monogamy should be easy if you're with the "right person." In language at times scientific, at times erotic, Brandon reminds us that our biology works against us. We must *learn* to feel pleasure in ongoing, monogamous unions. And she teaches us how with great exercises and wonderful advice. Dr. Brandon does us all a great service.

—**Aline P. Zoldbard,** PhD, author,
SexSmart: How Your Childhood Shapes Your Sexual Life and What to Do About It

Monogamy is an informative and thought-provoking look at modern sexuality. Author Marianne Brandon helps the reader explore the origins of monogamy, and the push and pull of our sexual instincts versus contemporary Western culture, to ultimately learn to love more fully.

—**Irwin Goldstein,** MD, Director of Sexual Medicine, Alvarado Hospital

An erudite and juicy guide to understanding the paradoxes of our biology, and achieving the perfect combination of a loving and sexually passionate marriage.

—**Rachel Herz,** PhD, author, *The Scent of Desire*